Case Study Research in Practice

Case Study Research in Practice

Helen Simons

Los Angeles | London | New Delhi
Singapore | Washington DC

© Helen Simons 2009

First published 2009

Reprinted 2010

Apart from any fair dealing for the purposes of research or private study, or criticism or review, as permitted under the Copyright, Designs and Patents Act, 1988, this publication may be reproduced, stored or transmitted in any form, or by any means, only with the prior permission in writing of the publishers, or in the case of reprographic reproduction, in accordance with the terms of licences issued by the Copyright Licensing Agency. Enquiries concerning reproduction outside those terms should be sent to the publishers.

SAGE Publications Ltd
1 Oliver's Yard
55 City Road
London EC1Y 1SP

SAGE Publications Inc.
2455 Teller Road
Thousand Oaks, California 91320

SAGE Publications India Pvt Ltd
B 1/I 1 Mohan Cooperative Industrial Area
Mathura Road, Post Bag 7
New Delhi 110 044

SAGE Publications Asia-Pacific Pte Ltd
33 Pekin Street #02-01
Far East Square
Singapore 048763

Library of Congress Control Number 2008929580

British Library Cataloguing in Publication data

A catalogue record for this book is available from the British Library

ISBN 978-0-7619-6423-0
ISBN 978-0-7619-6424-7 (pbk)

Typeset by C&M Digitals (P) Ltd, Chennai, India
Printed and bound in Great Britain by
CPI Antony Rowe, Chippenham, Wiltshire
Printed on paper from sustainable resources

For my past students and all who follow in their path.

CONTENTS

Acknowledgements	ix
Prologue	1
Introduction	3
SECTION I GETTING STARTED	11
1 Evolution and Concept of Case Study Research	13
2 Planning, Designing, Gaining Access	28
3 Listen, Look, Document: Methods in Case Study Research	43
SECTION II IN THE FIELD	67
4 Who Are They? Studying Others	69
5 Who Are We? Studying Our 'Self'	81
6 Whose Data Are They? Ethics in Case Study Research	96
Mid-term Letter	112
SECTION III MAKING SENSE	115
7 Begin at the Beginning: Analysis and Interpretation	117
8 From Data to Story: Examples in Practice	135
SECTION IV TELLING THE STORY	145
9 Start at Any Point: Reporting and Writing	147
10 Dispelling Myths in Case Study Research	162
Epilogue	171
Bibliography	173
Index	182
About the Author	190

ACKNOWLEDGEMENTS

Case study research and its development is a social process. I have been fortunate to have been part of a community of scholars whose conversations and challenges over the years have contributed immensely to my understanding of case study research and helped shape my practice.

Some of my debts will be obvious, some less so, and there are some to whom I owe special thanks. I am deeply grateful to Barry MacDonald, CARE, and Bob Stake, CIRCE, champions of case study research at a time when it was uncharted territory in educational evaluation and research, for the opportunitites to develop the theory and practice of case study reserach; to other colleagues in these centres at various times – Rob Walker, Nigel Norris, John Elliott, Saville Kushner, Ernie House – for their colleagueship and shared field experience; and to all Cambridge conference colleagues for the stimulating dialogue exploring the changing field of evaluation.

I would also like to thank several generations of research students whose questions and discussion in seminars prompted me to write this book. In particular I thank Jane Payler, Rosie Flewitt, Elena Ioannidou and Susan Duke, who took time from their current busy lecturing and research lives to read the manuscript in draft. Your suggestions have greatly improved the text.

So many friends have also been immense support. It is not possible to name them all, but I do want to thank those who read the manuscript in part or whole in draft, Ruth Thomson, Sue Ebury, Veronique Chown, Claus Moser, and Judy Hicks, a colleague in collaborative arts inquiry, who read the entire manuscript with me and offered her astute critique and wisdom. Many supported in other ways with their patience in my temporary retreat from social life, and awarenesss of what it takes to finally get a manuscript to press. Conversations at critical times with Jennifer Greene, Georgie Parry-Crooke, Veronique, Judy and Sue gave me the impetus to complete. Their love and support have sustained me through the process.

I also thank Claire Lipscomb and Vanessa Hawood at Sage for their prompt and helpful responses to my queries and Patrick Brindle, Senior Editor at SAGE, for his gentle persuasion and unfailing support.

There are many more too numerous mention to whom I am equally grateful but who for confidentiality reasons I cannot name. To those who have been part of the cases I have studied, I owe a special debt and thanks. Case study research relies on the generosity and honesty of individuals in the case. I would like to acknowledge that my understanding of the approach has been greatly informed by their participation and challenges in the field, which have led to many of the reflections in this book.

PROLOGUE

This book is about the theory and practice of case study research. It tells how to construct, conduct and communicate the story of the case that is the subject of the research. 'Story' provides an integrating metaphor for the process of case study described in this book and the underlying narrative structure of the case. Every institution or programme has a story to tell about its origin, its development, its achievements at a particular time. Case study documents and interprets the complexity of that experience in its specific socio-political context.

Underlying this account of the process is the story of my experience as a case study researcher in education and related professional fields. I have written with students in mind, inspired by questions they have often asked about case study research and to dispel some myths that have arisen around the practice. Laura, a research student,[1] raised some of these concerns in the following letter.

Dear Helen

I wonder if you can help. I would like to undertake a case study for my thesis. I looked in the university library for good examples. What I found were many MA and PhD theses claiming to have conducted case study research, though it was not always clear what constituted a case study or what the case was. Some appeared to have taken an institution as a case, others an issue or a person. Quite a number had conducted a few interviews and observations in a setting and called it a case study. And several talked about case study as though it was a method in itself. Is this right? There was little evidence of having designed a study and analysed or interpreted the data and few mentioned ethics, which I think is rather important when people feature prominently in a case study.

I have further questions, which also worry my supervisor, concerning the extent to which I can generalize and theorize from the case and how to defend the accusations that case studies are 'too subjective' and not useful in policy-making. I am interested in these issues as I hope that my study will make a contribution to policy and practice. But these concerns can wait a little. The immediate help I require is with clarification of the concept, methods, design and analysis. How can I advance a legitimate case for case study that can be conducted with rigour and produce credible findings? Are there any references that would help? And how might I best get started?

Yours sincerely
Laura

Here is my reply.

Dear Laura

Thank you for your letter. The issues you raise are very familiar. Rather than try to squeeze an answer to your queries in a single response to your letter, I have decided to write a book to respond in more depth. Here is a brief outline of the contents.

Early chapters will focus on the concept and purpose of case study, design and methods. Here you will find the reference support you seek for the justification of the approach. The middle chapters will concentrate on the process itself, particularly the study of individuals, the 'self' as the main instrument of data gathering, and how to create and maintain ethical relationships in the field.

Further chapters address analysis and interpretation, reporting and writing in case study. Finally I will return to the issues you have raised on generalizing, theorizing, subjectivity and policy-making, and indicate how you can argue a case for each in the context of case study research.

How does this sound? Will this meet your needs?

Yours sincerely
Helen

With Laura's positive response to my outline, I began to write.

Note

1 Laura is a fictional student but the questions she raises in this letter are actual questions students have repeatedly asked in case study courses and in conducting a case study thesis.

INTRODUCTION

Concept of Case Study Research

Case study is a study of the singular, the particular, the unique. If you read Katherine Mansfield's short stories (Mansfield, 1987) you have the ideal prototype, in one sense, for case study. Mansfield's descriptions of incidents in everyday life closely resemble the 'thick description' (Geertz, 1973) and portrayal of particular events, circumstances and people advocated in case study research. However, there are different forms of case study and different reasons for their use.

My focus is on the evolution and practice of case study research in education and educational evaluation. Case study has a longer history of course. It has antecedents in the disciplines of sociology, anthropology, history and psychology and the professions of law and medicine, each of which has developed procedures for establishing the validity of case study for their respective purposes. The affinities with these disciplines are many in terms of methods, such as open-ended interviewing, participant observation and document analysis; and the focus on studying a single case in depth interpreted in a specific socio/cultural/political setting. I acknowledge these shared characteristics while at the same time explore the different procedures and justification for case study that arose in the context of educational research and evaluation in terms of its own logic and purpose.[1]

In the literature on case study different authors refer to case study as a method, a strategy, an approach, and not always consistently. I prefer the term 'approach', to indicate that case study has an overarching research intent and methodological (and political[2]) purpose, which affects what methods are chosen to gather data. 'Method' I reserve for techniques of research, such as interviewing and observing, 'strategy' for the processes (educational and ethical) by which we gain and maintain access to conduct, analyse and interpret the case. However, I recognize that others use these terms differently.

Purpose of Case Study Research

The primary purpose for undertaking a case study is to explore the particularity, the uniqueness, of the single case. Reference may be made to other cases – how else would we know what is unique? – but the essential task is to understand the distinctiveness of the individual case, what Lou Smith (1978) has referred to as a 'bounded system', MacDonald and Walker (1975) as an 'instance in action', and MacDonald[3] as an 'authenticated anecdote'. Each of these descriptors highlights a particular aspect of case study that I explore further in subsequent chapters – first, what is a case and what constitutes the boundary of a case; secondly, the 'lived experience' of particular individuals, programmes, projects; and thirdly, the unusual incident or vignette, carefully evidenced and validated, that offers insight into a specific instance or event. The 'authenticated anecdote' captures the idiosyncrasy of the particular, the need to provide evidence (an unauthenticated fragment will not do) and the inherent story-telling potential in the case study approach.

Focus of the Case

The case could be a person, a classroom, an institution, a programme, a policy, a system. Opinions differ on whether the net should be cast more widely to include, for example, processes, policies and events. Stake (1995) prefers to see the case as an integrated system focusing on specifics rather than generalities. 'The case is a specific, a complex, functioning thing' (p. 2). Merriam (1988: xiv) includes process. I am content with a wider focus to include policies and processes while retaining a commitment to the singularity and uniqueness of the policy or process.[4] Yin (1994) finds the focus on the specific object (a person or classroom) too broad, as 'Every study of entities qualifying as objects (e.g., people, organizations, and countries) would then be a case study regardless of the methodology used (e.g., psychological experiment, management survey, economic analysis)' (p. 17). This differentiates the concept of case study from those who draw their inspirations primarily from qualitative traditions, though Yin does not exclude qualitative methods from a study of the case.

Particular Perspective of Case Study Research

My focus in this book is on qualitative case study to understand the complexity of that 'instance in action', 'bounded system', or 'authenticated anecdote'. Subjective data are an integral part of the case. It is through analysis and interpretation of how people think, feel and act that many of the insights and understanding of the case are gained. It acknowledges that you are the main instrument in data gathering, interpretation and reporting. While this is significant in all forms of research, in a single case and with qualitative methods, the 'self' is more transparent, and it is important to monitor its impact on the research process and outcome. This is more than noting its inescapable influence in a preface. It is a rigorous exploration of how your values and actions shape data gathering and interpretation and how people and events in the field impact on you. You learn about yourself, in other words, as well as about the case.

Qualitative case study values multiple perspectives of stakeholders and participants, observation in naturally occurring circumstances, and interpretation in context. This is consonant with how I view the world and choose to understand it, that is, through the ways in which participants construct their worlds and how we and they interpret them. It is also influenced by the need, when I began case study research, to find alternative approaches to evaluating educational programmes to those that were drawn from a positivist, experimental tradition that assumed a different view of reality – one that was constant and could be measured objectively.

Two other perspectives are prominent. The first is the focus on education and the educative process of case study research. Education is the field in which most of the research cited in this book has been based, though examples are also drawn from cases in health and social care that have an educational focus. Education is also an aspiration in the conduct and dissemination of the case. Engagement in case study research should contribute to participants' self-knowledge and to their political knowledge of what it means to work in and between groups. Dissemination to audiences beyond the case allows others to learn from it to inform decision-making, policy and practice. This last aspiration resonates with a point both Merriam (1988: xiii) and Walker (1974: 77) have made in suggesting that qualitative case study is a particularly appropriate methodology for exploring problems of educational practice. Professional practitioners make judgements in concrete circumstances and 'naturally' explore 'instances in action'.

The second is the concept of the 'story of the case', which I alluded to in the Prologue. What I am referring to here, following House (1980),[5] is how we come to make sense of the case through determining its underlying structure and meaning. There is an ordering and understanding of events that tells a coherent story not in a chronological sense but through an integration of inferences and interpretations of events organized to tell a story of the whole (p. 104). This is not restricted to method – the story can be comprised of metaphors or statistics for example – and it can be implicit or explicit, but in order for implications to be drawn from the case, the story must be there (p. 111). It is also important to distinguish the 'story' from how it is told. Different ways to do this, including the use of documentary, poetic and dramatic forms, are explored in a later chapter.

While my perspective stresses understanding the qualitative nature of experience, it is important to acknowledge that case study research need not use only qualitative methods. Methodology does not define case study, as several authors have pointed out (Adelman et al., 1980; Stake, 1995; Yin, 1994), although it shapes the form of a particular study. It is possible to conduct a case study comprised of quantitative data, or from secondary sources as in a historical case study, and with a mix of methods.

The determining factors in deciding whether to use qualitative or quantitative methods are whether they facilitate an understanding of the particular case, what kind of inferences you can make from the data and how these are valued by different audiences for different purposes. The contemporary groundswell of interest in 'mixed methods' research (see, for example, Greene, 2007) addresses these different ways of making inferences from the data and combining/integrating them to inform policy and programme development. While case studies of the kind discussed in this book may be used in mixed method research, I do not pursue this angle here. My interest is the in-depth study of the single case using qualitative methods within a naturalistic paradigm.

How I Began

My story begins over thirty years ago in the late 1960s in Melbourne, Victoria, Australia, when case study in the field of educational research had yet to be established. My role, as an educational psychologist, was to advise schools on how to handle adolescents with learning or emotional difficulties. In the district in which I was based, an opportunity arose that changed the course of my professional life. The state of Victoria had recently adopted a new curriculum policy, which required a shift from a state-prescribed curriculum to the creation and implementation of a new integrated curriculum devised entirely by the school itself. I was interested in this development for the autonomy and responsibility it gave students and teachers to learn together and decided to explore how the initiative was interpreted in one particular school. I began to observe, not individual adolescents and their emotional or behavioural problems, but how the school as a whole managed the transition to a new curriculum and what effects it had on the principal, the teachers, the students, and on learning and teaching.

The dominant educational research paradigm at that time was experimental design, positing control groups with which to compare experimental groups in any new programme. Such a methodology was clearly inapplicable here. There were no control groups. The school was developing its own unique curriculum. My task became one of monitoring that development through a close description of how and what they did.

I did not set out to conduct a case study of that school or tell the story of that school's new venture. However, intuitively that is what happened as I watched, listened and documented how teachers planned and taught the new curriculum. I observed classrooms. I talked with teachers and students, alone or in groups, to see what they thought of the new curriculum in practice. I examined school records and any other documentation I could find to learn about the school before the change. These three methods, formally known as observation, interview and document analysis, are three of the major methods used in qualitative case study research.

When I moved to England I was fortunate to be able to continue to explore this way of documenting educational change, as Research Associate on the evaluation team of the Humanities Curriculum Project (HCP) based at the Centre for Applied Research in Education (CARE), University of East Anglia. The evaluation team was facing a similar problem of how to evaluate a broad aims programme – an innovative and unique curriculum – which was interpreted differently in different schools and for which no existing evaluation approaches were appropriate. The director of the evaluation, Barry MacDonald, decided to 'case' the schools to learn what he could from observing, listening and questioning how the project was played out in the cultures of different institutions. From here, it was a short step to developing the case study approach as a major element in the overall evaluation design. This had several components: a psychometric testing programme, a national survey of uptake of the innovation, and case studies of schools and the local education authorities in which they were located. I was the school case study researcher on the team. (For a full account of the evaluation design see MacDonald, 1971, [1973]).

Building on this experience I went on to conduct further case studies of other innovative programmes in education and health and social care. Several years later I began to explore the potential of case study for institutional development. This seemed a natural progression. External case study evaluation had shown that innovations were bound to fail if they did not allow for local cultural differences, did not acknowledge teachers and students as interpreters of curriculum, and ignored the politics of the institution. Schools had their own unique cultures that affected how innovations were received and implemented.

From my observations in the 'case' school mentioned above and several later cases, it also occurred to me that the qualitative methods of observing, interviewing and documentary analysis could be seen as an extension of the skills teachers use in teaching, when they observe, listen, question and make sense of documents and texts. These were the methods I used when I conducted my first case study. The parallel was obvious. Why should teachers and schools not conduct their own case study research? I decided to explore this avenue and in subsequent years, in addition to conducting external case study research of programmes and policies, provided research training for institutions to tell their own unique stories through case study research.

Concurrent with these developments at the practical level, I began to write about the theory and practice of case study research in education (Simons, 1971, 1981, [1977], 1987, 1996; Humble and Simons, 1978). These publications draw on the experience of conducting case studies and dilemmas encountered along the way. This book continues that practice of trying to capture experientially the theory and practice of case study research.

Structure of the Book

Given this focus, it seemed useful to organize the book in four sections to reflect the process of case study research from start to finish. There is a more complex reality in the doing of course. Chapters are interlinked and issues revisited in places to emphasize that the process is more iterative in practice than a linear structure suggests.

Case study memos throughout summarize essential features of each chapter to act as an aide-memoire for the process in practice. In many places I suggest several ways of reaching the same aim and offer choices to this end. This is deliberate. This is not a textbook to be followed in every detail. There is no right way to do case study research. While my preferences will be evident both in the main text and the memos, there are other decisions you can make. Stay open to what suits you and your research topic.

Section I: Getting Started

When we know *why* we want to conduct a case study, the *how* more easily follows. Chapter 1 examines how and why case study evolved in educational research and evaluation and discusses the concept of case study research that emerged in this context – its strengths and limitations. Chapter 2 explores issues of planning and design, how to gain access to the case and establish field relationships. Chapter 3 focuses on three methods commonly adopted in qualitative case study – interviewing, observing and document analysis – and presents practical guidance for data collection.

Section II: In the Field

Chapter 4, 'Who Are They?', draws attention to the central role of the person in case study research and the need to understand how individuals experience the programme, policy or organization. It suggests different ways of documenting the experience of individuals and the stories they tell. Chapter 5, 'Who Are We?', looks at the other side of the coin. It acknowledges that we are inevitably situated in the contexts we study and explores why case researchers need to be self-reflexive at all stages of the research process. It outlines processes for discovering different aspects of your 'self' in the specific case you are studying and for monitoring your subjectivity. Chapter 6, 'Whose Data Are They?', discusses the ethics of case study research. It presents the case for situated ethics, indicates how to establish and maintain trust in the field and gives examples of dilemmas that indicate the complexity of ethical decision-making in situated practice. Specific protocols are offered to guide ethical practice in the field.

Section III: Making Sense

The title of Chapter 7, 'Begin at the Beginning', reflects the fact that analysis and interpretation start at the outset and continue throughout the research process. It includes strategies for making sense of the data from different theoretical perspectives and a discussion of how to ensure the validity and credibility of your findings. Chapter 8, 'From Data to Story', offers examples of different analytic and interpretative strategies used in actual cases.

Section IV: Telling the Story

'Start at Any Point', the title of Chapter 9, indicates that telling a story of what you have found may have a quite different sequence from the one that led to your analysis and interpretation. It outlines different forms of reporting, including documentary, narrative and journalistic, and explores the boundaries between fiction and ways of telling the story that ensure the authenticity of the research data is retained. It also offers guidance on how to enhance your writing skills. Chapter 10 addresses the issues raised in the initial letter from Laura concerning generalizing, theorizing and policy-making in case study research, through attempting to dispel frequently cited myths around the practice. The Epilogue and final memo summarize key issues in case study research and extend a challenge to Laura and her fellow students to take the story on.

Notes

1 Case studies also exist in the fields of management, organizational development and policy studies but these are not my focus here. Nor are case studies generated solely for teaching purposes and which may or may not be based on authentic experience, case precedents, as in law, or individual case reports, as in psychology, social work or medicine.

2 Not all case study research has a political purpose. This is a reference to the democratic focus of my case study practice in evaluation and the intent in this context to provide evidence to facilitate decision-making professionally and publicly.
3 Personal communication, April 1974.
4 See Simons et al. (1998) for a case study of a national policy curriculum initiative.
5 In the context of evaluation, House (1980) has advocated that for minimum coherence every evaluation should tell a story. 'There must be either an explicit or tacit sequence of events (or more accurately, an interpretation of events) for the reader to use as a guide to valuing' (p. 102). This coherence extends to the use of imagery, dramatic structures and other aesthetic elements that appeal to emotional as well as cognitive ways of knowing. His argument is that both the story and the aesthetic elements contribute to overall coherence and that greater coherence makes the evaluation report more credible (pp. 104–105).

Section I
GETTING STARTED

1
EVOLUTION AND CONCEPT OF CASE STUDY RESEARCH

This chapter explores *how* and *why* case study came to be a significant research approach for the study of social and educational programmes and outlines different conceptions and types of case study, its strengths and limitations. If getting started practically is your main interest, you might choose to miss the early history, though part of the reasoning for the case study approach is embedded within it. I start by locating the emergence of case study in education within a broader social science and professional trend towards qualitative inquiry that has emerged over the past forty years.

The Move to Qualitative Inquiry

In the late 1960s and 1970s in the UK and the USA case study developed a significant following in educational research and evaluation for understanding the experience of curriculum innovation. Predominant models at that time, such as the objectives model and systems analysis, had failed to provide evidence to develop the programmes and adequately explain success or failure. Alternatives were needed that included participant perspectives, were responsive to audience needs, attentive to the process and dynamics of implementation and interpretation of events in their socio-political contexts. Case study was one of a number of approaches that embodied these features in reaching an understanding of specific curriculum projects. At that time it was necessary to argue the case for alternative models to those drawn from positivist research.[1] Now case study is widely accepted as a research approach for evaluating complex educational innovations in specific contexts (Simons, 1980) and social and educational phenomena in general (Merriam, 1988; Stake, 1995).

This development of case study in educational research and evaluation, which is explored in more detail in the next section of this chapter, was paralleled by a renaissance of ethnographic research in sociology and of humanistic research in psychology, all part of that broad movement of qualitative inquiry in the social sciences that has evolved over the past forty years, and which Denzin and Lincoln, writing in 1994, referred to as 'a quiet methodological revolution' (p. ix). The practice of case study research (as distinct from professional case histories) has also extended to other practice professions, particularly nursing (Treacy and Hyde, 1999), health care (Dowell et al., 1995), social work (Shaw and Gould, 2001) and medicine (Greenhalgh, 1999; Greenhalgh and Worrall, 1997).

As a result of this 'quiet methodological revolution' we now have an extensive methodological literature on qualitative inquiry: see Denzin and Lincoln (1994) for a comprehensive account of the various forms and processes of qualitative research; Guba and Lincoln (1985, 1989) for arguments justifying qualitative inquiry *vis-à-vis* other forms of inquiry; and Silverman (2000) and Flick (1998), to note just two examples of many, for specific qualitative research methodological texts. See also Flick (2007) for the Sage eight-volume set of qualitative research texts. Given the wealth of this literature, I do not repeat here all the arguments that were necessary to advocate the case for qualitative case study as distinct from positivist forms of research in the study of social settings.

Case study, in common with other forms of qualitative inquiry, shares many of the same epistemological arguments and methods of fieldwork adopted in sociological and anthropological traditions. It cannot, however, be equated with qualitative research. Much qualitative research is not case study and case study can incorporate methods other than qualitative. While acknowledging this shared tradition, the focus in this chapter is on how we can characterize case study and its potential as a research approach, starting with the reasons why this development was necessary in educational evaluation.

Evolution of Case Study Research in Educational Evaluation[2]

Locating current practice of case study in this historical context is important for two reasons. First, as I have already indicated, the researcher is the main instrument in collecting and interpreting data. So it is with creating text. It is important to indicate in what contexts I have conducted case study so you can see what has influenced my understanding and shaped my practice. Secondly, it is easy to forget the origins for the growth of case study research now that we are familiar with its practice over several decades. It is useful to recall what problems it was designed to solve and why existing models at the time were inappropriate or inadequate to the task. Many of these problems still exist and many of the models advocated then are re-emerging as dominant approaches for conducting research in education (see Lather, 2004; Lincoln and Canella, 2004).

In the late 1960s and 1970s, in the context of evaluation, the task was to determine the effects of social and education programmes in order to inform decision-making and improve social and educational action. Evaluations were primarily experimental, quasi-experimental and survey, utilizing quantitative outcome measures of programme effectiveness (House, 1993: 5). Such approches failed to capture the complexity of these programmes in practice and provide adequate evidence as basis for action (Norris, 1993; Simons, 1987).

Many programmes were specific and innovative. No comparative control groups could be established to make sense of an experimental design, no benchmarks of 'normal' practice existed with which to compare the innovation, and focusing on pre/post testing as the sole indicator of the worth of the programme clearly fell short of representing the programme in action. It was not sufficient to indicate solely what learning gains were achieved by testing learning outcomes. Developers, stakeholders and other audiences needed to know how results were achieved, why some succeeded where others did not, and what the key factors were in the particular setting that led to the precise outcomes. Without such explanation results were inadequate to inform development, policy or practice and were potentially unfair.

Broadening the database – multiple data/multiple perspectives

In the USA, Stake (1967a) was the first to suggest that evaluators needed to widen their database and to rethink the role of evaluation itself. In his introduction to the inaugural issue of AERA Monographs on Evaluation, Stake wrote of the need for evaluators to tell the programme story, setting in motion a 'reconceptualisation of the evaluation task in terms of more idiographic traditions of research, and away from the idea of curriculum developments as poorly designed experiments in student learning' (Simons, 1987: 9).

Stake's 'countenance' paper, published in the same year (Stake 1967b), was aptly titled to reflect the changing face of evaluation. Here he drew attention to the need to include antecedent data, data about transactions and judgements, and data on outcomes in order to '*tell the programme story*'. Further papers argued for portrayal of the programme *vis-à-vis* analysis (Stake, 1972) and the need to be responsive to issues identified by stakeholders and participants iteratively throughout the evaluation (Stake, 1975).

In the UK around the same time, it was also evident that different data were needed to understand how curriculum programmes fared in action. In the evaluation of the Humanities Curriculum Project, MacDonald (1971) was developing the case study approach to capture the complexity of innovation and meet the needs of decision-makers. Having found from early fieldwork that generalizations derived from previous studies of schools and innovation did not fit, he set about documenting how the programme was implemented in the particular context of each institution – interviewing key players, observing classrooms, capturing images of the context, exploring the surrounding milieu. In doing so, he paid attention to the culture of the institution, its previous history, styles of teaching, patterns of staff mobility, experience and confidence, staff–student relationships and student reception of the new curricula as well as their achievements.

This early foray into how the project played out in particular schools led him to formulate a rationale for the case study design element of the evaluation that took account of the variability of human action in institutions and the different influences that determine it, the interrelationships of acts and consequences, the judgements of those within, and the possible different perceptions of the goals and purposes of the programme held by those who designed the programme and those who implemented it. From here it was a short step to conducting detailed case studies that provided evidence of these effects in context to inform decision-making and explain success or failure.

Both these authors were forerunners of the evaluation case study movement in educational evaluation in their respective countries. MacDonald was later to be joined at CARE by Rob Walker, who contributed to further development of case study research, particularly in rethinking the use of case study in educational settings, and exploring methodological innovations in observation (video and film, for example), use of photographs and novel formats for reporting. From these early beginnings, these authors began to articulate and theorize the concept of case study in educational evaluation and research (MacDonald, 1971; MacDonald and Walker, 1974, 1975; Stake, 1980, [1978], 1995; Walker, 1974).

Around the same time in the mid-1970s support for the case study approach in educational evaluation came from two unexpected quarters and 1975 seemed to be a critical year. Donald Campbell, an experimentalist and measurement specialist, in the 1960s had limited the use of case study to exploratory studies and questioned their scientific value because of the lack of control and high probability of bias (Campbell and Stanley, 1966: 6–7). Yet in 1975, in an exploratory paper, '"Degrees of freedom" and the case study' (also published, with minor editorial change, in Cook and Reichardt, see Campbell, 1979), he had modified this view to recognize his early 'strong rejection of the single case study' (Campbell, 1979: 56) and the contribution of qualitative knowing to social action.[3]

In 1975 also, Lee Cronbach published a paper in which he argued that the two disciplines of scientific psychology (experimental and correlational research) were inadequate to meet contemporary needs for knowledge of social programmes, failing to account for contextual factors of time and place and the uncontrolled nature of complex social situations. Indicating a need for descriptive studies, Cronbach suggested that instead of making generalization the ruling consideration in our research we reverse our priorities and observe and interpret effects in context (p. 123). 'As he [the observer] goes from situation to situation, his first task is to describe and interpret the effect anew in each locale, perhaps taking into account factors unique to that locale … That is, generalization comes late, and the exception is taken as seriously as the rule' (p. 125).

These observations from two leading psychologists of what was needed to understand social programmes gave further warrant for pursuing the case study approach in educational evaluation.

Further Evolution of the Case Study Approach

The Nuffield conferences

This early development of case study research was taken forward in a number of conferences over the next thirty years between US and UK evaluators sponsored primarily by the Nuffield Foundation to explore alternative styles of evaluation. The first conference was devoted to reasons for the emergence of alternative styles, the second to case study itself and the third to naturalistic inquiry, the umbrella term that came to be adopted to cover a range of different qualitative approaches. These included case study (MacDonald and Walker, 1975), responsive evaluation (Stake, 1975), transactional evaluation (Rippey, 1973), illuminative evaluation (Parlett and Hamilton, 1976). What these approaches had in common was a focus on documenting complexity, interpreting in context, observing in natural social conditions and communicating in the natural language of participants. Later conferences focused on policy implications, assessment and appraisal, and the postmodern trend. These Nuffield conferences are well documented and mark the developmental path of alternative approaches to evaluation (see Elliott and Kushner (2007) for an extensive account of their outcomes and publications).

Case study was one way of conceptualizing an alternative methodological approach to evaluating a *particular* programme or policy. Parlett and Hamilton (1976), the authors of illuminative evaluation, conceptualized this methodological shift as a move away from an agricultural botany model (related to experimental design and pre/post testing) to a social-anthropological model. While not advocating a case study approach, illuminative evaluation, with its emphasis on contextual understanding, people and places, and qualitative methods, had a strong affinity with the case study approach for understanding educational innovation in naturalistic settings.

Political dimension

Beyond methodology, but closely connected with it, were other reasons for a shift to case study related to the purpose and role of evaluation in a democratic society. I want now to explore this dimension further to illustrate how the methodology and political purpose are linked. The purposes are many but are generally recognized to fall into three broad categories – accountability, development (of the institution or agency) and knowledge. The major role is to inform and promote public decision-making (Chelimsky, 2006; Greene, 2000). In exploring this link with methodology, there are three particular points to keep in mind about the nature of the evaluation field.

First, evaluation is about judgement, determining the merit or worth of a programme. Different methodologies consider the role of judgement in different ways. So there are methodological choices to make about how to determine worth (and these have political implications), and there are political decisions to make about whose role it is to do that. Is it for evaluators to decide the worth of a programme on the basis of evidence and their scientific judgement? Is it for audiences in relation to decisions they have to make or problems to solve? Or is it for the wider public to whom the results are disseminated to facilitate their contribution to policy debate?

Secondly, evaluation is inherently political, concerned with the distribution of power and the allocation of resources and opportunities in society. Evaluation has consequences for who gets what, whose interests are served in an evaluation, who stands to gain or lose by the findings of an evaluation. Thirdly, to be fair and offer a sound basis for informed action, evaluation is, or should be, independent of particular interests. It should be an impartial information service to all stakeholders, participants and the public on the value of the policy or programme to enable them to contribute to informed policy-making and debate (Simons, 2006: 245–246).

In the developing alternative evaluation tradition there was a growing awareness of the need for a shift in the power of research relationships away from regarding the evaluator as the sole judge of what was worthwhile to acknowledge the perspectives of participants in the case and the judgements of those who have decisions to make in policy or practice contexts. This shift in the locus of judgement was articulated by MacDonald (1976) in his political model of democratic evaluation, which emphasizes participant judgement and engagement in the process of evaluation and dissemination to a range of audiences. It is also reflected in Stake's (1975) concept of responsive evaluation which, as its name suggests, is responsive to stakeholder and participant identification of issues and refinement and validation throughout the evaluation.

The case study approach is useful in this context. It involves and is accessible to multiple audiences. Using qualitative methods, it can document participant and stakeholder perspectives, engage them in the process, and represent different interests and values in the programme. Case study reports that are issue-focused, comprised of naturalistic observations, interview data and written in the language of participants allow access to findings that others can recognize and use as a basis for informed action. There was, as Kushner (2000) has put it, 'a natural fit between this political ethic and case study methodologies' (p. 6). This is why, as I have argued elsewhere (Simons, 1980), case study in the context of evaluation is far from a straight 'lift' from the idiographic traditions of social science. It has to be seen within the complex nexus of political, methodological and epistemological convictions that constitute the field of evaluation (Simons, 1987: 62).

The fact that this shift in methodology and the role of evaluation in society occurred on both sides of the Atlantic at the same time, initially without knowledge of the other, indicates that it was not simply a one-off response to a local or national need. It represented a major sea-change in how evaluation could be conceived to contribute to social and political action. To some, it signified a more direct participatory, if not transformative, role for certain groups in society (see, for instance, Greene, 1994; Lincoln, 1995).

This then is a brief outline of how and why case study came to prominence in the field of evaluation and why the alternative forms of evaluation evolved to evaluate innovative curriculum programmes. For further discussion on the evolution of case study in evaluation see Simons (1987) and on the history of qualitative evaluation in general, Greene and McClintock (1991), Guba and Lincoln (1981, 1989), Patton (1997) and House (1993). Further challenges have arisen through the practice of case study research and these will be considered in later chapters.

Definitions and Types of Case Study Research

The previous section focused on case study in the context of evaluation. From this point on I shall refer to case study research more broadly – that process of conducting systematic, critical inquiry into a phenomenon of choice and generating understanding to contribute to cumulative public knowledge of the topic. This is a different purpose from the role of evaluation in democratic society outlined above, though some forms of research, such as action research and participatory research, share similar aspirations. For the most part I will be discussing the conduct of case study research of programmes, projects, organizations and policies, not persons, although in Chapter 4 I explore the role of individuals within the case and in Chapter 5, the reflexive role of the case researcher herself.

Seeking to define what is a case study

Case study, as several authors have pointed out (Gomm et al., 2004; Merriam, 1988; Stake 1995), has different meanings for different people and in different disciplines. In seeking to characterize what case study is, some authors start by comparing it with other social research approaches. For example, Gomm et al. (2004: 2–4) note that the term is employed to identify a specific form of inquiry which contrasts with the experiment or social survey on several dimensions, the most important of which are the number of cases investigated and the amount of detailed information collected about each. Other features of comparison include the degree of control over the variables/issues investigated, the kind of data and the way they are analysed, and how inferences are drawn. In case study, the data are often unstructured, the analysis qualitative and the aim is to understand the case itself rather than generalize to a whole population (pp. 2–4).

Others start by indicating what case study research is not. Adelman et al. (1980), for instance, indicate that case studies should not be equated with observational studies (which would rule out historical case studies), are not simply pre-experimental (understandings are significant in their own right) and are not defined by methodology (many methods can be used) (p. 48). Merriam (1988) notes its difference from case work, case method (as a teaching device), case history and case work (in social work and medicine, for example) (p. 15).

This exploration is helpful in clarifying the scope and focus of case study. In the next section I try to characterize the concept more distinctively, so we have a clear sense of what it is before examining the process and to help you justify a case study research approach for your thesis or project. While precise definitions are difficult because of the variation in use described above, below are four characterizations of the concept from leading proponents of case study research.

Definitions of case study

The first is from Stake (1995). 'Case study is the study of the particularity and complexity of a single case, coming to understand its activity within important circumstances' (p. xi). In outlining his view of case study, Stake indicates that he draws from naturalistic, holistic, ethnographic, phenomenological and biographic research methods. He does not pay as much attention to quantitative case studies that emphasize a battery of measurements or to case studies designed for teaching purposes, such as in law and business. These, he says, are special topics deserving books of their own. His focus is on disciplined, qualitative inquiry into the single case. 'The qualitative researcher emphasizes episodes of nuance, the sequentiality of happenings in context, the wholeness of the individual' (p. xii).

In referring to different purposes for case study and different disciplines that use the term, Stake reminds us of two important points. First, that it is important if you choose case study as your research approach to acknowledge the tradition you are drawing upon. Secondly, that case study is not synonymous with qualitative methods. This was noted earlier but is worth emphasizing here. It is a common misunderstanding. While case studies of the kind I am discussing in this book tend to use qualitative methods, this does not define them. What defines a case study is its singularity – of the phenomenon being studied. Choice of method is related but it is a different point.

The second definition is from MacDonald and Walker (1975).

> Case study is the examination of an instance in action. The choice of the word 'instance' is significant in this definition, because it implies a goal of generalisation. We might say that case study is that form of research where n = 1, only that would be misleading, because the case study method lies outside the discourse of mathematical experimentalism that has dominated Anglo-American educational research. (p. 2)

What MacDonald and Walker are drawing attention to here is the tradition of social science research that acknowledges the possibility of generalizing from the particular, where studying the particular in depth can yield insights of universal significance. In highlighting the process through which such insights emerge, they indicate that case study calls for a 'fusion of the styles of the artist and the scientist' (p. 3). 'Case study is the way of the artist, who achieves greatness when, through the portrayal of a single instance locked in time and circumstance, he communicates enduring truths about the human condition. For both the scientist and artist content and intent emerge in form' (p. 3). Inspirations for these authors stem primarily from a qualitative social science tradition, and they aspire to artistic and literary forms of re-presenting and communicating findings.

The third definition, from Merriam (1988), is similar to the two above in its emphasis on the qualitative, the particular and the singular, as well as drawing attention to a major mode of reasoning in making sense of data. 'The qualitative case study can be defined as an intensive, holistic description and analysis of a single entity, phenomenon or social unit. Case studies are particularistic, descriptive, and heuristic and rely heavily on inductive reasoning in handling multiple data sources' (p. 16).

In this fourth definition, Yin (1994) continues the practice noted earlier of describing the characteristics of case study compared with other research strategies and what each can achieve.

> *A case study is an empirical inquiry that*
> - investigates a contemporary phenomenon within its real-life context, especially when
> - the boundaries between phenomenon and context are not clearly evident. (p. 13)

However, because it is not always possible to distinguish between phenomenon and context in 'real-life' situations, he points out that other characteristics become part of the technical definition. A case study inquiry would explore many variables of interest, rely on multiple sources of evidence and 'prior development of theoretical propositions to guide the collection of data' (p. 13). In this definition, case study is not defined by object or particularity but is a comprehensive research strategy, incorporating specific data collection and analysis approaches to investigate phenomena in real-life contexts.

I have selected these four definitions of case study to illustrate different emphases. What they have in common is a commitment to studying a situation or phenomenon in its 'real life' context, to understanding complexity, and to defining case study other than by methods (qualitative or otherwise). Differences relate to philosophical, methodological and epistemological preferences.

My own definition of case study is similar to the first two above though I phrase it slightly differently and extend it to include the purpose and research focus. Case study is an in-depth exploration from multiple perspectives of the complexity and uniqueness of a particular project, policy, institution, programme or system in a 'real life' context. It is research-based, inclusive of different methods and is evidence-led. The primary purpose is to generate in-depth understanding of a specific topic (as in a thesis), programme, policy, institution or system to generate knowledge and/or inform policy development, professional practice and civil or community action.[4]

Types of Case Study

Intrinsic, instrumental, collective

Stake (1995) distinguishes three types of case study: *intrinsic*, where a case is studied for the intrinsic interest in the case itself; *instrumental*, where a case is chosen to explore an issue or research question determined on some other ground, that is, the case is chosen to gain insight or understanding into something else; and *collective*, where several cases are studied to form a collective understanding of the issue or question (pp. 3–4). The point of making these distinctions, he says, is not because it is useful to sort case studies into categories but because the methods used will be different depending upon intrinsic or instrumental interests (p. 4). The same is true for the brief descriptions that follow of other types of case study. Methods will differ according to the type and the purpose for conducting the case study.

Further types and categories

To these three types we may add those indicated by Bassey (1999), in a reconstruction of educational case study, where he categorizes case studies as theory-seeking and theory-testing, story-telling and picture-drawing, and evaluative; and those by Merriam (1988), who characterizes types of case study from their discipline framework but also by the nature of how they are written up – descriptive, interpretative, evaluative. Yin (1994), in the context of evaluation research, notes five categories – explanatory, descriptive, illustrative, exploratory and 'meta-evaluation' – that is, a study of an evaluation study. The most important of these, he says, is explanatory, 'to *explain* the causal links in real-life interventions that are too complex for the survey or experimental strategies' (p. 15). It is not my intention here to discuss all these types in detail – the descriptors, for the most part, are self-evident – nor examine overlaps between them (see Bassey, 1999 for discussion of their similarities). I do, however, wish to highlight three of a more general kind.

Theory-led or theory-generated case study

Theory-led case study has different meanings. Theory-led can mean exploring, or even exemplifying, a case through a particular theoretical perspective or, as in programme evaluation case study, exploring at the outset what the theory of the programme is – what it is aspiring to achieve in order to focus and design the evaluation. If taking this approach, it is important to stay open to eliciting what the actual theory of the case may be in practice. This is not the same as testing a specific theory or taking a specific theoretical lens to the study. It is determining a specific theory of the programme to guide data collection in the case.

Theory-generated refers to generating theory arising from the data itself, whether this is through a classic grounded theory approach (Glaser and Strauss, 1967), a constructivist grounded theory approach (Charmaz, 2006) or some other interpretative lens that leads to an eventual theory of the case.

Evaluation case study

Evaluation case study of public programmes has several imperatives. These relate to the discussion on the political dimension raised earlier. An evaluation case study needs, first and foremost, to discern the value of the programme or project that constitutes the case. How you do this will depend on which political stance you choose. It could be solely your judgement of value based on the evidence, or, if adopting a democratic or social justice perspective, it would include how different people and interest groups valued the programme. Within a democratic perspective you would also engage participants in the process and ensure that the final case study was disseminated to audiences beyond the programme.

Secondly, given the role of evaluation to inform decision-making, an evaluation case study needs to be responsive to multiple stakeholder and audience information needs and maintain effective negotiations with key participants throughout the process. In funded evaluation of public programmes, this may extend to stakeholders and programme commissioners having a say in what issues are explored and which methodologies are used.

Thirdly, as many evaluation studies have consequences for who gets what in society when resources are reallocated on the basis of evaluation findings, it is important to include and balance all interests fairly and justly in the programme.

Ethnographic case study

Ethnographic case study has its origins in an anthropological or sociological tradition. This type of case study uses qualitative methods, such as participant observation, to gain close-up descriptions of the context and is concerned to understand the case in relation to a theory or theories of culture. It can be conducted in different timescales, in familiar or unfamiliar cultures and increasingly uses a wider range of methods than in classic ethnography. In this sense it differs from ethnographic research *per se*, which traditionally has involved long-time immersion in the field in societies beyond our own, even though it is now widely conducted in familiar as well as 'strange' cultures. In contemporary educational and social research shorter ethnographic studies are sometimes referred to as micro-ethnography (see, for example, Ball, 1987) to distinguish them from a full ethnography. However, these are not necessarily case studies in the sense of a bounded system, or 'instance in action' as described earlier. While sharing methods in common with classic ethnography, such as participant observation and interviewing, ethnographic case studies focus on a *particular* project or programme, though still aspiring to understand the case in its socio-cultural context and with concepts of culture in mind.

Summary of Strengths and Limitations

From the conduct of case study research over several decades, it is possible to summarize its key strengths and note what problems or limitations people perceive or have experienced in practice.

Strengths

- Case study using qualitative methods in particular enables the experience and complexity of programmes and policies to be studied in depth and interpreted in the precise socio-political contexts in which programmes and policies are enacted.
- Case study can document multiple perspectives, explore contested viewpoints, demonstrate the influence of key actors and interactions between them in telling a story of the programme or policy in action. It can explain how and why things happened.
- Case study is useful for exploring and understanding the process and dynamics of change. Through closely describing, documenting and interpreting events as they unfold in the 'real life' setting, it can determine the factors that were critical in the implementation of a programme or policy and analyse patterns and links between them.
- Case study is flexible, that is, neither time-dependent nor constrained by method. It can be conducted in a few days, months or over several years and be written up in different forms and lengths appropriate to the timescale. It is responsive to shifts in focus and the unanticipated consequences of programmes in action. It can include a range of methods, whatever is most appropriate in understanding the case.
- Case studies written in accessible language, including vignettes and cameos of people in the case, direct observation of events, incidents and settings, allows audiences of case study reports to vicariously experience what was observed and utilize their tacit knowledge in understanding its significance.
- Case study has the potential to engage participants in the research process. This is both a political and epistemological point. It signals a potential shift in the power base of who controls knowledge and recognizes the importance of co-constructing perceived reality through the relationships and joint understandings we create in the field. It also provides an opportunity for researchers to take a self-reflexive approach to understanding the case and themselves.

Potential limitations

To provide balance and signal some issues that will be discussed in later chapters, I indicate here what some have seen as potential weaknesses of the case study approach. Often these centre on the mass of data accumulated that is difficult to process, reports that are too long and detailed for stakeholders to read and narratives that over-persuade.

Reflecting on his practice of case study in curriculum research, Walker (1986) has noted three issues which caused him to think again about claims for this approach – the uncontrolled intervention that case study research is in the lives of others, the distorted picture it can give of the way things are, and its essential conservatism – the case study is locked in time while the people in it have moved on.

Further concerns focus around the personal involvement and/or subjectivity of the researcher, the way in which inferences are drawn from the single case and the validity and usefulness of the findings to inform policy.

I appreciate and recognize these concerns, yet I do not see all of them as necessarily limitations of the approach. It is often a question of how they are perceived and interpreted. Several are addressed in subsequent chapters. Suggestions for how to make sense of the mass of data are offered in Chapters 7 and 8; how to improve reporting so it is accessible and authentic in Chapter 9; how to be sensitive to our interventions in people's lives in Chapter 6. Exploring and disciplining subjectivity is discussed in Chapter 5, and the issues of how to draw inferences and use case study to inform policy-making in Chapter 10. However, there are five brief points I wish to make at this point.

First, in the conception of case study discussed in this book, the subjectivity of the researcher is an inevitable part of the frame. It is not seen as a problem but rather, appropriately monitored and disciplined, as essential in understanding and interpreting the case. Too much personal involvement, however, can be a problem and this is examined in Chapter 5.

Secondly, while the reports we write cannot capture (hold) the reality as lived (and in this sense are always historical), there is much we can do to highlight the timing of the study, the partial nature of interpretations and the conditions of their construction so readers can make their own judgements about their relevance and significance.

Thirdly, there are a number of ways to make inferences from a case or cases that are applicable to other contexts. These are not stated as formal propositions or generalizations as in random sample surveys or experimental design research. They stem from a qualitative database and appeal more to tacit and situated understanding for their link to other cases and settings.

Fourthly, the usefulness of findings for policy determination is partly dependent upon acceptance of the different ways in which validity is established and findings are communicated in case study research.

Finally, it is important to state that in many situations in which case study research is conducted, formal generalization for policy-making is not the aim. The aim is particularization – to present a rich portrayal of a single setting to inform practice, establish the value of the case and/or add to knowledge of a specific topic. These issues of subjectivity, generalization and utility for policy-making are explored further in the final chapter. Now it is time to get started. The next two chapters focus respectively on the practicalities of planning and designing the case and choosing methods for your study.

Case Study Memo 1 Concept, Type and Justification for Case Study Research

- Think through the different types and purposes of case study and the origins from which each stems. This should strengthen how you justify the type you choose.
- Decide what kind of case study you will conduct for what purpose, and what issues or questions it will help you address.
- Acknowledge the particular tradition in which you are locating your case study.
- Justify why your choice is the best approach for the topic and purpose of your research.
- Demonstrate an awareness of any potential difficulties you might encounter and how you would address these in your research.
- Do not spend too much time arguing why you have not chosen other research approaches. This may be helpful to a degree. However, the more important point is to present a convincing argument for why case study research is most appropriate for your research topic.
- Consider the timescale you have in which to conduct the study and what difference this makes to the type you choose, for example ethnographic, evaluative, theory-based or intrinsic, instrumental, collective.
- Think about the political implications of the type you choose and the consequences for those in the case – who will benefit, who might not.
- Reflect on what type of case study report your main audience would find useful, for example, descriptive, interpretative, evaluative, explanatory.
- If considering case study for your thesis, decide whether it will be part of your thesis or the whole and how you would justify your decision. Think carefully about whether collective case study is viable. Students frequently opt for two cases thinking that comparison is helpful. It can be, but often is not needed. One case in depth may give you the information you need.

Notes

1. The shortfalls of methodologies stemming from a positivist tradition for evaluating and understanding social programmes are outlined in the manifesto from the first Cambridge conference (MacDonald and Parlett, 1973), which brought together US and UK evaluators to explore alternative forms of evaluation. The manifesto also indicated what changes in methodology were required at that time for future effective evaluation.
2. In this section I have drawn on Chapter 1 in Simons (1987), which outlines how the field of evaluation evolved. My focus here is only on those factors that led to the need for a case study research approach.
3. It is important to note that in this 1975 paper, '"Degrees of freedom" and the case study', Campbell was writing in the context of comparative political studies, where he regarded the single cultural study as the dominant mode of inquiry. While not entirely persuaded of qualitative forms of knowing, Campbell acknowledges both in this paper and elsewhere (Campbell, 1976, 1979) the lack of attention to qualitative evidence in quantitative evaluation studies and that science depends upon qualitative, common-sense knowing even though at best it goes beyond this. In the conclusion to his 1975 paper he states that methodologists 'must achieve an applied epistemology which integrates both [quantitative and qualitative forms of knowing]. I am indebted to Nigel Norris for this understanding.

Those who discuss the early use of triangulation in social research often draw attention to Campbell's early work in integrating these different forms of knowing (see, for example, Greene, 2007; Stake, 1995).

4   For further discussion of the concept of case study and reasons for its emergence as a research approach in educational research and evaluation, see Simons (1980).

Further Readings

Bassey, M. (1999) *Case Study Research in Educational Settings*. Buckingham: Open University Press.

An examination of case study in educational settings locating the concept within educational research and exploring concepts of generalization and theory development. Chapter 3 provides an overview of how others have defined case study and Chapter 6 presents the author's own reconstruction of educational case study, with a useful checklist of key characteristics (see p. 58).

Gomm, R., Hammersley, M. and Foster, P. (eds) (2004) *Case Study Method: Key Issues, Key Texts*. London: Sage.

This edited collection covers more than the concept of case study, the focus of this section of readings, but it is included here for two reasons. It has an excellent extended annotated bibliography of major texts on case study (pp. 250–70), including those listed here. Its division into two major sections on case study and generalizability and case study and theory outline much of the debate around these topics. It will be useful to be aware of this throughout the process and in deciding what position to take on these issues.

Merriam, S.B. (1988) *Case Study Research in Education: A Qualitative Approach*. San Francisco, CA: Jossey–Bass.

Focuses specifically on the field of education and qualitative case study, with an interest in what can be learned from the case study approach for professional practice. Chapters 1 and 2 focus respectively on defining the concept, types and uses of case study research, its strengths and limitations as a research design.

Ragin, C. (1992) 'Cases of "What is Case?"', in C. Ragin and H. Becker (eds), *What is a Case: Exploring the Foundations of Social Enquiry*. Cambridge: Cambridge University Press. pp. 1–17.

Outlines four different approaches to defining what a case is – by object, through discovery (within the case), theoretical constructs that emerge from the study, and by convention or consensus of a common concept.

Simons, H. (ed.) (1980) *Towards a Science of the Singular: Essays about Case Study in Educational Research and Evaluation*. Occasional Publications No. 10. Norwich: University of East Anglia, Centre for Applied Research in Education.

The first five chapters demarcate the distinctiveness of case study compared with other forms of social inquiry. Later chapters focus on ethics and reporting in case study.

Stake, R.E. (1995) *The Art of Case Study Research*. Thousand Oaks, CA: Sage.

Explores the central precepts and process of qualitative case study with illustrated examples from an actual case. Chapter 1 provides a succinct conceptualization of the distinctiveness of case study research drawing a distinction between three main types – intrinsic, instrumental and collective case study.

Yin, R.K. (1994) *Case Study Research: Design and Methods.* London: Sage.
An examination of case study as a research strategy. The introduction and first chapter indicates the range of research situations for which case study is appropriate compared with other research methods.

2

PLANNING, DESIGNING, GAINING ACCESS

What determines how you choose a case and what methods you adopt to explore it? How might you focus your research topic? What kind of relationship do you hope to establish with participants? And what do you need to do to ensure that you get off to a good start in the field? These are the questions this chapter explores. It offers guidance for choosing a case, identifying key questions, selecting methods, choosing a role and gaining access to the field.

Preliminary Planning

Quite a lot of planning is needed before you choose a case, or if the case is a given, in determining how the case study will be designed and conducted. This includes getting a deeper understanding of your topic, the merits of different methods and thinking about how you will relate to participants in the field.

A major preliminary consideration is deciding whether the case study design is in fact appropriate for the phenomenon or topic you wish to explore. If you need help with this, Yin (1994) has a useful guideline. He indicates that case studies are likely to be 'the preferred strategy when "how" or "why" questions are being posed, when the investigator has little control over events and when the focus is on a contemporary phenomenon within some real-life context' (p. 1). I am assuming you have been through this stage and decided case study is the appropriate approach for your topic and that what we can now explore is how to define and design the case itself.[1]

Defining the case

In deciding on a case study design you will have refined to some degree the nature of the problem or activity you wish to investigate. You may have come to this through a reading of the relevant literature, identifying issues in a study conducted by someone else, or through your own thinking. You do not need to circumscribe the study precisely but it does need to go beyond a general interest in the topic to a specific statement of the research focus. This is often referred to as the 'research problem', not in the sense of something that is difficult but rather something that is challenging, unknown or contested. Identifying what this is sharpens the focus and you can then choose the unit of analysis – the case – that best enables you to explore the problem.

However, formulating a 'research problem' is not the only way to decide what the case is. Leaving aside the issue of where the case is a given, it may be that you will choose a case in which you have an intrinsic interest. Here there is often no statement of a problem but a general intent to understand what is happening in the case.

Boundaries of the case

Another way of defining the case is to decide what constitutes the 'bounded system'. This is a single unit of analysis – a class, institution, project, or programme. In some cases there may be sub-elements and instances within it. For example, in a collective case study of the impact of curriculum innovation,[2] the overall case was the medium-term impact of centrally developed curriculum projects, the sub-elements were case studies of four schools and, within each of these, explorations of the uptake of the same four projects. Each school was written up as a case. Yet each also served as a database for the overarching case – the impact of centrally developed curriculum projects.

Opinions differ on whether it is necessary to define the boundary of the case at the beginning of your research. Personally, I think it helps to think through what you think your study is a case of. However, you need to be aware that this may change once you enter the field and gain a realistic sense of where to draw the boundary to most effectively research the topic you are exploring. You may need to conceptualize the case differently to match what you find. The boundaries may also shift in the course of conducting the study and once you begin the analysis.

In the following example, the boundary of the case had to shift from the school to the local education authority (LEA) in which the school was located. Case studies were part of a national evaluation of a major curriculum project that was dependent for its successful implementation in schools on financial and advisory support from a local education authority (LEA).[3] The school was chosen as the unit of analysis as this was where the curriculum was being implemented and it also provided the context in which to interpret student test results – another element in the research design. However, early fieldwork indicated that in order to understand why the curriculum appeared to be more successful in some schools and LEAs than others, the boundary of the case needed to shift from the school to explore the possible differential support of the local education authority. The case studies then became studies of the implementation of curriculum innovation in each associated local education authority.

There are various factors to consider in setting the boundaries of your case. These extend beyond physical location, such as a classroom or an institution, to include people, policies and histories. Is a school, for example, comprised of teachers and students only? Or does it include parents and teaching assistants? Is a policy defined only through its documentation or does it include the history and motivations of those who conceived it and the interpretation of those who implemented it? Is it possible to understand the function of a particular institution without an understanding of its previous history?

While boundaries can usually be set early on, in some instances, especially when unintended major political shifts require a refocus, the final boundary can only be established towards the end of the study.

Selecting a Case

In choosing a case there are a number of factors to take into account – type of case you wish to conduct, where it is located, what will yield most understanding, travel costs and time. In some contexts – in commissioned evaluation studies for instance – there may be no choice to make. The case – the particular project or programme – is a given, although if it is a large programme there may be cases to select within it. The brief may also have circumscribed regions or sites in which cases need to be located.

Where you have an open choice, the case can be selected for intrinsic or instrumental reasons. One example of the former is the case I mentioned in the introduction which I decided to document, while employed in another capacity, to see what I could learn about the new curriculum programme in action. This case was of intrinsic interest to me. It could be seen by someone interested in curriculum reform to be instrumental to understanding curriculum change in this school and district or indeed in general. However, I did not set out with an instrumental intent – to study the curriculum change – but rather to learn about the dynamics of this particular school in transition.

If conducting an instrumental case study, you may choose any one of a number of cases to explore the issue you are investigating. Take the following example, of a student who studied the Greek Cypriot dialect in a Cypriot school. To explore this issue, Elena could have chosen any school in Cyprus with a density of dialect speakers. The point was to gain an understanding of language acquisition and use taking account of the context but not to conduct a detailed intrinsic study of the school itself. In selecting a school to research in this example, the number of children speaking dialect was clearly a critical factor. Further criteria that may be helpful in selecting an instrumental case study include geographical location, willingness of institutions and people to be studied, and opportunity – near where you live.

When choosing a case to study it is not necessary to seek one that is 'typical' of other cases. This is something of a holy grail in a pure sense. Each case is unique so no one *is* typical of another – though there may be commonalities between cases in similar contexts. Nevertheless, there is often a push for typicality on the assumption that this will have greater potential for transferability or provide a sounder basis for extrapolation of findings to other contexts. This is not necessarily the case. As Stake (1995) has pointed out, 'Sometimes a "typical" case works well but often an unusual case helps illustrate matters we overlook in typical cases ... The first criterion should be to maximize what we can learn' (p. 4) and some cases, he suggests, serve better than others in this respect.

If you are conducting a collective case study, you might select cases from different geographical areas to explore any regional or institutional cultural differences between how the issues are experienced in each. For example, in one collective case study I was involved in, case study schools were chosen from the North, South, East and West of England. This was not to ensure representativeness but to explain differences. Pilot case studies had indicated that no two schools were alike in the way the particular project was implemented and there were regional differences. Selecting cases in the main study from different areas enabled us to understand not only *how* the innovation was being implemented in each unique case and what *problems* were encountered, but also whether these were shared characteristics or could be attributed to *differences in demography or the institutional culture* of the schools.

Design of the Case

Emergent design

Having selected your case or cases, you need to think about designing the study. It is a common misconception that design is not necessary in an open-ended, flexible approach to research like case study: one simply goes into a case and starts to observe and interview. This is rarely a good strategy. Case study research, like any research, needs to be designed. In many types of case study the design is more emergent than preordinate. It provides a starting point.

It is possible to design a case study that has predetermined issues or issues on which data need be sought for some other purpose. This may be necessary in a collective case study where specific hypotheses are being explored or where the case researchers need to provide data on specific issues to facilitate cross-case analysis. However, cross-case analysis is also possible of case studies where significant issues arise in the process and caseworkers have taken individualistic approaches to the conduct and interpretation of the case (see Black and Atkin, 1996; Stake and Easley, 1978).

The kind of qualitative case study I am discussing in this book is characterized by open or emergent designs with the potential to shift focus in response to a growing understanding of the case, unanticipated events, or a change in emphasis by the stakeholders or case researcher. Factors to consider in designing your case include the identification of research questions or issues, the overall methodology, specific methods that will provide relevant data to inform the questions, criteria for choice of participants and ethical procedures to ensure participants are treated fairly.

Research questions

One way to start designing the case is to identify or refine your research questions. Take your time at this stage. Consider the theoretical presuppositions underlying the questions and think through whether they will provide an adequate frame for your case. This is not the same as starting with a pre-existing theoretical framework (which is discussed later in this chapter) or hypotheses to test a specific, existing theory. It is acknowledging that, even with an emergent design, the questions you ask will have inbuilt assumptions which it is important to be conscious of as they will impact on the data you collect and what they mean.

Do not generate too many questions. Quite often one, two or, at the most, three are sufficient. These give focus and shape to the study and facilitate choice of methods and analysis. At the same time, while helping to frame the study, do not be too attached to these questions. Other more significant ones may arise once fieldwork begins and you have more knowledge of the context.

Whatever questions you choose, it is important that these be conceptualized so that they are feasible to research and in the timescale you have. You also need to think about the potential for analysis and interpretation in the questions. Descriptive questions are fine for some purposes and often lead to an illuminating portrayal of case studies in specific contexts. These may be stand-alone studies where the evidence is embedded and interpreted within the case. They can also provide a basis for subsequent inductive analysis. However, questions that seek evidence for how or why something occurs provide a sharper focus that can facilitate later analysis and understanding. If you are conducting an explanatory case study, the how and why questions are what you want. If your primary intention is to produce a descriptive case study, open questions, which allow documentation of the case in all its particularity, will be helpful.

In addition to providing a frame for your study, the research questions act as a reminder of the focus of the research to keep you on track. You may return to these at the end to see how far the questions have been answered by the results or findings. However, this does not necessarily mean repeating the question and laying out the data and findings specifically in response to each. Such an approach is repetitive and can be boring to read. Stretch your imagination and think of alternative ways to answer the question without repeating the question! You will find some suggestions in Chapter 9 on alternative modes of reporting.

One final word on research questions. Do not confuse these with interview questions. This may seem an obvious point but frequently the two are conflated with the result that there is either little focus for the study or no adequate framing for analysis and interpretation. The purpose of interview questions is quite different and more particular. It is to explore in depth specific issues and perspectives to generate data, which will contribute, along with data obtained from other methods, to inform and answer the overall research questions.

Foreshadowed issues

An alternative way to provide an initial framing for your case is through foreshadowed issues. This concept recognizes that you rarely enter the field with little idea of potential relevant issues, even if you are conducting a descriptive case study with an open design. Your thinking will have been informed by reading relevant literature, other cases perhaps, and your own intelligence of the topic. I first came across this notion of foreshadowed issues in the work of Smith and Pohland (1974). 'Foreshadowed problems', the term they use, offer a guide as to what to explore but do not constrain the research process to these problems only.

In introducing the term, Smith and Pohland (1974) comment that people using qualitative research strategies disagree on 'the degree to which there should be *a* problem, *some* problem or *no* problem that initially guides the observer' (p. 38). Their position, they state, is strongly in accord with Malinowski's (1922) concept of 'foreshadowed problem'. For example, before beginning fieldwork for their rural highlands study, Smith and Pohland wrote a three-paragraph statement indicating their initial identification of the problem, outlining their intent, possible foci and 'foreshadowed problems'. However, the final product was only partially a result of the initial problem statement. 'The problem evolved as events in the real world played themselves out' (Smith and Pohland, 1974: 40).

It is now common practice to focus a case in this way. While Smith and Pohland chose to do this before beginning their systematic observation, others choose to define 'foreshadowed problems' on the basis of early fieldwork. The term I prefer is 'foreshadowed issues', which has the same intent but carries less of the connotation often associated with the word problem – something that is difficult. Whichever term you use, the purpose is the same – to establish some clarity at the outset but with the expectation that the foreshadowed issues may change or be redefined as you start data gathering and as knowledge of the field deepens. The reality is often different from what is foreseen.

In some forms of research and evaluation, such as responsive, participatory and democratic, the identification of research questions will also take into account issues identified by participants or stakeholders. These too may change in the course of the study. When this happens it is important to maintain a dialogue with participants and stakeholders to include their perspectives on any prospective changes to the questions and emerging 'new' issues.

The concept of progressive focusing (Parlett and Hamilton, 1976) is often used to describe this process of refining issues once in the field. It is a useful concept in an open or emergent design where the most significant issues may not be known in advance. While it begins at the design stage, it is a process for how you make sense of the data throughout your research. For this reason it is discussed further in Chapter 7.

Theoretical Framework

Students often ask if they should start with a theoretical framework or theory to guide collection of data and its analysis or whether it is more appropriate to generate a theory from the data. There are advantages and disadvantages with each approach. Having a theoretical framework at the beginning provides security, focus and makes analysis comparatively straightforward; the danger is that it can lead to a false consensus – making the data fit the framework – or failing to see the unexpected. Building a theory from the data has the advantage of being grounded in the 'lived' experience of participants in the case, leading to a unique understanding or potential theory of the case. The downside is it can take more time, and it is not always easy to make sense of and generate a theory from contrary, ambiguous, complex, qualitative data. There may, of course, be steps in-between. You could use an existing theory or begin to build a theoretical model to explain part of the data; or you could generate theoretical propositions that make sense of the data but do not constitute an overall theory. See Chapter 10 for further use of theory in case study research.

Choosing Methods

Three qualitative methods often used in case study research to facilitate in-depth analysis and understanding are interview, observation and document analysis, and these are discussed in the next chapter. However, there are many other methods you can choose, both qualitative and quantitative, to extend or deepen an understanding of the case. Qualitative methods include critical incidents, open letters, discourse analysis, narratives, video analysis, photographs, log entries, artefacts. Quantitative measures include small-scale surveys, patterns of examination results, questionnaires, descriptive statistics, content analysis.

Select methods for the potential to inform your research questions and not because they may be the most frequently used methods in case study or you have a predilection, say, for interviewing or observing. Seek support to go beyond your method comfort zone if you think methods with which you are less familiar may be useful. Ask your supervisor, an experienced researcher or a research colleague to guide you through using a different method. Search out case examples of the method in use. Or set up a small group of colleagues to experiment with using a different method and share your experience. Learn from each other. In order to check that you are choosing the most appropriate methods, ask yourself the following questions: Will these methods give me the data I need to answer my research questions? What other methods might offer a different take on the issues? What combination of methods might strengthen the validity of the study?

It is useful to draw a chart that shows which methods and sources are likely to yield the most relevant data in relation to which question. The chart in Figure 2.1 is an example from a research case study exploring the 'new' role of the nurse consultant in the National Health Service in England which was introduced in 2000. Sue, the researcher, chose not only to relate the methods to the research questions she was pursuing but also to ways of knowing (epistemology), the values promoted by different ways of knowing, and the key audiences likely to accept different value perspectives and methods. This was not the final design of the study. What it represented in an early stage of the research was a way of thinking about which methods were likely to yield which sort of data to answer certain questions and which audiences such data were likely to serve.

Sampling choices within methods

In addition to selecting relevant questions/issues and methods, there are design and sampling choices to make regarding people to interview and observe, events to observe, group interviews to conduct, relevant documents to search and the amount of time to spend on site. Where the study is small you can interview all the key actors in the case, but sampling decisions may still be required for other groups. While it is sometimes possible with groups of students, for example, to approximate a random or semi-random sample to interview, most often in case study, where the aim is to understand or gain insight into the case, the sampling will be purposive. You will choose people to interview who have a key role in the case and events to observe from which you are likely to learn most about the issue in question. Theoretical sampling may also be employed at a later stage to gather further data related to a developing theory of the case.

Epistemology	Primary values	Key audience	Preferred methods	Potential evaluation questions related to nurse consultant role
Post-positivism	Efficiency, accountability, cost-effectiveness, policy enlightenment	High-level policy and decision-makers, funders, social science community	Quantitative: experiments/quasi-experiments, surveys, causal modelling, cost–benefit analysis	Are the intended objectives of the nurse consultant role achieved? Are patient outcomes improved? Is nursing leadership enhanced? Can advantages of the role be achieved as effectively and at less cost by other staff?
Utilitarian pragmatism	Utility, practicality, managerial effectiveness	Mid-level programme managers and on-site administrators, funders	Mixed methods: surveys, interviews, observations, document analysis, panel reviews	What aspects of the nurse consultant role work well and which need improvement? Does the nurse consultant role enable the aims of modernization to be achieved? Are patient and staff satisfaction increased as a result of the role?
Interpretivism, constructivism	Pluralism, understanding, personal experience	Programme directors, staff, participants, social science community	Qualitative: case studies, open-ended interviews, observations, document reviews	How is the nurse consultant role experienced by stakeholders in the context of practice (e.g. Director of Nursing medical consultant)? What meanings are constructed about the role? How is it influenced by the context in which it is situated?
Critical social science	Emancipation, empowerment, social change, egalitarianism, critical enlightenment	Programme beneficiaries and their communities, social science community	Action oriented: qualitative methods, stakeholder participation, interpretative analysis	How does the nurse consultant role influence the power relationships between other nurses, doctors and patients/families?

Figure 2.1 Example of methods relevant to questions, different ways of knowing and audiences (from Duke, 2007; reproduced with permission)

If conducting a small-scale survey within the case, you could seek a random sample – of a year group in a secondary school, for example – if this was appropriate for understanding the research topic and feasible in terms of relationships in the site. But you may learn more, or more in depth, from a purposive sample of students. If conducting a small-scale survey, you also need to decide whether it is a one-off or to be repeated, whether the questions are closed or open-ended and to which groups it will be sent.

Relationships in the Field

The above design features need to be considered at the beginning so that when you enter the field to gain access and seek informed consent from prospective participants, you can be explicit about how much of any participant's time you are seeking, who else in the context you will be interviewing or observing and how the data will be recorded and analysed.

Clarity of research relationships

You will also want to be clear about the kind of research relationship you wish to establish with participants. I am using the word 'participant' here to signal that my preferred way of working is to engage people in the study in a shared experience that they can value, if not partly own. Such a perspective acknowledges that it is their experiences – their 'realities' – you will be documenting and interpreting, and gives a strong message that you will be researching *with* them, not simply gathering data on or about them for your own project.

This perspective is part of the theoretical, democratic stance I take to all research I conduct. It had its origins for me in the democratic model of evaluation.[4] Conducting case studies in this tradition involves engaging with stakeholders throughout the process, documenting their perspectives and judgements, negotiating meaning and interpretations with them, using accessible methods and language and communicating to audiences and beneficiaries beyond the case.

It is important to note that participatory and democratic forms of case study research do take a lot of time – to prepare reports, send drafts, negotiate with individuals and groups, incorporate responses where relevant and rewrite. I like working in this interactive way and am convinced of its validity and usefulness, so for me it is time well spent. You will need to decide what suits you and the culture in which you are conducting the research (whether a participatory form of research meets expectations and tolerance for negotiating data) and given the time that you have.

Choosing a Role

The role you take in documenting the case is likely to be connected to the type of case study you choose to conduct, your personal preferences for relating to people and methods for gaining data, and audiences for the study. The options are many. You can choose to conduct a case study from the point of view of a historian, a documentary film-maker, a teller of stories, interpreter of events, impartial observer, a collaborator, an educator, to name a few possibilities. While you may have an overall preference for one role or another, elements of different roles can be integrated at different stages in the research. One example is in the case study of policy-making noted in Chapter 8 in which I, with colleagues, mainly took the role of the impartial observer and documenter of events, but for one section of the case became the 'historian' to position the development of nurse education in the contemporaneous case study within the history of nurse education in the nation.

Early inspirations for me were Berger and Mohr's (1967) *A Fortunate Man: The Story of a Country Doctor*, Frederick Wiseman's documentary films and Studs Terkel's documentary journalism. In the first of these, Berger and Mohr convey, through a closely observed story of the day-to-day life of a doctor in a rural community, an understanding of the ills inherent in society as a whole. The story is full of close description of episodes and dialogue between the doctor and his patients illustrated with photographs. His intimate contact with patients and with the continued history of the area results in him being called a 'clerk of the records' (Berger and Mohr, 1967: back cover).

Wiseman's documentary films aspire to capture 'life as it is' in the institutions which he filmed. He does not provide a narration through the film. It is comprised of scenes and episodes skilfully edited from many hours of observational filming. Wiseman is clear that when constructing a film he is not creating an 'objective' record. His subjectivity is ever-present in choosing what scenes to shoot and in the editing process to produce a film.[5]

From the work of Studs Terkel (1967, 1970, 1975), which engaged ordinary men and women in talking about their lives, I gained an understanding of the power of unstructured interviewing as conversation, and the way he crafted individuals' stories from their accounts. I also followed his practice of audio-recording interviews, which he notes was necessary to achieve such in-depth accounts, even if the recorder was not always the interviewer's friend (referring to technical mishaps and how he handled these). The virtues and pitfalls of audio-recording are discussed in the next chapter.

The story, the documentary film and documentary journalism all aspire to record events as they occur or as individuals reflect on events in their lives, and capture subjective understandings of people and events. Plummer (2001) has described the aspiration well when he notes of Terkel's work that 'Terkel listens, records, transcribes and then publishes, with the minimum of comment and the maximum of content' (p. 55). In following these inspirations in case study research I was aspiring to be a 'clerk of the records', observing events in context, listening to participants' stories, documenting their perceptions and constructions of meaning in order to portray something of the participants' reality as they perceived it. Some might say, in the typology of Van Maanen (1988), I was aspiring to conduct a 'realist tale', though I did not use this term.

In thinking about the role/s you might choose, it may help to ask the following questions:

- Do I like to be a non-participant or a participant observer?
- Do I prefer a formal interview style or one that seeks to engage interviewees in telling their stories, either through deep listening or establishing a dialogue?

- Do I prefer to work with secondary data or documents unravelling the history of a programme or policy?
- Do I wish to conduct a collaborative case study or one that is external and independent?
- What are the benefits and drawbacks of different roles?
- Do I have the skills of the storyteller? or documentary film-maker? What else might I need to learn?
- What kind of role (and style of reporting) will my audience accept?

Case Study Memo 2 Planning and Designing a Case Study

- Decide what your study is a case study of and where the boundaries of the case lie, though be aware that these may change in the course of conducting the study.
- Define your initial statement of intent, 'foreshadowed problems', issues or research questions but if others arise that seem more appropriate once you are in the field, by all means refocus.
- Keep in mind that case study designs are emergent rather than preordinate. You can respond to the unanticipated, refine the issues and reframe the case.
- Specify the criteria by which you have selected the case; ensure that you can justify your choice in relation to what you can learn about your research topic.
- Identify research questions to frame the study. Do not confuse these with interview questions.
- Decide whether you will start with a theoretical framework or remain open to developing a theory in the process of conducting and analysing the case.
- Choose methods that will offer *relevant* information to address these questions/issues.
- Think about the possible roles you could adopt as case researcher. Decide which is most suitable for your purpose and audience, but take up others if useful at different stages, as long as they are consistent with agreements made with participants.
- Plan well ahead for your first field visit. Make sure you have piloted your interview/observation schedules, checked your recording equipment, and have plenty of notebooks and pens.
- Stay open to changes in design and methods as understanding in the field grows.
- Draw up schedules of interview questions or issues to be explored; pilot these with colleagues or a small sample within your case.
- Consider what ethical procedures are important to ensure the design is fair to all groups in the case and to establish rapport and trust. See also Case Study Memo 13 in Chapter 6 which comments further on ethical issues to consider in design.

Gaining Access

Before the site visit

The next step is to gain access. You will have written to the main gatekeeper in the setting you wish to research to seek an appointment to discuss the study and gain permission. This may or may not have been preceded by a telephone call seeking an 'in principle' agreement. Not everyone likes the telephone approach but for me this is the beginning of establishing the personal relationship that is so essential to good field relations. Voice matters. You can tell a lot from tone and reaction. The conversation also gives you the opportunity to counter any possible misapprehension right from the start. If the response is favourable, follow up immediately with a letter outlining further details. If not, you have saved a lot of time waiting for a response to a letter and can move to another site. Below is one example of a letter to a principal to follow up a telephone call that sought access to case study his school.

Example: An Access Letter

Dear Mr …

Thank you for responding so positively to my request to study your school. I am writing to confirm the arrangement we made by telephone last week for a preliminary visit to the school on the 20th October to discuss the details further.

You asked for a brief outline of the research in order to discuss with your staff. The overall purpose of the research is to ascertain the benefits to the students, and indeed to the school, of participating in this innovative project which aspires to raise the level of awareness of environmental issues throughout the curriculum. Essentially, I and my co-researcher are hoping to spend six weeks in the school spread over three terms, that is, two weeks per term. These two weeks would be in short site visits of two days at a time so as not to overburden staff or disrupt the ongoing work of the school. During these visits we hope to interview staff and students, observe classrooms which are involved in the project and any community projects in action with the aim of gaining an in-depth understanding of how this innovative curriculum is affecting the school and community.

I enclose a copy of the ethical protocol we talked about which will guide the collection and reporting of data. When I visit next week I will be pleased to discuss this and the outline of the research with your colleagues and answer any questions you and they may have.

Thank you again for agreeing to be a case study school. This is much appreciated.

I look forward to meeting you and to learning more about your school and the community's involvement in this project.

With many thanks
Yours sincerely

Keep the letter relatively short. At times I have written a shorter one, leaving the details of which groups to interview, for instance, to the first visit. Occasionally, when I detect from the telephone conversation the principal may have anxieties about interviewing students or observing classes, I have left raising these issues to the first visit. You need to use your judgement and write enough to be open and honest, yet not so detailed as to raise anxiety.

First visit

On your first site visit, beyond gaining access, the overriding aim is to establish an open working relationship with participants so that they feel the study will have some benefit for them and that any difficulties which arise can be discussed and handled amicably. What may help is a short – no longer than one page – document outlining the focus of the research and what participants can expect by way of contact with you and in relation to any data they offer as part of the study. They will also be curious about who else may be seen and observed. If you seek access to records, those who give consent will want to know for what purpose these are sought and ground rules established for their access and use. I recommend drawing up a short ethical protocol, which outlines the precise procedures for the collection and reporting of data, to discuss with them on this visit.

Persuasion to participate

Access may initially have to be sought through the head and/or senior management team of the organization. While you need to be sensitive to the organization's structure and processes, it is wise not to take access granted by a key gatekeeper to mean that it covers all in the organization. It is necessary to establish your own relationship and negotiate access with each participant. Think carefully about how you persuade people to participate. Here are a few suggestions:

- Invite them to participate in the research, pointing out the opportunity it offers them to state their views and defend their interests.
- Indicate that you are exploring the programme, not focusing on a close-up portrayal of them.
- Make it clear that you wish to engage in an ongoing dialogue to share understanding.
- Explain that a research case study could be useful for their own development and for accountability to the wider community.
- Think about what you might offer in return – transcripts, short report, a summary of findings or the case study in your thesis. However, do not over-promise what you cannot deliver within the scope of your resources.

Engagement in the research

You might also take some time to indicate how participants could become active in the study. Ways in which they can be involved include identifying issues, commenting upon interim drafts and interpretations, alerting you to changes in the implementation of a programme. They could also gather data in your absence through, for example, self-report on identified issues, journal entries, senior students interviewing junior students on specific issues. Not only will such participation facilitate the progress of the study, hopefully it will add to participants' own understanding of their case and of the research. In this sense, as I said in the introduction, case study should aspire to be educative for all taking part.

If involving participants actively in gaining data, it is helpful to offer practical suggestions for how this is to be collected and recorded. This is essential both to save them time and to ensure that any data collected by them can be integrated with that obtained by you. You could suggest they use the same or similar interview schedules or you could draw up a list of questions for senior students to ask of juniors, for example, or a list of issues for teachers to reflect upon in any self-report or journal they may keep. Alternatively, they may raise questions and issues you have not foreshadowed.

Review this process with participants quite early on to determine whether the data collected are relevant and useful. If you decide to go down this route, keep in mind that participants are likely to have full-time jobs and may have little spare capacity for data gathering, even if you convince them that taking part will add to their understanding of the topic and enhance their skills. You need to maintain a balance between involving them in the research and not being over-demanding of their time and energy.

Case Study Memo 3   Gaining Access

- Communicate the nature of the research clearly and discuss the procedures that will underpin the collection, analysis and reporting of data.
- Establish an open, transparent relationship with participants in the case, being neither a stranger nor a friend; be straightforward and seek the help of participants.
- Make clear who is in the sample – teachers, pupils, principal. There should be no surprises in the field, for example, of pupils being interviewed when permission was not sought for this possibility.
- Do not presume that a key gatekeeper has given access for all participants in an organization. Gain permission from all in the case and ensure they are equally well informed about the purpose and protocols of the study.
- Seek permission to interview each person. The same applies to observation. Always ask, never assume. Negotiate with individuals at every stage.
- Similarly, always ask permission to audio-record. Explain how the material will be used, where it will be stored, whether anyone else will have access to it, and whether data will be anonymized or attributed in reports.
- Think carefully how you will gain informed consent; follow procedures that may be necessary in the institution in which you work, but keep in mind that informed consent also has to be honoured in the process of the research.
- Indicate what opportunities participants will have to edit what they have said or comment on the fairness and accuracy of how they are portrayed.
- Formulate these points into a set of practical ethical procedures to indicate how data will be sought, used and disseminated, when and to whom. Keep these short – no more than one page. Short statements are easier for participants to endorse than a long list.
- Alternatively, present the points in a question and answer format, answering questions you think participants or the focus of the study will raise.

(Continued)

(Continued)

- Through your initial contact and explanations, inspire confidence. Leave participants feeling that you will treat them fairly and that they will gain understanding about themselves, their case, and the research from working with you.

Notes

1. If you are still at the stage of deciding whether a case study approach is appropriate for the phenomenon you wish to study, see Merriam (1988: 6–9) for a useful discussion on key questions to consider in deciding whether this design is what you need compared with an experimental or a survey design.
2. This was the Safari project (Success and Failure and Recent Innovation), funded by the Ford Foundation in 1973 to explore the medium-term effects of centrally developed curriculum projects (MacDonald and Walker, 1974, 1976 and Norris, 1977).
3. The project was The Humanities Curriculum Project, funded by the Schools Council from 1967 to 1972. The total design of the evaluation is in MacDonald (1971) and the report of the evaluation in Humble and Simons (1978).
4. The democratic model of evaluation was envisioned by MacDonald (1976) as a counter to prevailing models of evaluation in the early 1970s which he perceived as more autocratic or bureaucratic in intent and to redress the power imbalance in research between researcher and researched. Its major aspiration is to effect a balance in the process of research between a person's right to privacy and the public's right to know. This involved procedures both for giving participants in research control over how their data were used and ensuring that reports were disseminated to a wide range of audiences to inform their decision-making.
5. Personal communication and interview, 29 November 1975.

Further Readings

Flick, U. (1998) *An Introduction to Qualitative Research*. London: Sage. Chapters 5 and 6, pp. 49–62.
Chapter 5 examines different types of research question and how to refine them to ensure the research is possible to conduct; Chapter 6 explores how to enter the field, gain access to institutions and individuals and the different roles you can adopt in the field.

Janesick, V.J. (2003) 'The choreography of qualitative research design: Minutes, improvisations and crystallization', in N.K. Denzin and Y.S. Lincoln (eds), *Strategies of Qualitative Inquiry*. London: Sage. pp. 46–79.
Through the use of metaphor, explores how we can design qualitative research that has both the rigor and fluidity of dance. Starting with an idea and preliminary questions or movements, the researcher, like the dancer, improvises as the research proceeds. Covers the warm-up period and design decisions that need to be made both at the start and throughout.

Mason, J. (1996) *Qualitative Researching*. London: Sage. Chapter 2, pp. 9–34.
Through asking a series of critical questions, explores the need for design in qualitative research and discusses how to refine your topic, formulate research questions and link data sources and methods to research questions.

3

LISTEN, LOOK, DOCUMENT: METHODS IN CASE STUDY RESEARCH

In this chapter I discuss three methods commonly used in case study research – interviewing, observing and document analysis. The chapter is divided into two parts. The first focuses on interviewing, the second on observation and document analysis. Though I use all three methods in case study, I have a strong preference for interviewing. Compared with other methods, interviews enable me to get to core issues in the case more quickly and in greater depth, to probe motivations, to ask follow-up questions and to facilitate individuals telling their stories. Transcripts of interviews offer a basis for later analysis and a spur to further reflection by participants. For each of the methods – interviewing and observing – in this chapter, there are two case study memos. The first provides a summary of key issues, the second suggestions for practising your skills in the method. There is also a summary memo on how to record and report the interview.

INTERVIEWING

Aims and Purposes of In-depth Interviewing

Most texts on qualitative research provide guidance on different types of interviewing – from structured to unstructured – purposes for each, and the kinds of questions to ask in different types (Patton, 1980; Rubin and Rubin, 1995). My focus here is on the in-depth research interview, sometimes also called unstructured or open-ended.

In-depth interviewing has four major purposes. One is to document the interviewee's perspective on the topic or, as Patton puts it, 'to find out what is in and on someone else's mind' (1980: 196). A second is the active engagement and learning it can promote for interviewer and interviewee in identifying and analysing issues. Third is the inherent flexibility it offers to change direction to pursue emergent issues, to probe a topic or deepen a response, and to engage in dialogue with participants. Fourth is the potential for uncovering and representing unobserved feeling and events that cannot be observed. In interview people often reveal more than can be detected or reliably assumed from observing a situation. This can be insightful for both the interviewer and the interviewee. On reading transcripts, interviewees have often commented, 'I have never said that to anyone before', 'I did not realize how articulate I was about that issue', 'I am surprised how strongly I feel about that'. At other times it may be discomforting – 'I wished I had not said that', 'I know I said that but I would prefer it not to go any further'. The unstructured, interpersonal interview encourages an openness that can lead to unexpected disclosure of issues interviewees would have preferred to keep private. It is important to be mindful of this in the process and in reporting. This issue is discussed further in Chapter 6 in discussing ethical procedures that give participants control over data they offer in research.

Interviews as Conversations

In marking a shift towards a more interactive style of interviewing many authors (Burgess, 1984; Kvale, 1996; Patton, 1980; Rubin and Rubin, 1995; Simons, 1981) have likened the interview process to a conversation to indicate informality, friendliness and an attempt to equalize the relationship between interviewer and interviewee. Burgess (1984) talks about 'conversations with a purpose' (p. 102), Rubin and Rubin (1995) 'guided conversations' (see Chapter 6) and 'building conversational partnerships (see Chapter 5), Kvale (1996) 'knowledge as conversation'.

The analogy is not a perfect one and some have cast doubt on its relevance. 'Most of us are not very skilful conversationalists', says Denny (1978: 11), implying that reliance on one's natural conversational style in interview may have drawbacks as well as advantages. It is a skill we may need to learn. The purpose of research is also different. Rubin and Rubin (1995) note that in research you need to obtain more depth and detail on fewer topics than in ordinary conversation (p. 8). You also choose the topic, seek the interview and write up the study. However, an analogy need not be exact for it to have merit. It is the intention underlying the conversational interview we are striving for here. I think it is possible to distinguish responsibility for the research questions and management of the process from the aspiration in the concept of the 'conversational interview' to establish a more equitable relationship between interviewer and interviewee and create opportunity for active dialogue, co-constructed meanings and collaborative learning.

How interactive or personal should one be?

For the most part in conventional forms of research interviewing the process is one way; the interviewer is in control asking the questions or doing the listening, the participant is a passive knowledge-giver. The interview here is seen essentially as an instrumental exercise to gain data for the research. The interviewer refrains from giving information and answering participant questions, often out of a belief either that this is not her role or that it might interfere with the gathering of 'objective' data. Various authors (see, for example, Bellah et al., 1985; MacDonald, 1981; Oakley, 1981) have questioned the technical and indeed moral assumptions underlying this form of interviewing and explored a more interactive and personal approach in unstructured interviewing. But how interactive and personal should you be? Clearly you need to establish empathy and be responsive to participants' concerns. But should you answer interviewees' questions? Should you give information or simply receive? Should you share your experience? Should you accept or resist the offer of friendship? Quite how much informality is appropriate? Here are three different perspectives on this issue.

Oakley (1981) argues that 'finding out about people through interviewing is best achieved when the relationship is non-hierarchical and when the interviewer is prepared to invest his or her own personal identity in the relationship' (p. 41). In the context of interviewing women, often in their homes, at several stages in their transition to motherhood, Oakley found that interviewees asked her many questions that were difficult to avoid answering, given what she was asking of women at a stressful time in their lives. She also found that repeated interviewing over the 'intensely personal experiences of pregnancy, birth and motherhood' (p. 42) led to more personal involvement, often initiated by the interviewees themselves, which was also difficult to avoid.

Her response (based on pilot interviews and previous experience of interviewing women) was to answer their questions on the research as fully as possible and on her own experience honestly and to give information when she knew it or make a referral if not. There were three main reasons why Oakley decided to take this interactive responsive approach to interviewing in this study. First, she did not regard it as reasonable simply to see interviewees as sources of data. Secondly, she believed that giving the subjective situation of women more visibility was an important role for research in a patriarchal society (pp. 48–49). Thirdly, she had found from previous research that declining or deflecting answers was not helpful in promoting rapport, and that a different role, 'no intimacy without reciprocity' (p. 49), seemed especially important in longitudinal in-depth interviewing.

In deciding whether you might take such an interactive, responsive approach, it is important to keep in mind that in the above example the research focus was sensitive and 'personal', the interviewer was experienced, the interviews were preceded by nine months' participant observation in hospital settings, and the repeated interviews and the gap between them offered scope for developing trust and joint collaboration. Context matters. Not all settings evoke questions from the interviewee that require a personal response or that it would be morally indefensible not to answer.

Another approach to taking an interactive role in interview is that proposed by Bellah et al. (1985). However, these authors chose to be interactive in a different sense to achieve a different purpose. In their study exploring individualism and commitment in American life, they conceived the interview as a Socratic dialogue and deliberately brought their (that is, the researchers') perceptions and questions into the conversation.

> Though we did not seek to impose our ideas on those with whom we talked ... we did attempt to uncover assumptions, to make explicit what the person we were talking to might rather have left implicit. The interview as we employed it was active, Socratic. (p. 304)

The purpose of this style of interviewing was also to engage readers in the dialogue as much as interviewees:

> When data from such interviews are well presented, they stimulate the reader to enter the conversation, to argue with what is being said ... Active interviews create the possibility of *public* conversation and argument. (p. 305)

In evaluation research, MacDonald (1981) has also advocated an active interview process though with a different intent from the above. His focus is promoting a proactive and educative role for the interviewee. He cites the example of a weekend conference he and Rob Walker ran for young teachers on the theme 'To what extent is the person you are the teacher you are?' which generated a most perceptive evaluation by participants of their own institutions and practices.

Such a question, he argues, could be the basis of a much more 'personalised approach to interviewing in which the person being interviewed is invited to take an outsider's view of his [her] professional situation and subject it to evaluative scrutiny' (p. 8). This approach also entails a different relationship between the interviewer and interviewee and an even greater shift in the focus of control to the interviewee but the purpose is different. Here the interviewee is proactive in contributing to the research agenda but the prime aim is codifying and gaining an understanding of her own experience. The interview is still interactive but the interaction is more subtle. The role of the interviewer is to listen actively rather than question or answer questions, as in the first example above, or probe and encourage debate, as in the second.

Finally, if you are not persuaded by the perspectives of the authors quoted above, listen to the case for interviewing from Terry Denny in the preface to his case study of River Acres.[1]

> Seeing may be believing, but I need more. I never see the picture worth a thousand words. It occurs to me that a very few words can represent a thousand pictures; can represent unobservable feelings; can reveal tomorrow's hopes and yesterday's fears which shape today's actions. My story is largely teachers' words. Students, parents, administrators and others with something to say about River Acres contribute to its telling. But it's mostly a story of and by teachers. It wasn't supposed to turn out this way. The deeper I went, the more I needed a place to park my mind to keep it out of trouble. I found it in the teachers' words.
>
> I began my study by looking at science instruction and then interviewing teachers and students about what they did, why they did it. Hour after hour I saw teachers working, doing what teachers always have done. Students fell into their rightful places, too. Frequently after an observation and interview, a teacher would say something in a few sentences that summed up several hours of observing for me. (Denny, 1977: 1–2)

Conducting the In-depth Research Interview

> There is no single right way of interviewing, no single correct format that is appropriate for all situations, and no single way of wording questions that will always work. The particular situation, the needs of the interviewee, and the personal style of the interviewer all come together to create a unique situation for each interview. (Patton, 1980: 252)

If Patton is right, and I think he is, that 'there is no single right way of interviewing', then I cannot outline how to conduct an interview that will be appropriate in all contexts, though I can indicate some ways I have approached the task. More suggestions are in Case Study Memo 4 and the Further Readings.

Establishing rapport

Establishing rapport is essential for the generation of in-depth data. You need to create a contemporary context, often in little time, in which interviewees feel comfortable to express their innermost thoughts and feelings. Some authors suggest 'icebreakers' – speaking about something other than the precise research topic – are useful to set the interviewee at ease. Rarely do I find these helpful. In my view, this delays actual participation. My preference is to establish rapport directly in relation to the purpose of the study through a brief explanation of the research, clarity of purpose and procedures, openness and presence. There is no need to say a lot to get the interviewee started. It may simply be a statement of the research focus. Denny (1978) has the best response I know on this issue: 'It surprises me to this day just how far plain, dull truth can carry one in the field: "I am working to get some sense of what it is to teach and learn here in River Acres." It worked every time.' (p. 7)

Active listening

Once rapport is established and the interview started, listen actively to '*hear the meaning* of what is being said ... [the] interpretations, and understandings that give shape to the worlds of the interviewees' (Rubin and Rubin, 1995: 7). This is a skill that requires patience and restraint and frequently needs to be learned. In the beginning it is often difficult not to ask questions, especially if you are anxious about gaining data. But do not rush to question. One of the biggest faults in interviewing is intervening too soon, cutting off interviewees before they get to the heart of their story. Resist this temptation. Listen carefully and learn.

At the same time do not allow interviewees to dominate the interview entirely and take you off track from gaining relevant data for your research. Some interviewees are expert at fobbing off unwanted questions or deflecting the interviewer from information that they do not wish to reveal but which is critical for the study. One of the greatest challenges for the interviewer is to know when to listen and when to question. This will vary according to the purpose of the research, at different stages in the research and the level of tolerance the participant has for engaging in open-ended inquiry.

Open questioning

In the following case, where the task was to document the process of curriculum change in a school context that was unfamiliar to me, I adopted an open, unstructured interview style. At the beginning, to gain an understanding of the culture, I asked open questions. For example, what changes have taken place here lately? Tell me how the staff/students describe this institution? Why is there a low turnover of staff? When trying to understand the experience of teaching I asked teachers 'if I was in your class the other day, what would I have seen?' or 'describe a "high" moment in your teaching here?' When aspiring to get at the values of the organization I used probes such as 'name three characteristics that sum up this institution for you' or 'help me understand what it means to work here'.

In other cases, where the purpose of the study is more precise and interviewees are senior executives, policy-makers or heads of institutions, there may be little tolerance for unstructured questions, though the flexibility and openness of the research interview can be maintained. In circumstances like these, it is helpful (and it is often requested) to send a short list of questions in advance. This has a dual purpose. It is useful for the participant to prepare for the interview, and it can demonstrate your knowledge of the policy issues you are seeking to understand. It may also help prevent the 'fobbing off' syndrome and allow you to challenge the interviewee, if it seems apposite to do so, as you will have established your credibility with knowledge of the key issues. In this way you can aspire to equalize the relationship and engage in that 'conversation with a purpose' or Socratic dialogue.

The proactive interview

When you are aspiring to engage participants in analysing their own practices, the listening stance is essential. Your role is to facilitate reflection on their practice. Simple probes such as 'have you thought about?' 'why?', 'in what way?', 'for instance, give me an example', will help participants to analyse more deeply. Sometimes a silent acknowledgement, nod, smile or gesture is all that is needed to encourage the person to continue. Photographs are useful in this context – to facilitate rapport and help establish field relationships (Collier, 1967); to provide a stimulus for interviewees to tell their story (MacDonald, 1981); to offer them an opportunity to construct or reconstruct their worlds (Hicks and Simons, 2006; Walker, 1993). Photographs are particularly helpful where individuals feel anxious about having little to say and you wish to avoid an expected response to please the interviewer.

More focused questioning

While unstructured interviewing is my preferred approach for gaining in-depth data, there are times when sharp, focused, quick questioning is a useful adjunct. Sometimes this is at the end of a series of interviews when you are seeking closure but still have gaps to fill, hypotheses to check, themes to confirm or data to corroborate.

Art other times it is to connect with the interviewee – for example, a busy person with limited time, an impatient person, or one reluctant to be interviewed. On one occasion I was trying to adopt an unstructured interview approach with a deputy head in a school. He was slightly nervous about being interviewed as he did not think that he had much to say. When I started with an open invitation to tell me about his experience of the innovation that was the focus of the case, he could not relate to it.

This may have been because he was not interested but I suspect it was because I had not focused sufficiently. In the event he responded with 'ask me a question'!

Time

Unstructured interviewing takes time, especially when unanticipated issues arise. The length of time varies depending on availability of interviewees, precise purpose of the interview and the nature of the topic. I always allow an hour to two hours to create interpersonal trust and generate in-depth understanding. Often when I have asked for an hour an interviewee has said 'we will not need this long'. Yet, once started, has spoken for over two hours. The exceptions have been telephone interviews and interviews with students in school who have been released from class and are sometimes reluctant to speak. This latter problem can stem from uncertainty of expectations, seeing the interviewer in the same authority position as the teacher, fear of reprisal, or loyalty to the teacher or the school. (See Simons (1981) for further exploration of this issue and tactics for overcoming the problem.)

Group Interviews

Group interviews are economical and have several advantages: they can be less threatening to any one individual; they enable you to get a sense of the degree of agreement on issues and they provide a cross-check on the consistency of perspectives and statements of certain individuals. However, there are some downsides. Watch out for 'group think' or dominant individuals taking over the interview and preventing diverse responses. With different people trying to have their say, the interview may be difficult to control to retain a focus on the research topic. Group interviews can also be difficult to transcribe. Hearing different voices is not easy; checking consistency and attribution can be a problem.

I have found group interviews helpful when interviewing students in school, where it would be well-nigh impossible to conduct many single interviews in depth. This may seem contrary to what I have said above about the initial reluctance of students to speak. However, once they are reassured the interview is confidential, how the data will be used, that they will not be named and that you will not be reporting to teachers, this changes and they are often keen to contribute. Students have insightful perspectives and observations to make on their own learning and context. The problems noted above still exist, but are less problematic if, in reporting, you are presenting a general student perspective.

Non Face-to-Face Interviews

I prefer face-to-face interviews, but you can extend the interview process through the post by asking interviewees to reflect in your absence on further questions and preliminary interpretations written in a short report. This can be seen as an extension of the proactive interview discussed above. It has the advantage of allowing interviewees to discuss issues in your absence without having to please you (the interviewer). It also gives them time for in-depth reflection and gives meaning to any promises you may have made to record their perceptions accurately. If the face-to-face interview questions caught interviewees off guard and they subsequently found what they said was not accurate or revealed more than they intended, this is a useful corrective.[2] I found this a useful strategy when conducting a case study in a short timescale – seven days on site and a month to write up spread over a year – both to facilitate the school's interpretation and analysis and to gain more data. For further reading on the virtue of extended interviewing and data gathering by post see Simons (1987: 114–125).

Telephone interviews can also serve a number of useful purposes. With broadband connections these are relatively inexpensive as well as keeping travel costs down. You can often interview a larger number of respondents by telephone. To be effective telephone interviews need to be fairly focused and notes written at the time or immediately afterwards. It is helpful to audio-record, though simply because you are distant and the recording facility not evident do not forget to ask permission. Telephone interviews are also useful to maintain continuity with key informants or participants you may be profiling in depth over time. Asking participants to keep a research journal reflecting on key issues in your absence may serve the same purpose but the telephone offers a more personal connection. It can be intrusive, if not sensitively handled, but is economical in cost and time.

Case Study Memo 4 The Process of In-depth Interviewing

- State the purpose and focus of the interview clearly and succinctly.
- Keep questions short and simple. Avoid complicated preambles and questions with several prongs which leave interviewees not knowing how to respond to what aspect of the question.
- Avoid offering alternatives in questions: Is it this that you think? Or this ...? Or this ...? Such a tactic tends to lead to yes or no answers and little in-depth understanding unless the prompt is the basis of previous analysis and is seeking confirmation.
- Listen actively and learn.
- Remember that listening is not simply letting interviewees talk. This could mean letting them ramble and gaining little relevant data for your research. Maintain focus through eye contact, body language, the odd word, phrase or question.
- Try not to interrupt interviewees to agree with their point of view or summarize too soon. These are tactics we sometimes fall into if we are anxious that an interviewee is going off-track or time is running out.
- The process of regarding the interview as a conversation encourages engagement by interviewees. However, if you talk too much you may learn less. It may

also disempower interviewees if, after persuading them that you are interested in hearing their views, you then proceed to give your own!
- Refocus and sharpen interview questions as you proceed.
- Be responsive to additional questions provoked by an interviewee's story.
- Do not aspire to a false objectivity by assuming you can standardize the questions and that each person will understand them in the same way.
- Use the interpersonal nature of this style of interviewing to generate in-depth data.
- Plan your exit interview carefully. It may be the final opportunity to gain crucial data relevant to an understanding of the case. Follow-up telephone calls can be made but these are best reserved for the unexpected, which may arise in the final stages of analysis and reporting.
- Remember to write and thank the person interviewed after the interview.

Case Study Memo 5 — Developing Skills in In-depth Interviewing

- Listen without interruption for five minutes to a colleague telling you about a key event that shaped the person she is today.
- Restate the key concepts in that person's story while she listens to you for five minutes without interruption.
- Audio-record the five-minute listening episode.
- Write the story.
- Compare the written account with the recording to see which is a more accurate and meaningful reading of what occurred.
- Prepare a list of questions and try them out on friends or colleagues to see whether they are likely to give you useful data for your research.
- Listen to a recorded interview. Note how many times you interrupt the interviewee, how many leading questions and/or closed questions you ask and how many questions end with a yes or no. These responses all lessen scope for understanding and analysis.
- Record an interview and examine where biases appear in your questioning.
- Share a transcript with colleagues and ask them to check your questions for bias.
- Invite a colleague or fellow researcher to interview you and write up the interview. This will give you experience of what it is like to be an interviewee and to receive an account of what you have said.

Audio-recording or Note-taking?

Advantages of audio-recording

Whether to audio-record or take notes in interviews is one of the questions students frequently ask about interviewing. Audio-recording has a number of advantages.

First, it ensures accuracy of reportage and adds to the veracity of reporting.[3] Readers can be assured that the interviewee actually said these words. Secondly, it frees you from having to write everything down so you can concentrate on the social interpersonal nature of the interview process and respond fully to the interviewee.

Thirdly, audio-recording allows you to check your recall and recording skills, not to mention hearing and memory. You can compare data obtained from a recording with the data obtained from taking notes. To take one example: when interviewing a principal reflecting about his role, he indicated that he saw himself as 'authoritarian' – at least, this is what I wrote down. However, on checking the recording I found that what he said was that he was very much 'in authority', quite a different perception. The recording here provided a useful check on accuracy but also on misreporting and fairness. In mishearing what the principal said, I was possibly supporting a 'story' I was developing that coincided with how teachers in the school perceived him – as authoritarian. For the above reasons I always record interviews where I can.

If individuals do not wish to be recorded, this should be respected, though you may wish to ask their reasons to see if any anxieties can be allayed. Some are concerned about what they sound like and wish to hear their voices. A short play back at the end or the beginning seems to satisfy this curiosity. It is common for students to request such play back, though other interviewees do as well. One senior civil servant I interviewed in a policy study asked for a pre-run of one or two answers to the first question to see how his response sounded. Having heard his first two responses we erased them and started the formal recorded interview again with the same question.

Disadvantages of audio-recording

Audio-recording has downsides as well. Recording can lull you into a false sense of security and to not paying enough attention to the issues at the time. Thinking that you can always return to the recording later, you may not concentrate sufficiently in the interview or document the main issues in order to deepen questioning as you proceed. Equipment can also fail, leaving you vulnerable to having no data at all if you are not also taking notes.

Audio-recordings are time-consuming to transcribe. For one hour of recorded interview, add five for transcribing and many more for analysing. Few of us can afford to pay for transcription at this ratio. Transcription by someone else, in any event, does not necessarily save you time. You still have to check the transcript for meaning. A person unfamiliar with the research topic or context may not be able to pick up the correct word, nuance of language, dialects and accents.

But the greatest drawback, if relying on transcription by others, is the time that elapses between transcription and analysis. The longer it takes for transcriptions to be completed, the harder it may be to recall the exact nuances of the interview and the meaning and tone of what the interviewee said.

Note-taking

To avoid the above pitfalls, I always take notes as well as audio-record. Taking notes means I can keep track of the research process and evolving understanding. I can highlight issues to query in subsequent interviews, signpost parts of the interview that are important to transcribe, provide a starting point for early analysis and interpretation and document elements of the process – tone, gesture, degree of comfort – that seem relevant and to which I can return to contextualize meaning. Note-taking also eases the social process by breaking sustained eye contact with the interviewee. For further reading on the virtues of audio-recording *vis-à-vis* note-taking in interviews see MacDonald and Sanger (1982).

Case Study Memo 6   Recording and Reporting the Interview

- Always take notes, even if audio-recording, to signpost issues to query in subsequent interviews and to provide a starting point for early analysis.
- If recording, ensure that your digital recording equipment has sufficient space and an effective microphone.
- Listen to what is said once the recording is switched off. This often provides a critical clue or insight.
- Beware of relying on later transcription of recordings, whether by yourself or others. The time involved, given a ratio of 5:1 for a one hour interview, is extensive; it may also delay the process of analysis.
- Write field notes as soon as possible after the interview. Note issues to follow up, key points it might be useful to transcribe, observations of body language, mood and anything unexpected that arose. Make sure you record the precise date and time. This may prove to be relevant in the analysis.
- Include in your field notes observations on participant reactions and your reflections on the field experience. Note early hunches, hypotheses or interpretative asides on the meaning of the data you have gathered.
- If you are using someone else to transcribe audio-recordings make sure that you listen to them as well to pick up nuances of language and recall contextual clues to meaning.
- Do not use the interview to obtain basic data. This can be gained more easily by asking participants to fill in a short data sheet or questionnaire at the end.
- If asking individuals to respond to a transcript or to a report of their interview data, outline the criteria by which you wish them to respond. Free-floating responses are rarely helpful and may threaten the focus of the research by setting it off on a different track.
- Make clear why their response is being sought – to ensure that the information reported is accurate, that perspectives are reported fairly in context, to seek further data, and/or to establish or reaffirm co-operation.

This next memo points out some of the political issues that may arise in the field which require sensitive handling. Field relations and how to manage them are discussed further in Section II, where how to portray persons and negotiate data are discussed. The memo is included here to alert you to potential issues that could occur in the field before you start interviewing or observing.

Case Study Memo 7   Managing Field Relations

- Always enter and exit the field consistently and respectfully, even if you have had a hard time!
- Refrain from showing any anger, annoyance, frustration you may feel in the field. Wait until safely off-base or defuse in field notes and discussion with a colleague.
- If any participants breach agreed procedures, quietly remind them of what these are and re-establish the boundaries and principles of the research.
- Fieldwork is tiring. Make sure you are fit. Do not attempt too many interviews in one day. This is important, whether you are audio-recording or not, to allow time to make field notes and prepare for the next round of data gathering.
- Do not fall into the trap of colluding with any participant who wishes to persuade you that his or her story should take preference over others. Try to maintain a consistent and impartial stance.
- If participants try to deflect you from the research task by taking over or ignoring your questioning do not override with your agenda. Accept for a time, acknowledge their help, then redirect the conversation back to your questions.
- When participants feel discomforted by the research or do not like emerging findings, they often find ways to disempower you, even discrediting your skills or knowledge. 'You do not understand the culture' is a common phrase employed. A useful way to counteract such an accusation or prevent it arising is to build into the research procedures a critical friend, who is credible to the site but independent of it, with whom one can check nuances of language, historical antecedents or contemporary social and policy issues.
- Do not become embroiled in political issues within the site that were there before your research began, even if the research has made them more visible. Your role is to document and record. Resist pressure to give data for political ends.
- Remember to leave the site with participants feeling that they have learned something from being involved in the research and that they would welcome you or another researcher back.

OBSERVATION AND DOCUMENT ANALYSIS

Observation

Observation has a long tradition in social research and has been written about extensively. See Further Readings for elaboration of the advantages and limitations of the method. It is useful in case study research, where we have to closely observe a specific case and/or interpret findings gained from other sources or methods in context. Observation is present throughout the whole research process from the moment you enter the field until you leave. Through observing, you can tell if you are welcome, who is anxious, who the key players are in the informal structure, and whether there are any unspoken rules. Sometimes noted through the body language of participants, these informal observations help you interpret the ethos and may prove important later when interpreting the meaning of the data. So from the outset make notes of what you see and observe even though you may not be clear at the time why you have noted what you did.

Reasons for Observing

Beyond these important informal observations in the process, there are five reasons why formal observation is a companion method to interview in case study research. The first is that through observing you can gain a comprehensive 'picture' of the site, a 'sense of the setting' which cannot be obtained solely by speaking with people.

Secondly, documenting observed incidents and events provides 'rich description' and a basis for further analysis and interpretation. Thirdly, through observing you can discover the norms and values which are part of an institution's or programme's culture or sub-culture. These can often be detected through the rules of the organization, the artefacts displayed, interactions between people and communications with the external world.

Fourthly, given that interview privileges the articulate, observation offers another way of capturing the experience of those who are less articulate. It does not entirely meet this point, however, and you need to be alert to other ways of 'giving voice', to the possibility of misinterpreting observations, especially in cultures and contexts with which you are less familiar, and to the potential patronizing element in the very notion of 'giving voice' to others. Finally, observations provide a cross-check on data obtained in interviews. This is sometimes seen as strengthening the validity of the account, but there are other issues to consider here in terms of how you can justifiably combine or integrate methods. These are discussed further in triangulation of methods in Chapter 7.

Process of Observing

Like interviewing, observing may be seen on a continuum from structured to unstructured or, in field settings, complete participant observation to non-participant observation. In many case studies the norm is somewhere in between. In some forms of observing the choice is made through predetermined categories and classifications built into instruments that already exist or which are developed for the particular study. This is then what is searched for in the setting. Structured forms of observing are useful in contexts where particular hypotheses are being explored, a specific observation tool has been developed, the context is circumscribed and where several observers are involved in covering many settings. Many forms of classroom observation rely on such structured observational schedules.

Unstructured observing tends to be direct and naturalistic – not constrained by preordinate designs or intent, documenting or interpreting issues/incidents in the particular context in naturally occurring circumstances. Observations are primarily descriptive, interpretative to a degree, use both intuitive and rational means of capturing the essence of what is observed and are reported in accessible language. It is this form of observation that is most adopted in case study research to document an incident or event, explain the culture or aspects of the culture, or provide the basis for interpretation of data obtained by other means.

Choosing what to observe

In unstructured observing we have choices to make about what is observed. There is no predetermined schedule and we cannot observe everything in a case. How do you choose? Your research topic and intrinsic interest provides a focus but you may need to reflect further whether any foreshadowed issues or theories you have of how the programme or organization works might direct your observation.

One might conclude from this that it is important to be as conscious as one can about what guides selection of what to observe. Yet there is also a place for recording the free-floating, apparently random observations we make in particular settings. This may provide a basis for later examining different theoretical precepts we hold that are built into our observations. It may also lead to stories we do not know we can tell and provide a stimulus for further understanding (Sanger, 1996: 4). The Gestalt concept of the field is helpful here, the interaction between the foreground – what we choose to observe – and the background – what is there anyway. What we place in the foreground is what is of significance to us at any one moment, and this may change many times in the course of the study. In thinking about what to observe and how you know it is significant, there are a number of points to keep in mind.

Audience and purpose
First is the audience and the purpose for your study. If your research is sponsored by a government department or national agency, there are certain events you may have to observe and you may have to conform to a certain style of reporting those observations. If you have an open brief or aspiration to present a portrayal case study to give people an experience of what it was like to be on site, you have more choice both of what to observe and how to record. You might, for example, write a short vignette, of the kind Bob Stake once sent me on a postcard from Brazil when he was studying rural schools there.

> Example: A Vignette – Postcard from Brazil
>
> *Dear Helen – Have enjoyed the resort, 'radioactive' sand at this place, and just now have returned from a week visiting rural schools down the coast and into the mountains. Saw 21 1 room schools, Gr 1–4. Many pretty sad. Barren rooms, the dust and trash ever present. Teachers have workbooks for kids but no books, little paper. They carry water for the toilets, have no electricity, sometimes not even a woodstove to cook the pasta and beans govt. sends. County coordinator makes up final exam, sells it (15c) to kids to cover office expenses, teachers buy when kids can't afford it. Kids have to get 80% right to pass to next grade, so some kids get more than 4 years of education. Yet spirits are high. Bob.*
>
> (Simons, 1998: 145)

Staying open

Secondly, we need to be constantly aware that we do not fall into the trap of simply confirming what we know already: 'We look where we expect to find rather than opening ourselves to any possibility that might turn up' (Sanger, 1996: 5). As we noted in relation to interviewing, we have to balance foreshadowed issues with staying open to the unexpected. This is sometimes difficult as we are not always aware how our previous knowledge can get in the way. In Chapter 8 there is an example of how my previous knowledge became a bias in a school case study I conducted and how I tried to counteract this once it had been pointed out by the school. I had indeed looked where I expected to find and failed to stay open to what was unique for them.

In observation workshops I have run, the hardest task has been to get participants to suspend previous knowledge and judgements to observe and record what is *actually* in a setting. Asked to produce a written ten-minute descriptive observation of a student in a class, participants (first time round) invariably produced, not a closely 'observed' account of what transpired in those ten-minutes, but a pathology of the student, detailing, for example, her background, judgements of her character, comparisons with siblings, comments from her teachers. Clouded with pre-formed judgement (for which there was no evidence), what little description there was provided no basis for analysis or interpretation of what happened in those ten minutes. To some extent this was a question of language – using abstract concepts rather than factual or descriptive words. But it was also that participants failed to 'see' what was in the setting and to 'observe' what was significant in those ten minutes. Background and prior knowledge dominated.

In another case when nurses were asked to observe a patient for ten minutes when on ward duty, the outcome was similar. In their written observations, there was more pre-formed judgement than descriptive observation. However, such an outcome was more understandable in the different context of the hospital setting. Detailed histories are part of the craft of caring for patients, but so, too, is careful observation, for instance, of their blood pressure, state of breathing and emotional state.

Seeing differently
Thirdly, when observing we have to make a conscious effort to see differently. Looking through a familiar lens, as in the examples above, can prevent you observing what is there and revealing what is significant. Stake and Kerr (1994), in their paper 'Rene Magritte, constructivism, and the researcher as interpreter', make the strongest case I know for challenging us to see differently in drawing attention to the way in which Magritte's paintings confront our expectations.

The challenge – to see differently – is to directly experience the phenomenon we are seeking to understand and to re-present our interpretations of that experience, insofar as this is possible, in ways that others can directly engage with that experience. This means experimenting with different forms of reporting to persuade or provoke our audiences to see differently, but keeping in mind that our images are always personally and socially constructed and incomplete (Stake and Kerr, 1994: 2–3). In noting that we have choices to make about how we construct meaning, Stake and Kerr (1994) also draw our attention to the danger of misrepresenting direct experience through the categories and indicators we choose to investigate and interpret the social world.

Observations over time
Fourthly, both Sanger (1996) and Walker (1993) point to the importance of observations over time in understanding or misunderstanding the complexity of observed events. Often the meaning of an observation is not contemporaneous. It is embedded in events, stories, incidents that preceded the particular observed event. Frequently we cannot tell the exact meaning without knowledge of the context and history before our arrival on the scene. Linking interview closely with observation helps ensure that our observations are not misrepresentations; we can pursue in interview meanings that are not obvious in what we have observed.

Examples of Different Forms of Observation

The two observations that follow illustrate different ways of observing and recording observations. They are not the only forms you can choose. I have chosen these particular examples to illustrate and reaffirm three features of naturalistic observation noted earlier – that context matters, timing matters and close description matters if we are to adequately observe what is happening in naturally occurring circumstances. The first example is illustrative of the importance of observing over time or having antecedent data to contextualize meaning. It is also a commentary on the inappropriateness of a structured model of classroom interaction analysis – the Flanders' system – for interpreting open classroom settings.[4] The second is a detailed narrative descriptive observation of a critical incident in a hospital ward.

LISTEN, LOOK, DOCUMENT

> Example 1:   Observation to Contextualize Meaning
>
> In a project observing teacher-pupil interactions in primary school classrooms aspiring to use the Flanders' system of analysing classroom interaction, Walker and Adelman (1975) found that in many classrooms the talk that they observed and recorded did not fit the categories in the Flanders' system. It was not simply a case of seeking new categories, they pointed out, but calling for a new concept of talk, which depended for its meaning and significance on the shared meanings in the specific culture of the classroom. These are often hidden from the casual observer. Walker and Adelman (1975) comment, 'In some classrooms it is often those local, immediate and personal meanings that are educationally most significant – and any research technique that designs them out of consideration runs the risk of completely misunderstanding and misrepresenting the reality' (p. 74). To illustrate this point they offered the following dramatic example. In one classroom they observed, a student called out 'strawberries, strawberries' after another student had been rebuked by the teacher for not doing his homework adequately. All the class laughed, except the observer who could not see the joke. The observer discovered later that the meaning of the use of the word 'strawberries' was related to previous shared interactions between the teacher and pupil in this class and the teacher's wit: 'Your work is like strawberries. Good as far as it goes, but it doesn't last nearly long enough.'
>
> (Walker and Adelman, 1975: 74)

The observer in the above example could not have known what had transpired earlier and the jokey nature and good-humoured relationship that the teacher had built up with this class and so was at risk of simply not getting the meaning at all or, worse, misapprehending what was happening at that moment in the class. The story is a reminder that context is crucial in making sense of what we observe but so, too, is history. One-off contemporaneous observations run the risk of misrepresentation. We may need to be a participant observer over a period of time to develop appropriate meanings and insight in any particular setting. Alternatively, we may need to interview several people in the setting to pursue antecedent meanings and examine these in relation to observations made at the time.

The second example is an excerpt from an eight-page descriptive narrative observation documenting a ward incident in caring for a terminally ill patient. Sue, a nurse consultant in palliative care, wrote this observation as part of the research she was conducting of her own practice in this role. This excerpt is the beginning section only. Entitled 'Caring for June and Her Daughter', the observation was written after the event, as many observations are, even if notes are taken at the time. It could not be otherwise, given that Sue was managing the incident she was observing in a delicate setting where June was dying. However, it does record the incident as close to the 'truth' of what happened as experienced and observed by Sue. For the complete account of the incident transposed into poetic form see Duke (2007).

Example 2:   Descriptive Narrative Observation

It is 11a.m. on a Friday and I have seen six of the patients whom I need to review and completed a tutorial with one of the clinical nurse specialists (CNS) on pain management. I have three other patients to see before the end of the morning. I am working with Sally, a nurse learning to be a CNS in palliative care. June is a sixty-four year old person with end stage liver disease. She has been described to me as someone with a strong sense of autonomy. When I arrive on the ward I am told that June has become paranoid overnight, as a result of toxins from her liver. Bill is the ward nurse caring for June.

Bill ... explains that June ... has just telephoned the fire brigade from the public telephone on the ward and asked them to come and get her as the nurses are trying to harm her... I go to see June ... June is standing still, in the middle of the ward in her dressing gown. Her arms are drawn tight across her chest, her index fingers laying over each other in a sign of a cross. Her eyes are narrowed ... and scornful. Her dressing gown cord is tied tight around her wrist. I notice that her case is packed on her bed. I introduce myself as a specialist nurse and she accuses me of lying ... saying that I am poisoning her. I answer quietly; gently explaining again who I am and that I have not met her before. She says I am a witch come to make her come back from the dead when she dies ... The conversation continues like this for a couple more turns and then I say to her that it must be very frightening to believe that people are trying to harm you. She replies 'Yes it is'.

... My concern has risen. June is very frightened and this draws me to help her and yet I know that the only way I can do this is to sedate her, and this will compromise her wish to be in control. This wish is still strong within her paranoia – her determination to protect herself from the harm that she perceives is threatening her ... June is still well enough in her body to be standing and walking and I am really concerned about sedating someone in this situation. I telephone the medical consultant I work with and leave a message for her to telephone me ... June's daughter arrives and is shaking with tears. I kneel down beside her, putting my hand on hers and explain who I am. I ask if she would like to talk to me and she nods. She tells her mum that she will be back in a couple of minutes and her mum warns her to be careful as 'they [Sally and I] will try and get you too'.

... I sit alongside [June's daughter] ... listen to her explain how shocked she is by her mum's condition, how quickly things are happening, how she had promised to look after her mum at home, for her not to die in hospital, but how she would not be able to cope with her like this. I agree and say that we need to care for her and that I am seeking advice about how best to do this ... that usually we do this by giving someone some rest, through sedation. She sees that this ... will give her mum some dignity: 'she would be horrified if she knew that she was like this, this just isn't her'... She explains that her brothers were not planning to come down and see their mum this weekend but perhaps they should come and I agree. She asks whether it would be better if they come today and I affirm this. She makes a plan to go to get her mum some lunch from the hospital shop and to telephone her brothers. Sally and I update Bill, and go for some lunch and some help.

The narrative continues to detail the incident which results in the nurse consultant having to sedate the patient and the difficult emotional toll this has for all concerned – the patient, her daughter, Sally and the nurse consultant herself.

In this narrative observation, facts are documented, the emotional states of key people in the scenario are reported, and decisions are carefully recorded. What I gain from reading this (and I have had the privilege of reading the full version) is a real sense of the delicacy of the situation, the dilemma the nurse consultant faces having to balance 'managing' the situation with respect for the patient's autonomy, concern for the stress the incident raises for the patient's family, nursing staff and herself, and overall, an emotional and cognitive understanding of what it means to work daily in palliative care.

You may well have gained something different from reading this short excerpt and bring a different lens to it. My purpose in offering this example is to indicate the power of the descriptive narrative both for immediate insight and subsequent analysis. In the case in question, the researcher went on to analyse and interpret the incident in terms of 'emotional labour', the changing landscape of the role and context of care, role complexity, and her developing identity as a nurse consultant.

Observing with Video

Observing with video has been used for some time to record classroom observations for immediate and subsequent analysis. (See, for example, Walker and Adelman, 1975.) Its prime virtue is that it can take us beyond the spoken word and the researcher's observations of situations (which are open to attribution of motives and dominance of the researcher's constructs) to provide an 'objective' record. The record can be used both to cross-corroborate interpretations from other sources and for subsequent analysis by the researcher, with or without the participants, of the setting captured on film. It can also be used with other groups to test the validity of the interpretations.

With the increasingly sophisticated technological means of recording now available, observing with video may well become a more popular form of observation in case study. As with other methods, the usual ethical protocols of gaining access and permission need to be employed and you need to be aware that there are still ethical problems to be overcome if excerpts from a video are to be used in any published account.

This method is particularly useful in observing participants whose language skills are still developing. Flewitt (2003), for instance, used video in studying the communication strategies of three-year-old children at home and in a pre-school playgroup and Payler (2005) in exploring socio-cultural influences on the learning processes of four-year-old children in a pre-school and reception class. In exploring topics like these with young children, video observation can capture many of the non-verbal cues to meaning, body positioning, facial expression and interactions between children and their peers or teachers. While non-verbal cues are helpful in interpreting interviews, in settings such as these, where interview is not a viable option (or a limited one), they take on a greater significance in making sense.

When Should I Choose Observation as a Method?

The final point I want to make on observation to help guide your choice of method is to reiterate that observing is not only a complex process but a difficult one, at risk from our unconscious selection of what is significant and what is not.

We do not always notice. Our familiarity constrains us. Not quite knowing where to focus, we opt for recognizable categories to document what we see, and there is a danger here, as already noted of not capturing what is in the particular setting or misrepresenting what is there. In order to avoid this, we have to consciously prepare to observe but at the same time remain open to the unexpected. Asking the following questions may help you decide whether to choose observation as a major method.

- Do I need to observe and document what is happening to understand the context better or refine my research questions?
- Can I get the data I need to answer the questions by some other means?
- Do I wish to observe to present a documented account for subsequent analysis, whether by myself or others?
- What data will observation provide that other methods cannot?
- What might video/audio observations offer over other observation methods?
- Do I have the time and skill to deconstruct video observations?
- Do I rush to judgement or have I the patience to watch and learn?

Observation may take more time than interviewing. It can also be difficult making sense of a 'messy' reality through observation alone, unless you are immersed in the field for a long time. However, as the descriptive narrative example above demonstrates, observation is a powerful tool for understanding and eliciting the nuances of incidents and relationships in the 'lived experience' of people in particular situations and contexts.

Case Study Memo 8   Observation

- Think carefully about why you want to observe and what you will gain from this that you cannot from other methods.
- Choose the type of observation in relation to audience and purpose.
- Decide whether you will focus on specific events or people or whether you will stay open to what appears interesting in the case.
- Keep your research questions in the background, but stay alert to what may inform your understanding of them.
- Keep your judgements to yourself as you observe; notice what is actually there.
- Write observations that allow others to gain insight into the situation or event; that is, describe as closely as you can what happens.
- Note conversations, incidents, interactions, dialogue and timing.
- Include only the detail that enhances 'thick description' and understanding of the event/situation described; avoid irrelevant particulars simply because they are there.
- Avoid importing into the observation pre-formed judgements that are not backed by evidence of direct observation.
- Check your observations, if possible, with participants in the case, not necessarily to cross-corroborate – we observe with different lenses – but to gain their perspective and deepen your understanding.

Case Study Memo 9   **Improving your observational skills**

- Observe a child in a classroom, a person in a restaurant, or a university tutor teaching, for ten minutes and write a description of what you see.
- Read this through and see if you have in fact described what happened in those ten minutes.
- Note any value-laden comments and see if there is any evidence in the description for those judgements.
- Explore the text you have created for any unjustified attributed motivation to the persons observed.
- Examine the description for any unarticulated or emerging hypotheses you may be exploring.
- Note what you chose not to observe.
- If any value-laden judgements, motivations or hypotheses are evident that are not justified, rewrite the description stating only what you observed.
- Compare the two accounts, observe and evaluate the difference.

Use of Documents

Formal document analysis tends to be used less than interview and observation in case study research and its potential for adding depth to a case has not perhaps been fully exploited. However, there are many ways in which documents can be used in case study to portray and enrich the context and contribute to an analysis of issues. I am using the word 'document' widely to mean not only formal policy documents or public records but anything written or produced about the context or site. This can include documents that formally represent the organization, such as prospectuses, annual reports, audit reports, equal opportunity statements, vision statements, rules and regulations, examination results, and informal documents like newspapers, bulletins, memos, all of which may contain clues as to how the organization envisages itself or how the programme has evolved.

If your case is a class, or a group, this method may seem less relevant, and in some cases it is possible to come to a unique understanding of the culture of that classroom without reference to policy documents of the school. In other cases, an understanding of what happens in a classroom or a hospital ward may be intimately linked to the culture of the institution of which it is a part and the larger grouping beyond the institution whose policies they enact. A common example here is where a school's practices have to be in line with local authority policies or where hospital practices need to accord with the latest policy documents of the National Health Service. In cases like these, an analysis of the relevant policy documents in the larger unit may be necessary to help you understand the reasons and context for the policy as well as how it is being implemented in practice.

Written documents may be searched for clues to understanding the culture of organizations, the values underlying policies, and the beliefs and attitudes of the writer. Visual documents constitute another kind of documentation and there may be photographs and artefacts of various kinds which hold clues to understanding. Photographs can also be a major lens through which the culture of an institution is analysed and portrayed (Prosser, 2000).

It is always worthwhile when beginning a study to consider what documents already exist which may be relevant to your case. Analysis of tables of examination results can yield patterns of response. Informal memos may carry as many clues about the culture of the organization as formal documents outlining aims, objectives and vision. I am not suggesting any one of these written statements is significant in itself. However, collectively the values they impart may add meaning in the context of the study and depending upon its purpose.

Document analysis is often a helpful precursor to observing and interviewing, to suggest issues it may be useful to explore in the case and to provide a context for interpretation of interview and observational data. It is also a major method that can be employed. The following three cases illustrate different ways of using documentary analysis as a major method in case study research.

In this first case, Fry et al. (1991) used document analysis as the primary method in analysing and comparing the values (implicit and explicit) in the reporting of historical events in two textbooks, one in English and one in Russian, for the teaching of history in English and Russian schools. The second, Stake's (1986) case study of the evaluation of the 'Cities-in-Schools' (CIS) programme, integrated several sources of public documents and interviews with key people in the case. The third, a case study of nurse education and training in Ireland (Simons et al., 1998), used secondary, documentary sources to tell a short history of nurse education, which formed the background for a contemporary case study of a new programme (comprised of interviews, observations and documents).

The Further Readings offer guidance on how you might proceed should you decide to analyse documents as a major method or part of the methodology in your case.

Notes

1 River Acres (a pseudonym) is one of eleven case studies that formed the 'Case Studies in Science Education' project, funded by the US National Science Foundation (Stake and Easley, 1978).
2 There may be times where you might choose not to offer individuals an opportunity to reflect on their interview response if, for example, what you are aspiring to capture are people's unrehearsed reactions to events or spontaneous feelings. However, in many contexts in which we conduct case study research, giving interviewees opportunity to reflect on what they have said is common practice and adds to the accuracy and validity of the account.
3 Not all interviewers agree that veracity is enhanced by reporting participants' words. Rob Walker was the first to point out to me that a reported account of an interview that integrates many contextual and socially interactive factors may get closer to the meaning intended by the interviewee than words alone.
4 Walker and Adelman (1975: 74) suggest that the Flanders' system, which uses pre-existing categories to observe teacher–pupil interaction in the classroom, has an implicit theory of instruction embedded in it based on a question–answer sequence favouring a transmission mode of teaching. While useful as an observation tool to observe formal classrooms, it is less useful, they indicate, for analysing and interpreting open-ended classrooms or classrooms where relationships, context and change are central features of the teaching–learning process.

Further Readings

On interviewing

Kvale, S. (1996) *Interviews: An Introduction to Qualitative Research Interviewing*. Thousand Oaks, CA: Sage.

An extensive account of the theory and practice of the interpretative research interview also seen as a form of conversation. It has chapters on the seven stages of an interview investigation, on ethics, on the quality and validity of the interview and how to analyse and write up interviews to ensure readability.

MacDonald, B. and Sanger, J. (1982) 'Just for the record? Notes towards a theory of interviewing in evaluation', in E.R. House (ed.), *Evaluation Studies Review Annual*, Vol. 7 pp. 175–197. Beverly Hills, CA: Sage.

A detailed discussion of the case for and weaknesses in audio-recording and note taking of unstructured interviewing in evaluation. The summary table on pp. 189–194 is particularly useful for illustrating the strengths and weaknesses of each approach in the generation, processing and reporting of data in terms of their effectiveness, fairness and validity.

Rubin, H.J. and Rubin, L.S. (1995) *Qualitative Interviewing: The Art of Hearing Data*. Thousand Oaks, CA: Sage.

An accessible book on the concept, process and analysis of qualitative interviews seen as guided conversations. Includes how to design and structure qualitative interviews, hear and judge what people say, build conversational partnerships and conduct cultural interviews and interviews under unusual circumstances.

Simons, H. (1981) 'Conversation piece: the practice of interviewing in case study research', in C. Adelman (ed.) *Uttering Muttering*, pp. 139–150. London: Grant McIntyre.

A reflective account of the process and negotiation of unstructured interviewing in case study research, including interviewing students in schools.

On the use of photographs

Collier, J., Jnr (1967) *Visual Anthropology: Photography as a Research Method*. New York: Holt, Rinehart & Winston.

A classic text from visual anthropology exploring the use of photographs in social research.

Prosser, J. (2000) 'The moral maze of image ethics', in H. Simons and R. Usher (eds), *Situated Ethics in Educational Research*, pp. 116–132. London: Routledge/Falmer.

An examination of the ethics of using photographs, film and video-recording to observe. Located within a discussion of the role and function of image-based research in qualitative educational research.

Walker, R. (1993) 'Finding a silent voice for the researcher: using photographs in evaluation and research', in M. Schratz (ed.), *Qualitative Voices in Educational Research*, pp. 72–92. Lewes: The Falmer Press.

On the virtue of using photographs in social research both in the process of interviewing and understanding individuals' construction of their worlds.

On observation and documents

Many books on qualitative research include sections on the different forms of observation (including photograph and film) and the use of documents (see, for example, Punch, 1998: 184–191; Flick, 1998: 135–66). Flick, in Chapter 14, also has useful suggestions for how you record, take notes and document field data. The selected readings below are a more extended exploration of each topic.

Adler, P.A. and Adler, P. (1994) 'Observational techniques', in N.K. Denzin and Y.S. Lincoln (eds), *Handbook of Qualitative Research*, pp. 377–392. Thousand Oaks, CA: Sage.

Focuses particularly on naturalistic observation as a major method within a broader theoretical and historical discussion of the use of observation in social research. It includes a discussion of the essential features of naturalistic observation, the different roles you can take, different stages in observing, how to establish validity and reliability, and ethical issues raised by the method.

McCulloch, G. (2004) *Documentary Research in Education, History and the Social Sciences*. London: Routledge/Falmer.

A useful book on the methodology of using documents in social research, acknowledging their social and historical construction, the need to understand documents in context, with reference to their authors, and the potential link between the past and present. It looks at primary, secondary and online documents, archives and records, printed media and personal documents, and how to analyse and assess their reliability and validity. See also Prior (2004) and Scott (1990) if you are particularly interested in public, official documents, and Plummer (2001) for analysis of personal documents.

Plummer, K. (2001) *Documents of Life. 2: Invitation to a Critical Humanism*. London: Sage.

A classic text exploring the argument for and practice of using documents written by people and by others about them in social research. Has a focus on life stories and life histories but there is much more here, particularly in Chapters 2 and 3, that is relevant to the case study researcher who uses diaries, letters, stories, journalistic accounts, photographs, artefacts, video and film in their repertoire of methods. See also Plummer (1983).

Sanger, J. (1996) *The Compleat Observer? A Field Research Guide to Observation*. London: The Falmer Press.

Focusing entirely on observation, this is a reflective and closely observed study of observation with practical guidance on how to think about observing and how to observe.

Section II
IN THE FIELD

4

WHO ARE THEY? STUDYING OTHERS

> Her audience measured Sylvia Ashton-Warner by its own standards and was bewildered; Sylvia Ashton-Warner conducted her life on her own unique terms and it is only on those terms that her life begins to make sense. (Hood, 1989)

This observation from the Prologue to a biography of Sylvia Ashton-Warner highlights the importance of trying to capture the uniqueness of the people we study from their inner knowing, not by the external categories we employ to bring order to our observations or assess the worth of a person's contribution to social or educational life. How to do this is a most complex task and beyond the scope of this book. Nevertheless, it would be odd if a book focused on the singular did not draw attention to a study of an individual in the case, whether the case is an institution, programme or system, or where the whole case is a person; for example, in the study of one teacher's teaching over a year (Louden, 1991) or the study by a principal of his own educational journey (Loader, 1997).

Why Study Individuals?

There are three main reasons why some study of individuals within a case is central. First is the need to understand programmes and policies through the perspectives of those who enact them. Whatever the focus of the particular case, in educational and social research people feature prominently. They are the key protagonists in classroom transactions, in developing policies and translating these into practice. Policies and programmes are devised by people and implemented by people. They are not person-proof in the sense they can be interpreted the same way in each context. Even if a common standard and equal access is the aim, people reinterpret, subvert and adapt policies to their own settings and in relation to their own needs and experience. Secondly, case study research, particularly with an orientation to be educative, is an interactive social process. Study of transactions and the relationships individuals create in the field is essential to document the 'lived experience' of the programme. Thirdly, interpreting individuals' experience of a programme or aspects of their lives in specific socio-political contexts helps to understand not only how socio-political factors influence the actions of individuals but the impact of these factors on the individual and the case itself.

Scope and Focus

In drawing attention to a focus on individuals in case study research I am not suggesting that the case study researcher conduct biography or autobiography. While there are similarities between case study and these disciplines in terms of the focus on particular persons, narrative as a form of telling, and sensitivity to contexts and time, auto/biography has its own literary tradition and a logic and method of inquiry that serves its particular purpose of the interpretation of lives within social settings (Denzin, 1989; Erban, 1998). There are similar common features with life stories and life histories. However, these too have antecedents in a different tradition, the disciplines of anthropology and sociology, which have a different logic and purpose – the study of a life in its socio-cultural and historical setting (see, for example, Goodson and Sikes, 2001).

Purpose for Studying Individuals in Case Study Research

In undertaking portrayals of individuals within case study research our task is more modest and more specific. The purpose is to understand how the experience and actions of a single person or persons contribute to an understanding of the case. In reaching an understanding of individuals in a case you may need to document something of a person's professional and personal biography but by no means all. For instance, you may need to know why key people in the case were prominent, why they acted the way they did in the particular circumstances and what lay behind their judgements and perspectives. Exploring individuals' histories and the social context of their experience offers clues to such understanding and helps you interpret the meaning and effect of their role and experience in the case. But you do not have to give a full story of their lives or even an extensive narrative. Relevance to the research purpose is the critical factor here. You need to make a professional judgement about the appropriateness of any aspects of personal history or biography in the context of the specific case and in relation to its prime focus. It is also important to keep in mind that, while all experience is socially situated, there is no inevitable connection between our past experiences and contemporary actions in case study research.

In his book *Personalizing Evaluation*, which promotes an argument for evaluating social and educational programmes primarily through individuals' experience, Kushner (2000) makes a similar case for not equating a study of individuals within case study research with biography or autobiography. He cites two reasons. First, understanding the experience of individuals in case study does not mean 'losing the social program as the principal focus for evaluation analysis and critique' (p. 12). Individuals' stories are not discrete; they intersect and interrelate in the analysis of the case. Secondly, the methodological tools of biography and life history cannot replace methodology in the field of evaluation. What Kushner is referring to here is the institutional and political dimension of evaluation that is inherent in its methodology and which we noted in Chapter 1. He draws on the work of MacDonald (1977), whom he notes first argued for studying persons in context in his paper 'The portrayal of persons as evaluation data', to emphasize that what we are seeking to understand in case study evaluation is 'people in their contemporary institutional contexts rather than merely in the context of their lives' (Kushner, 2000: 12). In other words, how individuals 'live out', negotiate their role and experience in a case study of a social programme within the power structures of the case and in relation to one another. How, then, might we begin to portray individuals within case study research in their contemporary institutional contexts?

Portraying Individuals in Case Study Research

Using historical and biographical data

The first and obvious use of biographical detail in case study research is locating the background and significant features of key personnel for the reader to see how these may have influenced the case. These are the kind of personal history details – such as role, gender, age, previous experience and qualifications – that frame many a questionnaire and provide a basis for sampling and subsequent analysis of the relevance of different groups.

Some details of the context of the case, organizational ethos and history may also be required to situate the role of key individuals in contributing to the character of the organization and evolution of its policies and practices. However, as with personal history details, it is only necessary to include those contextual details that facilitate an understanding of the person's role and experience in the case. Many school case studies I read contain several pages of context detailing, for example, the catchment area, school population, curriculum and assessment practices, not all of which is relevant to the specific case. Early on you may document more than survives in the final account. It is not always possible at the outset to know exactly what will best frame the study. But as the story of the case, and the relevance of the person within it, becomes clear, so will decisions on what to include and exclude.

In one school case study I conducted of a school's experience of a centrally developed curriculum project,[1] I wrote a portrayal of the principal to frame the study because a strong view emerged in fieldwork that the school was '*his* school', determined and controlled by him. The portrayal drew on biographical detail, contextual details on the history and development of the school, observations staff made of the principal, his interview comments, and my observations. Initially it was five pages long. Much of this in the end was not relevant to my purpose in using the portrayal to begin the study, though I did not know this at the outset.

As I came to understand more about the role of curriculum development within the school, I edited the portrayal to one page to frame the particular story I wanted to tell. I left in details about the principal's academic status, reference to other research studies, the ten headteachers the school spawned in fifteen years, and the head's significant role in the district. These details were both factual and a reason for the school's public confidence and ease in accepting yet another researcher.

What I left out were details of the school population, the achievement of pupils, of school uniform and of curriculum organization (that came later in the study). I tried only to convey those characteristics that offered an immediate insight into why the school was characterized by so many within it as '*his*' and why it was so successful and public. This helped set the scene for understanding the reasons the school had fully engaged with national curriculum projects and why it was so open to being a case study.

Writing in case study is the subject of Chapter 9 and I will have more to say there about how to construct a portrayal that will engage the reader. But I do want to signpost here that when you are thinking about portraying an individual to start the case, consider the style as well as the detail. Maybe start with a quotation, a scene from the staffroom, an incident in class that gives an insight into the theme of the portrayal and why it is important in the case. This should engage the reader and set the scene for the story of the case.

Cameos

The second use of biographical detail is the short sketch of a protagonist which gives the reader a sense of who the person is. I am speaking here not merely of factual data – such as birthdates, location and career roles – but observations that give the reader a quick insight into the person and his/her potential importance in the story. Like a cameo portrait contained in a small frame.

The cameo is a short, succinct, glimpse of a person often captured through the use of metaphor, image and simile. It is brief, yet in a sense complete, for the precise purpose it serves of giving the reader an immediate 'feel' for the person. Katherine Mansfield epitomizes the use of the cameo in many of her closely observed portraits of daily life (Mansfield, 1987). Her stories are fiction, yet we have much to learn from how she observes social life.

From the biographical tradition, Judith Thurman (1984), in her biography of Karen Blixen (who wrote under the name Isak Dinesen), presents one of the most striking cameos I have read. Take the following, for instance, which, early on in the biography, encapsulates the spirit of the child Karen Blixen.

Example: A Cameo

There are certain irreducibles in the character of Isak Dinesen, as in the character of each of us. Some children have a depth to their nature from birth – a passionate curiosity – while others are cautious, passive, or serene. While almost anything can happen to those original qualities – in particular they can easily be discouraged – they also define a mysterious ground of one's being that defies analysis. Tanne [Karen] was a proud, deeply feeling, touchy, and vital child. She was a dreamer from the beginning, and it was her fate to have that quality within her recognized and nourished by her father, who took his second-born as his favorite and gave her time the others did not

> share. In a sense she led a double life as a child – as one of three, and as herself, only.
> (Thurman, 1984: 45)

Later on the same page, Thurman makes a connection to Dinesen's work, capturing its essence as follows:

> *There is in Dinesen's work and thinking a frontier – more of a fixed circle, like an embroidery hoop – that separates the wild from the domestic. Within it there is firelight and women's voices, the steam of kettles, the clockwork of women's lives. Beyond it there are passions, spaces, grandeurs; there lie the wildernesses and the battlefields. Wilhelm led his daughter out of the domestic limbo and into the 'wild'. He took her for long walks in the woods or by the Sound; he willed her his great love of nature; he taught her to become observant, to distinguish among the wild flowers and the bird songs, to watch for the new moon, to name the grasses. He exercised her senses, made her conscious of them the way a hunter is, in imitation of his prey. This was a kind of second literacy that she says she acquired at about the same time she learned to read, and its discipline and pleasure were at least as important in her life as those of books.*
> (1984: 45)

In Chapter 9, on reporting and writing, we return to this description to examine the literary devices Thurman has used in constructing this cameo and how they are combined to distil and convey a sense of the child Karen Blixen was and the impact of the context of her upbringing on her work. The inclusion of the extract here is to illustrate the power of the cameo for portrayal of individuals.

Case profiles

Unlike the cameo, which achieves its power and communicative effect from its interpretative brevity, the case profile is a longer account of one person's experience that allows in-depth analysis over time. The profile is rich in evidence with observations, excerpts from interview, and reflections by the person concerned and by others who know his or her work. This means that profiles are often lengthy, ten to twenty pages. As part of a case, they are useful for giving readers insight into the direct experience of participants, often communicating more effectively than analysis of themes and issues. They can also help to structure the case in different ways. Starting with a profile (which could be revisited or extended throughout) highlights understanding the case through the person. Placing a profile in the centre of the case – moving from a general interpretation of issues to the particular person – serves to illustrate the issues, personalize understanding and enliven the text.

The case profile can take several forms. It can be an experiential account written either by the person or by you, the case researcher, from the point of view of the profiled person. Or it can be a more comprehensive profile constructed from a range of data such as interviews with the profiled person, his or her own testimony, your observations, results and products of the person's work, and observations of other significant figures in the profiled person's professional life.

For several examples of a case profile in a nurse education case study see Clarke (2007). The profiles in this study were comprised entirely from individuals' reflections over a period of two years on an innovative Diploma programme in nurse education and training. They were guided by questions seeking reflection on particular issues. While composed by the researcher, they represented individuals' own evaluations of their progress, together with some biographical detail about their previous experience.

Personal portrayals

In evaluation case study personal portrayals were introduced by MacDonald (1977) to give commissioners of innovative programmes a more informed basis for making decisions about who to fund.[2] While portrayals of persons are useful for gaining insight into the experience of any programme, they are particularly relevant where the norm in programme and project development is step funding, that is, where funds are allocated year by year on the basis of how well individual grantees of development money delivered the previous year.

His argument was that whatever the strength of an evaluation proposal, it was individuals who determined whether the programme achieved its aims. In such a context, it was important not only to present detailed accounts of their performance on the job, but also something of their character and qualities. It was the person being funded, not the proposal. In-depth portrayals provided a more comprehensive, informed basis for judgement as to who should be funded than either the proposal or mere gossip.

To construct these personal portrayals MacDonald suggested evaluators aspire to the techniques of 'new journalism' (Wolfe, 1973) to convey a sense of the person's influence and achievement ('life') in the programme. The role of 'new journalism' in enhancing our reporting skills in case study research is explored in Chapter 9. What I wish to emphasize here is the usefulness of the devices Wolfe suggested – namely scene-by-scene construction, dialogue, representation of events as seen by a third party and descriptive details that give the reader access to the 'status life' of the subject (Wolfe, 1973 cited in MacDonald, 1977) for portraying a sense of the person's 'life' in the programme. Portrayals using these devices not only reported what happened but gave insight into the attributes of the individuals, which influenced their achievements. The portrayals varied in how they were written but included information about a person's previous track record, data from interviews, observations of the person on task, and judgements of co-workers. They were written by the researcher and negotiated with the individuals concerned before they were disseminated as part of the evaluation.

Kushner's (2000) personal portrayals of individuals include more biographical details, interpretations of the person's experience of the programme and relevant concerns in their contemporary lives than the portrayals mentioned above, which focused more on performance and the qualities of the person in fulfilling the aims of the programme. In this sense they are much more personalized. His argument for bringing in relevant concerns in people's contemporary lives is that these are an inevitable part of who the person is. Participation in a curriculum or social programme is only one aspect of their contemporaneous life. Their aspirations and challenges in everyday life go well beyond any curriculum or social programme, though they may well have an influence upon it.[3]

Kushner's argument is persuasive. We have many roles to play in different situations and contexts and it is false to try to separate one's on-going life from the temporary experience of a programme. Yet I have a lingering reservation about the degree to which such personalization serves all the functions needed for comprehensive programme evaluation. I worry, too, that we may not always get the balance right between understanding individuals and their role and influence in the case (and any connection with their contemporary life) and the programme story itself; a complex analysis of the intersection of individual stories and interactions in the socio-political context of the case and the history and development of the programme.

Narrative and lived experience

In one way or another all portrayals of individuals in case study research are about lived experience. This is what they are trying to capture, whatever the specific focus of the study. The case for studying 'lived experience' has been well explicated by, among others, Clandinin and Connelly (1994), van Manen (1990) and Richardson (1997). Often this explication of lived experience is linked to story form or narrative. We have seen in the previous section how elements of a person's lived experience may be documented through cameos, profiles or portrayals as part of the analysis of a case study of a social or educational programme. In other contexts a more extended story or narrative may predominate or constitute the case itself.

Narrative may be construed differently but essentially it is a 'tale, story, recital of facts, esp. story told in the first person; kind of composition or talk which confines itself to these' (*Oxford English Dictionary*, 1982: 673). Narratives aspire to capture the experience as it was 'lived' in the particular context through rich description, observation and interpretation and to retain this connection in the telling of the story. This creates possibilities for others to vicariously experience what happened and/or to make their own connections.

The narrative may be written by the individual under study or by you, the case researcher, drawing on the individual's experience, data offered in interview and other evidence about the person. In social and educational research, narrative has a research history of its own that is well documented in the qualitative research literature (see, for example, Clandinin and Connelly, 1994; Reissman, 1993; Ricoeur, 1981). It has been used extensively in the health care field, particularly in the use of illness narratives (Frank, 1997), in education, in the study of teachers' lives (Clandinin and Connelly, 1994; Goodson and Sikes, 2001) and in evaluation (Abma, 1999). Here I draw attention to those aspects of narrative that are particularly relevant to the portrayal of persons in case study research.

Narrative and story

For Clandinin and Connelly (1994), narrative and story are the common way we communicate our experience:

> ... when persons note something of their experience, either to themselves or to others, they do so not by the mere recording of experience over time, but in storied form ... In effect, stories are the closest we can come to experience as we and others tell of our experience. A story has a sense of being full, a sense of coming out of a personal and social history. (p. 415)

This does not mean that stories are fixed in time. The telling of our stories is a 'lived' and changing experience: '...in the telling [we] reaffirm them, modify them and create new ones' (Clandinin and Connelly, 1994: 415). This is an educative process both for the person telling the story and for you as case researcher learning about the case. However, you still need to gauge the 'truth' status of the story and its significance and meaning for the specific case you are exploring, cross-checking with other sources and people where relevant.

Narrative for these authors is both phenomenon and method; they use *story* to denote the phenomenon – 'people by nature lead storied lives and tell stories of those lives' (p. 416) – and *narrative* for the inquiry itself, that is describing such lives and writing narratives of experience.

Anecdotal narrative

Like Clandinin and Connelly, van Manen (1990) also explores the interrelationship of lived experience and narrative. In *Researching Lived Experience,* he explicates an approach to research and writing, integrating the reality of people's lived experience, interpretation and narrative. His argument is that these three processes are intimately linked. It is through our writing that we come to interpret and theorize 'lived experience'. For him, too, a common method of communicating that everyday lived experience is the story form.

Van Manen highlights a specific narrative or story form, that of the anecdote (1990: 115–121), which is relevant for a study of the particular. Recall the 'authenticated anecdote' characterization of case study noted in the introductory chapter. The anecdote, says van Manen, is a special kind of story. It is the essence of an observation, a person's relationship with the world or, as the *Oxford Dictionary* puts it, 'the narrative of an incident or event as "being in itself interesting or striking"' (quoted by van Manen, 1990: 116). Anecdotes are not to be understood, he says, as *mere* illustrations to bolster a difficult or boring text, but as a methodological device 'to make comprehensible some notion that easily eludes us' (p. 116).

He outlines the historical origin of the anecdote, deriving from the Greek meaning 'things unpublished', to indicate that anecdotes were often private, sometimes used 'to characterize a way of thinking or a style or figure which was really too difficult to approach in a more direct manner' (p. 117). This is part of their appeal to biographers (and I would add case study workers) as a means of capturing the 'essence' and meaning of events and incidents that may not be possible with other methods. Anecdotes often tell us something germane about a person's inner world.

Historically, says van Manen, anecdotes have had low status in scholarly writings (in contrast to historical accounts or reports) and these negative connotations may still be heard today when we hear someone dismiss an account because '"it rests merely on anecdotal evidence"' (p. 118). Such an attitude, he says, fails to realize that 'the anecdote is to be valued for other than factual-empirical or factual-historical reasons ... an anecdote is rather like a poetic narrative which describes a universal truth' (p. 119). Relating this to the nature of knowledge, he comments: 'The paradoxical thing about anecdotal narrative is that it tells something *particular* while really addressing the *general* or the *universal*. And vice versa, at the hand of anecdote fundamental insights or truths are tested for their value in the contingent world of everyday experience' (p. 120).

It is this meaning of anecdote that is reflected in the description of case study as an 'authenticated anecdote' noted in the introductory chapter. Authenticated refers to the fact that it must be true, grounded in experience, corroborated by other evidence where relevant and credible for an understanding of the case. Its purpose is to offer insight into the idiosyncratic nature of particular events and experience that cannot be captured by other means. Its value lies in enabling us to understand how a study of the particular yields universal understanding (see also Simons, 1996).

Life stories

Life stories are a further means of documenting a person's lived experience in case study research. These are stories told by individuals, often in interview, about aspects of their lives relevant to the research topic. In the context of exploring life history research in educational settings, Goodson and Sikes (2001) discuss an important distinction between *life history* and *life story*. The 'life story' is related by the individual, the life history is constructed by the researcher employing further interview and documentary data (p. 17). The important point these authors are making in drawing this distinction is that 'life stories' are already removed from life experiences, 'They represent a partial, selective commentary on lived experience' (p. 16).

Moving from life stories to life history adds a further interpretation. While such a move to *life history* has potential danger in taking the story away from the direct experience of the individual and giving more power to the researcher to locate the *life story* in context, Goodson and Sikes nevertheless 'hold to the need for providing historical contexts for reading *life stories* ... without contextual commentary on issues of time and space, life stories remain uncoupled from the conditions of their social construction' (2001: 17).

The life history method Goodson and Sikes note suffered a decline after reaching its peak in the 1930s. However, in the past three decades it has become prominent again in many different fields of inquiry, including educational studies. This may be seen as part of that quiet methodological revolution I referred to in Chapter 1, which acknowledges subjective forms of inquiry and the social and individual construction of knowledge.

Relevance for case study of narrative and life story

While not advocating extensive life histories in case study research of programmes, projects and policies, the distinction between life history and life story raised above has an important point for case study. Life stories, or even glimpses of them, in a case study need to be located in the socio-political context in which the case is embedded and those aspects of an individual's life that impact in the case. This is not so much the macro social and historical context, but rather the socio-political circumstances of the specific case to help situate why the particular story is being told.

Life stories have a further function, which is the telling of the story itself. In the particular focus on case study explored in this book, the process involved in telling the story is an inevitable part of the educative intent. This often has an impact on the person beyond the particular experience related or their role and impact in the case. In the process of interviewing, as we saw in Chapter 3, the educative intent is built into the proactive interview where interviewees codify and come to understand their experience. For some purposes, then, it may not matter that a life story becomes a 'life history' or that the 'life story' be told to others. The educative purpose of engaging participants in telling their story has been met; the product and how to produce a narrative of it is a secondary consideration. For other purposes – for example, to understand the role of a key person in the case – it will be important to produce his/her narrative 'life story'. To understand the significance of a person's role in the evolution of a policy over several decades, it will be essential to locate his/her life story in the historical and socio-political context of the time.

Whose Life is it?

Ethics is the subject of Chapter 6. Yet I cannot leave this chapter without commenting briefly on how important the ethical dimension is in how we portray individuals whatever form we take to do this – cameo, case profile, portrayal, extended narrative, life story. In many instances, the usual conventions of informed consent, respondent validation and fair, accurate and relevant reporting will be sufficient to indicate that you have acted ethically.

But there are other contexts in which presenting a valid and fair account of a person's experience has a sharp edge, as for example, when the prime aim is evaluating competence in implementing a project or programme. With consequences for the person – of potential continuing employment or not – such portrayals are high stakes. This is not the same as individuals reflecting on their experience of the programme, as in the case profiles above, or telling their life story or aspects of their life story to contribute to an ethnographic case study of the social life of a specific community. To some extent, those who tell their stories give permission for their stories to be told and thereby take some responsibility for ensuring that any published account is valid and fair.

However, you, as the case researcher, are also responsible for constructing a fair account. When portrayals are written for the precise purpose of informing judgement by others or even as part of the story of the case, there is a danger of painting a particular (possibly judgemental) portrait of the person. The authority of the researcher's interpretation may take precedence over perspectives offered by participants. The way the portrayal is written may also influence the message that is conveyed.

In Chapter 9 we examine issues surrounding the power of language to persuade. Here I simply want to allude to the ethics which may be involved in how you write portrayals of persons. Negotiation of the portrayal with the person is sometimes thought to counteract any tendency to over-persuade, though it is not always as equal as the term suggests; the one who writes the script often has a more powerful impact on the text. Co-construction of the portrayal is perhaps the ideal. Yet this depends on how feasible it is to develop an equal partnership in the context in which we conduct case study. In creating texts (portrayals) of individuals we should not lose sight of the origin of elements of that text in their lives and the potential consequences publication could have on their professional lives and work.

Notes

1. The case study was part of the Safari study (Success and Failure and Recent Innovation). See note 2 in Chapter 2.
2. The particular evaluation where these portrayals were first used was UNCAL (an acronym for 'understanding computer assisted learning'). It was commissioned for three years from 1974 to 1977 to evaluate the National Development Programme in Computer Assisted Learning. For further exploration of portrayal in this evaluation and an example see MacDonald (1977: 57–64).
3. Kushner does not exclude the case worker from such personalization. It is part of his extended argument for exploring the experience of the programme through people in the case (2000: 118). The case worker's values, interactions and concerns in his/her contemporary life will also impact on the interpretation and analysis of the programme in action. This is not discussed further here as exploration of the role and influence of the case study worker in the case is the subject of Chapter 5.

Further Readings

Goodson, I.F. and Sikes, P. (2001) *Life History Research in Educational Settings: Learning from Lives*. Buckingham: Open University Press.
An account of the origins of the life history method, its decline and resurgence, and the use of life stories and life histories in educational research.

Kushner, S. (2000) *Personalizing Evaluation*. London: Sage.
Explores the case for understanding programme evaluation through the lens of the personal experience of individuals in the contemporaneous socio-political life of the programme, illustrated with many examples from the author's own practice context.

MacDonald, B. (1977) 'Portrayal of persons as evaluation data', in N. Norris (ed.) *Safari 2: Theory in Practice*. Occasional Publications No. 4. Norwich: University of East Anglia, Centre for Applied Research in Education.
An argument for the portrayal of individuals in case study evaluation and for enhancing the way we write such portrayals in order to communicate and inform decision-making in programme evaluation.

(Continued)

(Continued)

van Manen, M. (1990) *Researching Lived Experience: Human Science for an Action Sensitive Pedagogy*. New York: State University of New York.
An exploration of the nature of lived experience and the art of researching that experience. Offers a range of methods for writing about lived experience interrelated with interpretation and a most useful account of the values and advantages of anecdote as a methodological device.

5

WHO ARE WE? STUDYING OUR 'SELF'

Why Study Our 'Self' in Research?

Chapter 4 was concerned with studying others in case study research. This chapter focuses on you, the researcher, in the process of conducting the research. Much is written about how the research context may be changed by our interventions, rather less about how the research impacts on us, or, at least, gives us pause to think about who we are in any particular research context. The case and methodological basis for doing this is similar to the case for studying individuals in Chapter 4, but it has an extra ethical dimension. What right do we have, in fact, to study others if we do not also study ourselves?

To be fair to those within the case, we need to be clear how our values and judgements affect our portrayal of them. But we also need to examine how the specific context and topic of the research shapes the story we come to tell. This goes beyond acknowledgement of the inevitable situatedness of 'self' in research or spelling out one's values in a preface. It is demonstrating *when* and *how* different aspects of 'self' or different multiple 'I's, as Peshkin (1988) and Clandinin and Connelly (1994) have termed them, may surface in research and impact on the research and on you.[1] This is central to the validity of what we find.

Two caveats are necessary. In exploring our 'self' it is not implied that the 'self', or aspects of the 'self', are static or unchanging, or that they are always known. We have multiple selves which emerge at different times in relation to different life and research agendas. Peshkin (1988) uses the concept of 'situational subjectivity' to underscore this point and Coffey (1999) notes that 'Selves and identities are fragmented and connected; open to shifts and negotiations. They are ambiguous, the outcome of culturally available and defined interactions, actions, meanings and values' (p. 35).

Situating Oneself in the Research Process

The main reason for examining the 'self' in case study research is that you are an inescapable part of the situation you are studying. You are the main instrument of data gathering; it is you who observes, interviews, interacts with people in the field. Your world view, predilections and values will influence how you act so it is best to declare and observe how these interact in and with the case.

This seems an obvious point to make, yet Bentz and Shapiro (1998) a decade ago noted that 'Most research textbooks and courses do not bring the living reality of you, the researcher, into the discussion of research' (p. 4). However, there is now a substantial literature in social and educational research which advocates the location and monitoring of self in the research process (see, for example, Bentz and Shapiro, 1998; Coffey, 1999; Denzin, 1997; Fine, 1994; Richardson, 1997).

This process of situating the self is perceived differently by several authors. For Bentz and Shapiro (1998), the person is always at the centre of the process of inquiry, both in a psychological sense in terms of how personality and preferences shape the research and a philosophical sense 'in seeing research not as disembodied, programmed activity but rather as part of the way in which you engage with the world' (p. 5). These authors draw on the concept of a *lifeworld*² to emphasize that you as researcher are also an individual with a life, 'a personality, a social context, and various personal and practical challenges and conflicts' (p. 5), all of which affect the entire research process. Since our lifeworld – our lived experience – is part of who we are, Bentz and Shapiro (1998) say we should view the research process as a journey between ourselves and the text – that is, something to be interpreted and reinterpreted in the social process of research (p. 42).

In the context of discussing lived experience and narrative, Clandinin and Connelly (1994) make a similar point about the non-separation of a person's lifeworld and workworld. Referring to Sarason's (1988) autobiography, they note:

> It is not that he fails to make a distinction between his job as a psychologist and the rest of his life. Rather it is impossible to separate them in practice: He is a human being as a psychologist and he is a psychologist as a human being. Keeping this sense of the experiential whole is part of the study of narrative. (p. 415)

From a sociological perspective, Coffey (1999) makes a case for not separating our fieldwork selves from our daily life selves. In rejecting accounts of the research process that remove the connectedness of the fieldworker self from the context of study, she says that 'it is naïve and epistemologically wrong to deny the situatedness of the self as part of the cultural setting' (p. 22), noting that 'The fieldwork self is always, to some extent, shaped by the cultural context and social relations of the field' (p. 30).

These authors all make convincing arguments for studying the self in research – it is part of our lifeworld, it is inescapable, it is shaped by the context. The question is how you can do this and what might help in the process.

Concepts to Consider in Exploring the 'Self' in Research

Concept of self

There is no consensus of what constitutes the 'self' or how to study it in research. For the purpose of exploring how we might examine its impact, I take the self to mean that inner sense of knowing who we are and how we define what is important to us – those values, emotions and ways of thinking and being that affect how we live and act. In a research context, we could call this a 'research self', but this would be misleading. It is the interaction of a personal sense of self with the research and reflection on the dynamic this creates that is the important point. A 'research self' would be a temporary phenomenon; a 'personal self' may change but is more constant.[3]

Concepts from different disciplines

In thinking about how we can study this interaction and monitor its influence, I have found a number of concepts from specific disciplines useful. Two from psychology are particularly significant – 'dis-identification' and 'individuation'.[4]

The process of dis-identification – 'to observe oneself without becoming emotionally attached to what one sees' (Holly, 1993: 166) – is important in research because it enables us to step outside the customary ways we identify with our different sub-personalities, in which we often have a strong emotional investment, to see how these influence our social interactions. We have to dis-identify in order to see clearly.

Individuation draws attention to the fact that we develop certain aspects of ourselves and neglect others in establishing our place and identity in the world.

> Individuation means integrating and developing these various aspects of ourselves … The process of individuation is made possible when the individual stops trying to control what is unconscious and steps out of the way simply to observe those aspects of the self that seek to be recognized. (Von Franz, 1968: 165, cited by Holly, 1993: 167)

From sociology comes the important distinction Nias (1993) has raised in her discussion of symbolic interactionism in studying primary teachers' lives. This is between 'situational selves' and the 'substantial self', the former being positions we can take in different situations, the latter being that part of us which is difficult to change, rooted as it is in the conscious and unconscious past and the relationships which helped to shape it (p. 146).

Finally, in exploring the interaction of self and other, the concepts of holism and field theory from the Gestalt tradition are relevant (Clarkson, 1989). Field theory in particular highlights the interrelationship of the person with the surrounding field, reinforcing the importance not only of understanding a person (or a case) within the particular socio-cultural context but also discerning what is central (foreground) to understanding that person or case and what is field (background).

How to Identify Subjective 'I's[5]

What students have found particularly helpful for actually monitoring their subjectivity is the process of identifying subjective 'I's outlined by Alan Peshkin in his (1988) paper 'In search of subjectivity – One's own'.

Starting from the premise that subjectivity is inevitable in research, and therefore not something we can eliminate, Peshkin argues that we should actively seek it out in the process of research to see how it may be shaping the inquiry and outcomes. This refers to all researchers, whatever their reputation, or whatever methods – qualitative or quantitative – they use. He notes that social scientists in general 'claim that subjectivity is invariably present in their research, but they are not necessarily conscious of it nor attentive to it in a meaningful way' (p. 17). When they do systematically seek out their subjectivity, he argues, they uncover particular subsets of personal qualities evoked by studying a particular research topic. 'These qualities have the capacity to filter, skew, shape, block, transform, construe, and misconstrue what transpires from the outset of a research project to its culmination in a written statement' (p. 17).

It was in the course of writing up his study of a fundamentalist Christian school (Peshkin, 1986) that Peshkin became 'acutely aware' of his own subjectivity when he observed how differently he used the concept of community and school in this context from how he used them in a previous study where he wrote about them in far more positive terms. His observation on realizing this partiality puts the point well: 'Struck by this differential generosity (explained in Peshkin, 1985), I knew that "I had indeed discovered my subjectivity at work, caught red-handed with my values at the very end of my pen"' (Peshkin, 1985: 277, quoted in Peshkin, 1988: 18).

He drew two conclusions from this observation: first, that subjectivity can be seen as virtuous in the sense that you can see how your personal qualities interact with the data to present a distinctive contribution; secondly, that discovering your subjectivity in writing up is too late – he wanted to be mindful of 'its enabling and disabling potential' (p. 18) in the process. In his 1988 paper he set out to do precisely this, uncovering in his 'subjectivity audit', as he put it, six 'I's, and how they impacted on his study of a multi-ethnic high school. How did he know when his subjectivity was engaged? He looked, he said, for the cool spots, positive and negative feelings, experiences he wanted more of or to avoid, and when he felt moved to act beyond a research role. 'I had to monitor myself to sense how I was feeling' (1988: 18). Seeking out your subjectivity is more than a rational process. It is sensing when your emotions and feelings are engaged.

Examples of Identifying Subjectivity

The two examples below illustrate different aspects of this last point – it is when our emotions and feelings are aroused that we know our subjectivity is engaged. In this first example, the awareness came rather late in the process, though I was conscious earlier on that there might be difficulty at some point. In the second, one of my doctoral students, Elena, identified the strength of her subjective 'I's before she started fieldwork.[6]

Example 1: Uncovering Subjective Selves

In my own work, in one particular case study evaluation I uncovered three subjective selves, one of which surprised me rather sharply. Rather like Peshkin in *God's Choice*, I only discovered these at the end, not in the initial writing up but in the negotiation of a final report. These were the political self, the educative self and the justice self, aspirations which are central to my philosophy of field relations. In this case they were severely put to the test. The context was a European Union funded project (Simons (ed.), 1997) that involved a range of stakeholders in three different countries. Like many European projects, the evaluation had to operate within a management structure, which itself was subject to evaluation, and on which a range of participants were dependent for financial payment for their development work.

The particular event[7] that made me aware that these 'selves' were apparent and in conflict centred on a request from the managers of the programme that I remove parts of the final report which they deemed to be critical of them and attribute blame where *they* thought it lay. Had I agreed to these changes, the report would have both misrepresented the case and failed to fulfil the obligation to report fairly and accurately to a range of audiences about the value of the programme.

Negotiations took several months face-to-face and by email. In the process I did accede to certain changes of language to modify the tone in places, though not, of course, altering any participant quotations or interpretations agreed by other participants in the case. I reiterated the methodological and ethical procedures agreed by all at the outset concerning the clearing of data with participants and respecting multiple perspectives. I offered them right of reply in the report. None of these strategies found favour.

The managers persisted in wanting data removed. Having made several adjustments which I thought were reasonable, I resisted further changes because I thought these would threaten the validity of the report, and this had been agreed by all stakeholders. I also argued that it was not in their interests to be seen to censor a report and that we should aspire to learn from the differences in a way that was educative for all.

I was aware of two conflicts in doing this. First, that I was using one self – the 'educative' – to drive home and secure another – 'justice' – at the point that the integrity of the research was under threat. Secondly, I observed how my 'political' self came to dominate and match the politics of the site, particularly when asked to change words participants had actually said. This, of course, was not appropriate. But the stronger the management demanded that I make certain cuts, the more I resisted, even wondering at one point if I should bypass them and send the report direct to the sponsor. I told myself that if I did this I would be honouring the integrity of the research and respecting all participants within the case. However, I was aware (from my feelings) that there was clearly an element of power and control in how I was reacting. I was in danger of disempowering the 'educative' and 'justice' selves I feature highly in my aspirations.

In the second example below, Elena identified her subjective 'I's before starting fieldwork so she could monitor her subjectivity in the research process itself.[8] Her thesis topic was language and ethnic identity among Greek Cypriot students. The more she thought about which aspects of her 'self' would be relevant, the more confused she said she became. How precisely to identify them? What were their origins? What set of values gave rise to them? Some seemed to overlap or intersect and several triggered strong emotions and feelings. To try to make sense of this confusion, she wrote a narrative poem 'I do not know – I am confused' (Ioannidou, 2002). Expressing her feelings and emotions in this form helped her identify six subjective 'I's that would potentially influence her research.[9] The elements in the example below are illustrative of a process, not the full story. Observations in bold italics are Elena's reflections (noted in Ioannidou, 1999) on how these 'I's might influence her research.

Example 2: Identifying Subjective 'I's for a Study of
Language and Ethnicity

In this stanza from her poem, Elena identifies her **Statehood/Cypriot** 'I':

> I was born in a small island –
> somewhere in the Mediterranean –
> Raised as a Greek
> born and lived as a Cypriot
> I am (or think I am) a Greek Cypriot …

And reflects: *'I know that I will have to modify the Statehood/Cypriot 'I' and be able to manage it, both while I am writing about Greek–Turkish relations and when I begin fieldwork examining issues of identity in Cypriot schools.'* From a similar stanza she identifies the Ethnicity/Greek 'I' which leads her to recognize the allegiances she has in different ways to each of the categories, Cypriot, Greek and Greek Cypriot, and that the boundaries between ethnicity and statehood are not always clear. *'There are times when they are discrete, even contradictory, and at other times they are two faces of the same coin.'* Not unconnected to the Ethnicity/Greek 'I' is her commitment to the Dialect 'I' revealed in the following stanza:

> I speak Greek. A special kind of Greek.
> Cypriot Greek they call it.
> It is an ancient dialect of Greek
> survived through the centuries
> alive and authentic
> – a bit different from the Greek spoken in Athens –
> But I like that. Its uniqueness makes it special to me …

Reflecting further on the origins of this feeling, she observes:

Being a Greek Cypriot, and especially, a liberal, Greek Cypriot, I feel a special connection with the dialect of my island. The way we speak constitutes a symbol of our group identity. It reveals the uniqueness of Cyprus, a small island but an autonomous state, a combination of a state and a nation, of language and dialect. The truth is I do not want to see it in decline. I want it alive and authentic as it has remained for more than 8000 years.

Uncovering and eventually controlling the Dialect 'I' in my research is very important since it will accompany me when I go to schools for my fieldwork to investigate children's talk. I know that deep inside me I wish to discover

> *positive attitudes toward the dialect and also to actually see people using the dialect as much as they can.*
>
> The **Justice/War 'I'** was the one that evoked the most sensitive and intense emotions for Elena and in the poem she expressed her anger, disappointment and feelings of injustice at the violation of human rights in the case of Cyprus in the Turkish/Cypriot conflict. Though not perhaps as obvious as the first three in terms of her research focus on language and ethnicity, it nevertheless had a strong impact: '*How can I deal with this in my research? I cannot suppress it, I cannot ignore it … I still have to deal with matters of ethnicity and nationalism both for Greeks and Turks. What do I do?*' Further reflection on this in the poem led to the identification of the **Liberal 'I'** and belief in the possibility of finding a peaceful and fair solution for communities of the island. This offered a means of finding balance in the research process.
>
> Finally, the **Educator 'I'** was interlinked with several others, namely, the Dialect, the Liberal and the Statehood 'I's as they came to impact on the research topic – studying the dialect in Cypriot schools. Standard Modern Greek is the only language taught in schools, though the dialect is evident in breaks and informal settings. While this is clearly a politicized point, Elena's concern was that it is also a social and a pedagogical issue. As indicated in the Dialect 'I', she had a strong desire to see the dialect continue to be spoken. As a teacher (at the time working with young children) she had seen children, especially those from low income families, failing in school and being bullied and excluded simply because they could not 'speak proper' and cope with the transition of language.
>
> *The Educator 'I' is the one that will be very crucial in school fieldwork since it will help me notice all those incidents that someone who has not had such experience with schools may not be able to understand. I will go there both as an outsider and insider.*

It is clear from this brief extract that the subjective 'I's identified here are not independent. They have a common value system reaching back to Elena's commitment to and identification with her homeland. Yet each raised a different angle that she recognized she needed to be aware of in conducting research on language and ethnicity – to explore when they enhanced her understanding and when they might become a bias.

What is also significant about this example (though the full import of this can only be seen in the complete poem) is that it was primarily through the poem, in which Elena expressed strong emotions and feelings, that she came to see the significance of the different 'I's and the values that gave rise to them. I am not suggesting that reflection was not also important in reaching this understanding. Both cognitive and affective processes were involved. But what the poem offered was a succinct way of getting to the core of the issue through expressing emotions and revealing contradictions and dilemmas.

Processes for Monitoring Subjectivity

Documenting what you think and how you feel

The above examples are explorations of subjectivity at the beginning and end of research. But there are many, perhaps simpler, strategies you can adopt throughout the process itself. These are summarized in Case Study Memo 10. Some refer to actions you can take before you enter the field, others to reactions while you are there.

> **Case Study Memo 10   Exploring Subjectivity in the Process of Research**
>
> - List the values you think have influenced your choice of topic and compare these with those that emerge. This is not as easy as it may seem. We do not always know (or know how to state) our values in advance.
> - Explore any strong feelings associated with your research topic. Often people choose a topic in which they have an emotional investment (positive or negative). Becoming conscious of this is a first step in monitoring your subjectivity.
> - If a particular incident was the trigger for your interest, try writing a short description to identify the strength of feeling it conveys and any particular issues arising from it.
> - Choosing an image or series of images to capture feelings and thoughts about the experience can also help raise this awareness.
> - Write down a series of hypotheses or propositions you think may emerge from the research. Set these aside and later compare them with what you discovered in the field.
> - Record issues in images and metaphor, if you can, as this may help identification of your 'subjective selves'. Images frequently speak louder than words.
> - Note observations and reactions to people, politics, events and context.
> - Document critical incidents, especially those that arouse indignation or overwhelming approbation.
> - Record your thoughts, feelings, emotions and anything unexpected, surprising or unusual – on postcards, in a research log, field notes, or research diary. Note what or who annoys you, why you had difficulty empathizing with a certain person, what was so surprising that you needed to review your foreshadowed issues or questions.
> - Keep a researcher's diary or journal to identify values and 'subjective selves' and track unintended effects of these in the research. Return to this when you are writing up and report how your values and subsets of self have influenced your interpretation.
> - Reflect on what you have documented above in an ongoing research journal (Holly, 1989; Janesick, 1999) to see how your reactions are affecting progress of your research and how they may be influencing interpretation of the data.
> - Ensure that you distinguish between error and bias, eliminate the first and account for the second; document your conscious biases and indicate what

> procedures you followed to minimize them; ask a colleague to read a sample of your interview questions, observations and interpretations to check for any unconscious biases.
> - Note when your values, prior knowledge and judgements may be a bias and when they enhance an understanding of the case.

Experiment with artistic forms

In recent years, and in collaboration with colleagues, I have experimented with artistic forms in documenting and interpreting case study research and understanding the role of the 'self' within it (Hicks and Simons, 2006; Simons and McCormack, 2007). In this process, we have used poetry, story, painting, drawing, movement, photographs, clay and collage. Using artistic forms enables you to engage with the data holistically, employing both rational and intuitive modes of understanding. It also allows you to express ideas, feelings and emotions about the research that may not be possible with other methods. The arguments for integrating artistic forms in methodology throughout the research are explored further in Simons and McCormack (2007). Here are a few suggestions related to examining the 'self'.

Poetry is often a helpful starting point. Poems are immediate, accessible and compelling. Words are familiar. In poetic form, they can encapsulate feelings, emotions, doubts and dilemmas in a concise statement, reducing the distance between the writing 'I' and the experience for the reader (Woods, 2006: 51). What makes the poetic form effective as a means of understanding and communicating is that it engages researcher and reader in *feeling* the experience, not simply recording or reading it. The Japanese *haiku* (a short poem of 17 syllables (5, 7, 5) is powerful for capturing the essence of a specific feeling or point. Longer narrative poems are useful in exploring story lines and making sense of dilemmas and contradictions. Both have proved popular with students, the first perhaps because of its brevity and, on the face of it, easy access to the world of the poetic form. The poems you write may or may not be incorporated in the final research account, though see Duke (2007) for an example of using the poetic form both in the process of making sense of the data and in reporting the final story that made sense of the case.

Painting and drawing are less familiar processes for many of us. Precisely for this reason they are useful in exploring our 'selves' in research. They take us out of familiar modes of understanding, allowing images to surface through colour, texture and in spatial awareness. It is not necessary to be skilled in painting or drawing to use these forms. No judgements of the product are being made. The point is to access a different way of knowing through creative processes that engage the emotions and feelings and facilitate intuitive understanding of the data.

Collage is more familiar and has less of the inhibitions we may hold from how we were taught art at school or assumptions we may have of what constitutes painting and drawing. Sue, whose observational narrative was included in Chapter 3, was conducting research into her own practice. Working in palliative care, she was often involved in sensitive and emotionally taxing situations and, at the end of a long, tiring day, writing about her experience seemed just as taxing. However, making a collage enabled her to access another way of dealing with the feelings that accompany such 'emotional labour' and capturing the authenticity of the experience. Another student explored her values, predispositions and past experiences in searching for her research focus through a collage of photographs of significant people and stages of her life. In the shape of a butterfly, it was also a metaphor for the many changes she had had to make in her life and the difficulty of 'settling' on a final topic to research.

How far to involve the emotions? How personal to become?

Including the emotions in research is part of the argument for not separating the person, and the wholeness of the person, from the researcher. We do not cease to be who we are in the process of doing research and that includes how we feel as well as what we think. In the past decade there has been much more acknowledgement of the importance of including our feelings and emotions in research (Bochner, 1997; Denzin, 1997; Ellingson, 1998; Ellis, 1996; Richardson, 1997; Woods, 2006).

Not to include an awareness of the influence of our emotions and feelings is just as likely to affect the validity of the research as any other potential threat to validity. But how far should we go? Students have often asked this question in exploring the interplay of the 'personal' and subjectivity in case study research. Where does one draw the line between exploration of self in a holistic sense and how this affects the research and an overly self-conscious or self-referential account?

This is difficult to answer in the abstract. It depends upon the purpose of your research, the context and circumstances – what support you have from tutors and colleagues, for instance – your research topic and the degree to which you feel comfortable working with your emotions in research. It would have been difficult for Sue, studying her role as nurse tutor in palliative care, not to include how she felt in aspiring to represent her authentic experience. In other contexts, for example, a case study of the impact of a policy initiative in literacy or numeracy, it may be less appropriate and, if a funded study, possibly less welcome. You will need to decide on a case-by-case basis how far to go. Case Study Memo 11 raises a number of issues it may be helpful to consider in deciding where you stand on this issue.

Case Study Memo 11   Engaging the Emotions in Research

- Keep in mind that there is no schism between the cognitive and the affective. Both are needed. Emotions are not opposed to rationality.
- Record your emotions, reactions and feelings in a log or diary throughout the research. Note the issues that trouble you and those that provoke strong feelings – positive or negative.
- Consider using creative processes to access your emotions and feelings and a different way of knowing.
- In exploring emotions in research (whether yours or others) think about where your comfort zone is and how far you might wish to challenge this and through what process.

- Think about how prepared you are to handle any negative emotions which arise and what you might do to manage these, through reflection in a research diary, for example, or discussion with a critical friend.
- In listening to and documenting emotional reactions, be clear where the boundary is between research and therapy.
- Reflect on whether the research has become more about you than about the topic. Watch that you do not use the research to revisit old wounds or rescript your personal story. Remember whose story it is.
- Do not cross the boundary into a confessional tale that is unrelated to the research. Confessional tales may be fine for some purposes, but not, perhaps, for your policy case study.
- Consider when sharing your emotions is a sign of empathy and when an intrusion into the interviewee's story or deflection from the study itself.
- Think about how you can construct a narrative that maintains integrity to the emotional experience observed yet also contributes to knowledge and understanding for others.

Demonstrate reflexivity

The processes above are all part of demonstrating your reflexivity in the process of research. Indicating how these affect your interpretations and conclusions is a necessary next step. To be reflexive is to think about how your actions, values, beliefs, preferences and biases influence the research process and outcome. It is an active process, an intentional, conscious, looking back (whether contemporaneously or at different points in the research process) on the actions you take and decisions you make to deliberate how they influence your study. It is particularly important in qualitative case study where you are re-presenting the experience of others, constructing an interpretation of the reality you observed and the stories people told you. When you are the major research instrument, demonstrating reflexivity – your role and reaction in this process – is a critical factor in ensuring the validity of the study.

Making your reflexivity transparent in the process and writing up of the research has three particular advantages. First, as we have seen, it enables you to identify what subsets of your 'self' any particular research project evokes. Secondly, critically reflecting on the actions and decisions you take throughout the research process enables others to see how you came to the interpretations and conclusions you did. Readers can determine whether you have drawn justified inferences, maintained a line between descriptive and normative statements, and reported impartially or allowed your views to dominate at the expense of participants in the case. Thirdly, you can indicate what biases you detected in the research process and what steps you took to counteract these including citing one or two specific instances.

In Chapter 8, I point out how my biases showed in a school case study I conducted and indicate how I tried to resolve this to produce a more accurate, impartial account. In another case, I recall being under extreme pressure to be 'friends' with a participant. Frequent invitations to dinner, even to go on holiday at one point. The request for friendship was genuine, though accompanied by the demand in field interviews that she was telling *the* 'truth' about the programme in question. Seeking friendship felt somewhat manipulative in this context. It was easy to resist the 'truth' claim. In a case study with multiple stakeholders and in a context that was highly political, I had to represent the many interests and perspectives in the programme. In declining requests for more social interaction (friendship) than was appropriate in the context of this fieldwork, I was aware of Hortense Powdermaker's dictum that in fieldwork you are both 'stranger and friend' (cited by Walker, 1974: 92). In this context I tried to maintain an effective field presence by being friendly without becoming a friend (Ellis, 2007: 9).

In some fieldwork situations it may be appropriate to adopt a 'friendship as method' approach, as Tillmann-Healy (2003) has advocated. This would entail much more interaction, reciprocity and scrutiny by both researcher and participant of each other in the process of conducting the research to deepen experience and understanding. I can see the virtue of this approach in certain contexts, where a deeper understanding of the topic may not be possible by other means. However, it does require a particular disposition, skill and openness of both parties and it is not without its own ethical dilemmas, as Ellis (2007) has pointed out. In the political contexts in which I frequently conduct case study research, which requires representing the interest and values of different stakeholders, it would be hard to sustain, even if wise to embark on.

Writing in reflexivity

Writing in your reflexivity in the final case study requires particular skill if it is to demonstrate the effect your values and biases had on your interpretations without overburdening the text. The common practice of stating one's values in a preface (with the implied assumption these somehow influence the research) is a start but it is insufficient to judge the validity of the research. It does not indicate how the researcher *acted* in relation to those values in the conduct of the research. Evidence of this is essential but it results invariably in a longer account. If you have used the processes indicated in Case Study Memo 10, you will be able to go beyond the common disclaimer 'inevitably my values will have influenced the research' to demonstrate (with examples) the *specific* values that were present in your *particular* research project.

There are various ways to write your 'self' into the text. In your thesis you can present a reflexive analysis as a separate chapter or as part of the methodology chapter. I took the separate chapter route in two case studies I conducted (Simons, 1987), presenting a reflexive account, following documentation of the case itself, indicating how and why I acted as I did in each. The declared democratic framework and values from which I conducted the research was evident in the early chapters. However, the reflexive accounts explored my reaction to events in relation to serving those values and reasons for the decisions I took in the context and problem structure of the case.

Where you have documented your reflexivity throughout the case, you have further options for presenting this understanding in the text of the case study itself. One is to integrate relevant aspects in the narrative in different typescript from the main text (see Robinson (1998) for an example). A second is to write a reflective poem and intersperse this in the text (see Duke, 2007). A third is to present a dialogue between your interpretations and observations on what influenced them, either in the text itself in different typescript or as an ongoing commentary footnote. Further suggestions are noted in Case Study Memo 12.

Case Study Memo 12 Writing in the 'Self'

- Start with a quotation that fires something in you, or a poem. It may be one written by you or by someone else, though try experimenting with your own if this feels right.
- Describe a significant incident from your childhood, adulthood or professional life that relates to your research topic or the values you bring to the research.
- Indicate what stimulated your interest in this particular research topic: for example, 'I first became interested in exploring X when I noticed that …' 'In a classroom one day I observed that …' 'For several years I have been aware that …' Students sometimes worry about using the 'I' in research. It is helpful not to overdo this, of course, but foolish to deny when it is *you* making the choices, not some disembodied self.
- Identify any metaphors that encapsulate your experience and use one to structure the narrative.
- Take the metaphor of a professional or research journey to indicate what you might be feeling at different stages in your research, for example, 'climbing a mountain', 'swimming against the tide', 'cracking the code' or whatever springs to mind.
- Use an excerpt from the data or your reading that sparked a connection with something in you.
- Think whether a novel or other book you have read triggers an allegory or insightful connection to your research.
- Create a dialogue with your 'self' as you explore what influenced you at the outset and how you changed during the course of the research.
- Imagine and draw, if you are at ease with this medium, how you are feeling at different stages in your research.
- Note if any further 'subjective selves' emerge in the writing-up of your case from those identified at the beginning or throughout.
- Write a narrative of how your different subjective selves arose and interacted in the process of the research to confound, confuse or clarify the process.
- Think about whether you will write a separate reflexive narrative account alongside your case study or integrate relevant aspects of it into your portrayal of the case.
- Consider what for you would constitute an adequate reflexive analysis of the role of 'self' in the research process; what would be an overly conscious stance.
- Imagine that you are presenting your 'self' as a prologue to presenting your research at a conference. What would you say about the values that underpin your research?
- Ask a colleague to read your case study and examine whether your values have impacted unduly on the story you have told.

Is This For Me?

One of the reasons for studying the 'self' in research is to meet the ethical point raised at the beginning of this chapter that we need to reflect on who we are if we are to study the experience of others and not allow our predilections and values to intrude in unhelpful ways. Such reflection can be a disquieting process. We may not like what we find. It may reveal blind spots in our consciousness or hitherto unacknowledged biases. The task is quite demanding. It means being constantly vigilant for what irks us in our interactions with people and what persuasions we favour and endorse. It means staying flexible and open to interpretations that are different from our own and cool in the face of threats to our persona, not becoming defensive when criticized or retaliatory in response.

I recognize that this process of coming to know who we are in conducting research may not suit everyone. For those who wish to distance themselves from this personal exploration of the 'self' in research, case study research of the kind discussed in this book may not be your preferred approach. However, for those who choose this route, you will gain a clearer sense of where different subsets of your 'self' interact in your research. You will be able to distinguish between your story and the participants' stories, the impact of one upon the other, when and how these intersect, and what may legitimately be termed co-construction of meaning. You may also discover something new about your 'self' evoked by the particular research. But the prize, and the exciting prospect for me in this work, is the discernment it brings. Becoming conscious of how your beliefs and values impact in the research enables you to discern when your values hinder understanding or constitute a bias and when they facilitate insight and deep understanding. This is the art of monitoring subjectivity in case study research.

Notes

1. This is an important point for all forms of research. However, in quantitative research or research where questions are predetermined and built into designs that require consistency of application to yield reliable and valid results, there is less opportunity to explore how different aspects of the 'self' affect the research process and outcome.
2. Lifeworld is a concept from the philosophical perspective of phenomenology meaning the taken-for-grantedness of our social world in time and space and the natural environment, and in relationship with others – the common-sense experience of everyday life (Schutz and Luckman, 1973).
3. It is perhaps important to emphasize that I am not discussing 'self' in an in-depth psychological sense of how we acquire and maintain an 'adequate' self, or in the sense of a 'confessional tale' – a highly experiential account of how every action in the field affected you personally. My focus is educational – what we can learn from monitoring the interaction of 'self' in the research that has an impact on both.
4. Though these concepts are familiar to me from my training in psychology, I am indebted to Mary Louise Holly for indicating their relevance for a study of the self in research in her paper 'Educational research and professional development: On minds that watch themselves' (Holly, 1993).
5. Those who write about identifying subsets of the self in research use different terminology to describe this process. Peshkin (1988) speaks of multiple 'I's, Coffey (1999) 'fieldwork selves'. In the main I have retained their descriptors.

6   Further examples of how to become more conscious of the ways in which values and beliefs influence the research process can be found in Bentz and Shapiro (1998), Coffey (1999) and Holly (1993).
7   For a full account of this episode see Simons (2000).
8   I am grateful to Elena Ioannidou for giving permission to quote from her poem and experience of uncovering her subjective 'I's as an example for other case researchers studying their 'self' in research.
9   A seventh, the PhD candidate 'I', spoke of the tension in revealing one's emotions, ideology and values in research in an academic culture that might not reward such exploration. This is omitted here as it is less relevant than the others for illustrating the impact of the 'I's on the research topic, though the point it raises may have relevance for other students. You need to be clear if you choose to examine your subjectivity in this way that you have support from your supervisor and colleagues. It may not be for everyone.

Further Readings

Bentz, V.M and Shapiro, J.J. (1998) *Mindful Inquiry in Social Research*. Thousand Oaks, CA: Sage.
An in-depth exploration of different theoretical traditions that can guide your research journey. Less about specific ways of exploring the 'self', more about examining ways of knowing and how you might engage with different cultures of inquiry and the research task. Encourages you to question and also offers advice.

Coffey, A. (1999) *The Ethnographic Self: Field Work and Representation of Identity*. London: Sage.
An excellent book on the subject of locating and exploring the self in ethnographic research with detailed examples from the field illustrating how different researchers encountered their subjectivity in research. Also offers guidance on how to write the 'self' into research and re-present what we learned in the field.

Loader, D. (1997) *The Inner Principal*. London: The Falmer Press.
Details the writer's personal journey through a number of 'telling stories', analysing his various leadership roles. Starting from a particular emotional turning-point in his life – leaving a school where he had been principal for eighteen years – the stories vividly (through metaphor, poetry, reflection and narrative) portray his self-analysis of his feelings, visions, values and beliefs as he encounters different aspects of his role as a principal.

6

WHOSE DATA ARE THEY? ETHICS IN CASE STUDY RESEARCH

The Nature of Ethics – A Situated Practice

Ethics is how we behave or should behave in relation to the people with whom we interact. This means establishing throughout the research process a relationship with participants that respects human dignity and integrity and in which people can trust. Participants need to know they are being treated fairly and that if difficult issues arise, these can be discussed and resolved, meeting both participants' concerns and the researcher's obligation to produce public knowledge.

Ethics is also a situated practice inextricably connected with politics and requiring deliberation of many factors – social, personal and political – in the precise socio-political context of a specific case. This is not always a straightforward process, as House (1993) has pointed out:

> Ethical principles are abstract, and it is not always obvious how they should be applied in given situations ... Some of the most intractable ethical problems arise from conflicts among principles and the necessity of trading off one against the other. The balancing of such principles in concrete situations is the ultimate ethical act. (p. 168)

In this chapter I discuss some 'trade offs' I made in specific cases. But first I want to explore some general principles. I start with the fundamental principle of ethics – to do no harm, the nature of the dilemmas that often confront us in the field, and ethical issues we need to consider in designing case study research. I then explore principles and procedures for the conduct of the research within a democratic approach to ethics and offer some reflections on these in particular instances to illustrate my situated ethical practice.

Fundamental Principle – Doing No Harm

The fundamental ethical principle in research, whatever methodology you choose, is to 'do no harm'. This seems uncontroversial, and something with which we would all agree. However, it is not a straightforward concept. What constitutes harm is interpreted differently by different people and may be perceived differently by them at different times. These differences can result in pressure to adopt procedures and methods that are not always relevant to the research in question or failure to recognize the potential harm that may result from use of particular methodologies.

Our focus is case study research where people and their experiences are closely described and interpreted in unique contexts.[1] We need to establish in any particular context what 'doing no harm' means to individuals, to review this in the process of gaining data and be particularly mindful when reporting. In the process, when you have developed a relationship of trust over time, participants often speak quite openly about their experience, and may inadvertently reveal something they did not intend. You need to be sure that you do not unintentionally misuse this information and exploit a person's openness or vulnerability.

When it comes to reporting, participants should not feel let down, 'at risk', or disempowered when they see in written text experiences closely shared with you in the field. On seeing how they are portrayed in the written case, participants, even if anonymized, may take a different, possibly more negative, view of themselves from the one they initially held. We cannot control for such a change of view but awareness of the potential harm this could invoke strengthens the argument for an ethical stance that places high priority on the primacy of relationships in specific contexts (Christians, 2003; Gilligan, 1982; Noddings, 1984) rather than individual rights and universal principles. Where trust and respect have been created through establishing good relationships, difficulties that arise can be resolved cooperatively through mutual understanding and dialogue (Etherington, 2007; Schwandt, 1998; Torres and Preskill, 1999).

This concept of relational ethics helps us to see the principle of 'doing no harm' in a new light. While appreciating the ethical intent underlying this principle, I have often wished it was more positively stated to acknowledge an intention to research *with* people rather than avoid doing harm *to* them. Focusing too much on 'doing no harm' may prevent us seeing the potential in the research process to contribute positively to participants' experience – an aspiration that underpins the ethical stance outlined in this chapter.

Ethical Dilemmas

Ethical issues in the field, more often than not, present themselves as dilemmas – where two or more courses of action seem irreconcilable yet both seem to be right (House, 1993; Russell, 1993), and we have to make a judgement which to pursue. This will be guided by the ethical principles we have adopted and the ethical theory or theories we appeal to concerning how we relate to people in social and professional life. But it is our professional ethical judgement at the end of the day. In reaching a decision, where there is a conflict of principles, a number of questions run through my mind. In most cases this comes down to have I been fair?

- Who gains and who loses by the release of this information?
- What are the consequences for whom of each course of action?

- Which course of action is more justifiable in the context of the whole case?
- Will that person's career be ruined if I include that data or is it only a fear?
- Has the way I have reported data changed the participant's meaning?
- Have I fairly represented all legitimate interests?
- Have I balanced the authority of the most powerful stakeholders with the authority of knowledge of the practitioner?
- Have I ensured that the power I have, simply because I construct the case, has not diminished participants' perspectives?
- Can I justify my decision in a way all participants and stakeholders will accept?

In the following example, the dilemma I faced was how to maintain the integrity of the case (reporting what actually transpired) while at the same time being responsive to the concerns of the Director of a project who feared his career might be at risk when the report became public.

Example: An Ethical Dilemma

This example is from an evaluation case study of an innovative bilingual project in the UK funded by a local education authority.[2] The early history of the project had been problematic and there were expressed difficulties between the Director and the Manager who had appointed him. This led eventually to the Manager requesting the Director's resignation, believing that he was not doing an adequate job in the way the authority had envisaged the project. The dilemma arose when the Director objected to the way his potential dismissal was described in the interim case study report, claiming that his future career would be at risk if this became public. Yet this information and the ripple effects it created in the project were crucial to how the project was being implemented in schools, an observation with which the Director agreed.

My dilemma was whether to excise all reference to the Director's potential dismissal and remove his anxiety about the future (thereby failing to report accurately on the project) or whether to seek with him a way to report the issue in a way that *he* could see no harm. While empathizing with his concern over the potential threat to his future career, I negotiated how we might best present the issue which resulted in his resignation being sought. Together we found a way to modify the language of the narrative documenting the event, resulting in a slight overall change of tone. This did not alter the data and the importance of recording the issue, merely the way in which it was reported. Language is not value-free, of course, and the modification may have had other consequences, but it did lessen the potential adverse effect for the Director when the report became public.

Ethical Issues in Designing Case Study Research

Many ethical conflicts, according to a study by Morris and Cohn (1993), arise at the reporting stage, as in the case above. But ethical dilemmas also occur in the process. It may not be possible to anticipate precisely what these might be, but thinking through what ethical issues may arise gives you a head start. It may also be necessary to do this for your research proposal to be accepted by an ethical committee. Case Study Memo 13 outlines ethical issues to think about in designing research related to your specific topic, methodology, procedures, conduct and reporting.

Case Study Memo 13   Ethical Issues in Research Design

- Consider at the outset what ethical issues might arise in your particular case.
- Think through, in one or two instances, how these would be addressed.
- Be conscious of what kind of ethics you personally aspire to and what values you hold in relation to the research topic.
- Become familiar with any legislation that exists related to your topic and act within it.
- Think through the ethical implications of the methodology you choose – for example, does it respect participants' rights? Does it balance this with the responsibility for generating public knowledge? Does it provide scope for participants' ethical development if this is part of your purpose? Does it honour those who are less enfranchised? Does it respect cultural, gender and age differences?
- Pilot any potential methodological tools (for example, questionnaire or interview schedule) to ensure that questions are unobtrusive (though do not equate this with non-challenging) and culture-, gender- and age-sensitive.
- Think through how you might report individuals' in-depth experiences and what rights you will give them to edit or expand their data.
- Decide what position you will adopt on informed consent, confidentiality and anonymity, control over data, access before publication. Decisions on these issues will to some extent be determined by the choice you make as to whether you prefer to be guided by an ethical tradition that favours universal laws and principles, one that is more relational and situation-specific, or one that is democratic in intent and participatory in process and outcome.
- Draw up a brief set of ethical procedures to guide data collection and dissemination. Indicate how you will maintain respect for persons while making research public knowledge. Include a consideration of issues such as non-coercion (do you require an opt-out statement?), potential benefit to participants (what might they gain from this research? what might they learn?), and potential harm (what might they lose? what might be the consequences and for whom?).
- These procedures are important if you have to submit your research proposal to an ethical committee. It will not be possible to encapsulate all the ethical dilemmas that may arise, but it will demonstrate that you have thought about the issues and have some reference points for acting ethically in the field (Piper and Simons, 2005).

Beyond Ethical Committees and Institutional Review Boards

Often the first step in establishing an ethical approach to research is your journey through an ethical committee or Institutional Review Board (IRB), as they are termed in the USA. In recent years there has been an intensification of these institutional gatekeepers for social research. These committees seek oversight of research proposals before researchers enter the field, often requiring lengthy informed consent procedures and explanations of methodology. If you are conducting research in an institution, you need to follow such institutional procedures. However, these are limited as an *ethical process* for two reasons.

First, they are prospective only, outlining what should happen or what you intend to do. Rarely are they followed up by those who grant institutional permission to examine if they have been followed in the field. Secondly, they do not address the inherent nature of the ethical act itself, which is relational and field-based. It is not possible to govern ethical behaviour through forms and procedures. While principles and procedures are necessary to guide your actions in the field, these are just that — a guide to action.

It is important to be aware that in recent times there has been a tendency for some ethical committees or IRBs to over-step the boundaries of their legitimate role of ensuring human subjects' rights are protected towards controlling the kind of methodology that is allowed (Lincoln and Tierney, 2004; see also see Janesick, 2002; Simons, 2006). This can be quite direct in actually stipulating the methods researchers should use, or it may be demonstrated through favouring certain methodologies over others. In such a context, you may have more of a struggle to get your research accepted. This places even more of a burden on you to thoroughly justify your choice of methodology and to indicate that it may change in emergent designs. If it is challenged unduly or another methodology is prescribed by an ethical committee, seek your supervisor's help to argue why the approach you have chosen is most appropriate for your research topic.

Many research proposals include a general statement to the effect that the research will conform to the ethical principles of a professional association such as the British Educational Research Association (BERA) or the American Evaluation Association (AEA). To get closer to practice, I suggest you go further and spell out (through precise ethical procedures) how you will *act* in the field in relation to the people engaged in your research. Such procedures will still be prospective but they are a step closer to action.

Ethics in the Field

Establishing and maintaining trust

Once in the field, the first task is to build relationships and establish conditions of trust with the people you are studying. Trust is essential to good field relations but it cannot be assumed; it has to be created in the process of conducting the research. Formal procedures are necessary to this end, as Nias (1981) has persuasively argued, '… formal procedures and the interpersonal knowledge which they promote are not the anti-thesis of "trust" but the necessary conditions for it. Moreover they act upon each other. Formal procedures facilitate the growth of trust and help to ensure its survival' (p. 22).

Having created trust, you need to nurture it throughout by adhering consistently to procedures and scrutinizing your ethical judgements in the field. One learns from case to case. Yet each case is different and may need a unique response. Questions it may be helpful to ask include:

- Are my questions in interview sensitive, not too intrusive?
- When observing, am I invading participants' privacy? Or attributing motivations?
- When taking photographs or filming, do I have informed consent? What will be the likely reaction when participants see the photographs or video?
- Have I recorded participants' perspectives accurately?
- Am I documenting participants' stories or confirming my previous theories?
- Am I honouring participants' requests to keep information confidential?
- Have my biases led to unfair selection of data or interpretation?
- Have I portrayed participants fairly in reporting?

Ethical principles and procedures – a democratic stance

In my own practice I have been guided by a set of ethical principles and procedures that stem from a democratic ethic underpinned by principles of fairness, justice and equity. This was explained to some extent in Chapter 2, in discussing the role I prefer to adopt in case study research to promote engagement of participants and informed action for stakeholders and audiences. It renders problematic the question of who owns the data and draws attention to the need to aspire to a more equitable relationship between the researcher and the researched and the audiences the research seeks to inform. MacDonald and Walker (1975) began to address this issue over thirty years ago in a paper on the concept of case study in educational research by raising the following questions:

- To whose needs and interests does the research respond?
- Who owns the data (the researcher, the subject, the sponsor)?
- Who has access to the data (who is excluded or denied)?
- What is the status of the researcher's interpretations of events, *vis-à-vis* the interpretations made by others (who decides who tells the truth)?
- What obligations does the researcher owe to his [sic] subjects, his sponsors, his fellow professionals, others?
- Who is the research for? (p. 6).

Implicit in these questions is a concern not only for respecting individuals who contribute to the research but also those, beyond the case, who have a legitimate 'right to know'. MacDonald (1976) went on to articulate the political implications of this research stance in his model of democratic evaluation, a term he used to distinguish this practice from autocratic evaluation or bureaucratic evaluation models in currency at the time.[3]

What is relevant for this particular chapter is the way in which ethical principles are derived from the central aspiration of the democratic model – how to find an appropriate balance in research between the individual's right to privacy and the public's right to know. This aspiration is translated into a set of power-equalizing principles and procedures for conducting the research that:

- accords equal treatment to individuals and ideas;
- establishes a flow of information that is independent of hierarchical or powerful interests;
- maintains that no one has the right to exclude particular interests and values.

The actual ethical procedures, an example of which is given in Case Study Memo 14, centre on the interrelationship between the three key concepts in the democratic model – *confidentiality*, *negotiation* and *accessibility*. Confidentiality helps to secure the trust and conditions necessary to gather honest, valid data. Negotiation is the means through which data that are not harmful to individuals can be released for public knowledge. Accessibility refers to the need to communicate to audiences beyond the case in ways they understand.

Case Study Memo 14   Ethical Procedures for the Conduct of Case Study Research

- The purpose of the study and the anticipated audiences for the information will be made clear at the outset.
- Permission will be sought for access to documents, files and correspondence; these will not be copied without explicit permission.
- Informed consent will be sought for each person interviewed and observed; this includes pupils in schools, even if the school decides to seek permission from parents.
- Interviews will be conducted on the principle of confidentiality.
- Use of data will be negotiated with participants on specific criteria (for example, accuracy, fairness and relevance) and within specific timelines.
- Individuals will be asked at the end of the interview for permission to use the interview and if anything needs to be excluded.
- Interviewees will have an opportunity to see how their comments or observations about them are reported in the context of the case study and to edit and add in, if necessary, criteria of accuracy, relevance, fairness.
- No data will be reported that a participant asks to be kept in confidence.
- Direct quotation and attributed judgements in reports require the explicit permission of the respondent.
- Non-attributable information used in summarizing findings across projects or in raising general issues about the programme does not require specific clearance.

- Pseudonyms will be used in reporting individuals and institutions; staff may be referred to in role. While this does not guarantee anonymity, it reduces the likelihood that individuals and institutions will be identifiable.
- Where it is not possible to anonymize (that is, with public figures or particular institutions), clearance will be sought for comments that may be identifiable.
- Where difficulties arise, all parties should be open to apology and be prepared to negotiate an agreed way forward.

While several of these procedures – for example, gaining access, informed consent, pre-publication access – are familiar in many forms of social research, the democratic perspective gives more weight to:

- ongoing informed consent – checking throughout what is valid consent in the specific context with particular individuals and renegotiating if necessary;
- involving participants in identifying and refining issues, having a voice in how they are represented, and checking interpretations;
- negotiation of what data becomes public on criteria of accuracy, relevance and fairness, with several opportunities for participants to edit or add to how they and their views are re-presented in the case;
- engaging in 'deliberative dialogue' (House and Howe, 1999) with stakeholders on the focus and use of the research to maximize its utility.

For examples of exact procedures used in different case study projects see Simons (1984, 1989).

Reflections on Principles and Procedures

Informed consent

The traditional way in which informed consent is sought is through a form participants are asked to sign prior to being interviewed or taking part in the research. While it is important to follow this procedure if sought by an ethical committee, it is insufficient for good ethical practice and inappropriate in certain contexts. It is, at the very least, provisional. There are four specific issues here.

The first is how to provide sufficient information so that participants are adequately informed. This is particularly problematic in emergent designs, where knowledge of which issues will be studied is not always known at the outset. The second is the possible need to revisit the concept of informed consent and if necessary secure it again in relation to difficult issues that may arise in the field. This is sometime called *process consent* (Ramcharan and Cutcliffe, 2001), *rolling consent* (Simons, 2005), or *provisional consent* (Flewitt, 2005a). The third is to be aware that informed consent should be obtained from each person you seek to interview. Do not accept that informed consent given by a major stakeholder or gatekeeper of an institution, for instance, holds true for all participants in that institution.

Finally, it is important not to assume that the same approach to informed consent suits all circumstances. You need to decide in each case what constitutes valid consent. For example, gaining consent in certain indigenous cultures may mean meeting with the elders and deliberating collectively what will meet the values of the particular community. In the NHMRC (2003) guidelines, for example, the values of reciprocity, survival and protection, spirit and integrity underpin their cultural norms and specific ethical procedures. It may also mean agreeing the methodology to be used – questionnaires may not be appropriate, for instance, where an oral tradition is the norm[4] (Smith, 1997 cited in Mataira, 2003: 6) – offering payment for information given, and deciding how any profits would be shared (NHMRC, 2003).

Informed consent with children and other vulnerable groups

In a school setting it is often assumed that consent by the school (acting *in loco parentis*) or parental consent constitutes informed consent for children to be interviewed or observed. Where large samples are sought, this is common practice and certainly facilitates the process of the research. In case study research where fewer children are likely to be involved, this falls short, for me, of valid informed consent. I think we should aspire to treat children and young people in our cases according to the same ethical precepts we adopt in research with adults – do no harm, respect participants, do not lie, treat people fairly, gain informed consent, allow the right to withdraw.

The age of the children may make a difference, though we should be wary about making assumptions about what age is appropriate. Children can speak for themselves, sometimes most definitely. From quite an early age they are capable of giving informed consent and showing, verbally or non-verbally, when they are withdrawing consent. (See Alderson and Morrow (2003) for an overview of ethical and legal considerations in research with children and Flewitt (2005a) for an account of ethics in research with very young children.)

The same is true for other 'vulnerable' groups who may have less control over their circumstances, such as those who have a terminal or degenerative illness. Participants should still be asked, but making sure that the consent was informed may mean assessing with a carer what would constitute informed consent for the specific individual at a specific time. It might also be necessary to keep checking throughout the research (daily if necessary) to see whether the participant is still giving agreement – based upon the careful recording of that person's capacity and well-being and monitoring of the conditions under which process consent is given.

Giving voice and participant control

One reason for giving participants opportunities to edit their comments in the context in which they are reported is the power of the social dynamic of the in-depth interview. Frequently, interviewees have commented 'I cannot understand why I am telling you this', 'I don't know why I tell that man [speaking of a colleague] the things I do', 'I wished I had not said that'. Giving participants control over what information about them becomes public is a useful procedure in this context, though it may not be the only one to ensure no harm. There are still decisions you need to make about how to report these comments fairly.

Individuals also sometimes say things that *you* wish they had not said. This is more tricky. What do you do, for instance, with damaging comments interviewees make about colleagues which affect the research but which, if reported, would raise problems for all concerned? On reflection, interviewees might edit their judgements so they do no harm to others or to themselves, but if they do not, it is up to your professional judgement whether or not to include this material.

The dilemma here is that if you exclude the data you counteract the principle that individuals should have control over how information about them is used. It might also be seen as patronizing, even if it protects individuals from the approbation of others or repercussions on themselves. If you include it, you run the risk of causing harm to some individuals and disrupting the study. The issue here is not simply one for the individual. If the publishing of some data reflects badly upon an individual and it would create undue disturbance in the research setting, it may be wise both for the protection of that individual and the continuance of the study to omit those data.

Participant control over observations
Giving participants opportunity to check how they are portrayed in reports that are interpretative (based upon observations, interviews and documents) is not as straightforward as giving them an opportunity to respond to their interview scripts, but it is equally important. Observations are made by you, whether corroborated or not by interviews with the individual. You have added a layer of meaning in writing a portrayal. Given the risk of attributing motivations to a person from something observed and the power of the narrative in interpretation, it is essential to offer individuals an opportunity to see and respond to how observations of them are presented in case study reports.

Participant control in different cultures
The issue of giving voice and participant control may have different implications in cultures different from our own. In the context of researching a school set up by black workers in South Africa in a period in transition from apartheid, McKeever (2000) draws our attention to two important ethical considerations: first, that owning data was a collective not an individual concern; and secondly, that the primary audience for the research was not an academic one but the community itself.

Procedures she adopted to respect these differences included cataloguing documents as Workers' School documents and producing two texts, one for the university in her name and another, co-authored with the workers, to be sold for their benefit. The point she is making here is that the knowledge produced from the data owned by 'the people' in her story should not only be 'accessible' to, but also 'attributed' to them and, if profits are to be gained from such research, they should have a share, if not the sole rights (see also NHMRC, 2003).

Though these issues were raised in a particular context of post-colonial research, they do have wider resonance for case study research that aspires to be participatory, democratic and action-oriented. Gaining data from a collective means acknowledging collective participation and voice, and sharing ownership over any product.

Decoupling of confidentiality and anonymization

It is often assumed that anonymization deals with the need to protect the privacy and identity of individuals and assures confidentiality. Here I argue that these two concepts need to be decoupled and considered separately. While anonymization may protect the privacy of individuals to a degree when the research is published, this is not the same as honouring confidentiality in the research process. It is not a trade-off and it is certainly no guarantee to say we will interview you in confidence and anonymize you in reports, as though one takes care of the other.

Confidentiality

Offering confidentiality is a common principle at the beginning of the research, to gain trust and encourage participants to speak openly and honestly. It assures them that any information they reveal, which is sensitive, personal or problematic, that they wish to keep confidential, will be respected and that they will not be exposed.

At the same time there is a common understanding that findings will become public. It would be odd for participants to engage in a research study with the expectation that all information they give is retained in confidence. The principle of negotiation in democratic procedures is the means by which data obtained in confidence are checked with individuals for public release. This can take place at any stage but is particularly important at the reporting stage, as noted earlier. Participants can still request that data be retained in confidence if they think that how it is presented may affect them in harmful ways.

Honouring confidentiality also means staying alert in the process to issues individuals wish to keep private. They may state this in words – 'I would prefer it if you did not use this', 'this is in confidence' – or reflect it in their body language. It means not asking intrusive questions or pointing the camera where access has not been granted. In the final analysis, it means acknowledging that not all information obtained in interview or discovered about the person in the case becomes public.

Anonymization

Using pseudonyms – changing participant and institutional names – is a common principle in research reporting to anonymize individuals and offer them some protection of privacy. This principle has recently been challenged by Walford (2005), who argues that in small-scale studies there are good reasons for not adopting this principle: namely, that it is impossible to successfully anonymize – people can guess who the protagonists are — and that it is useful for the sites to be known both for others to verify the validity of accounts and to celebrate the life and work of communities. Kushner (2000) has also challenged the principle of anonymization, arguing that there is an ethical issue in denying identity (p. 65). Anonymity, he says, is as potentially damaging to people as naming them in our reports. The issue is a complex one, not simply a case of anonymize or not. It depends upon who the anonymization or non-anonymization serves, styles of reporting and reception by readers of our reports.

The case for anonymization

In most case study research I have conducted (the exception was a case study of an innovative programme in a government department that was impossible to anonymize), I have anonymized individuals and institutions in case study reports. I have done this even when the head of a school declared that he was content for the school to be named. My reasoning is threefold.

First, while it may be relatively easy for the head of an organization if the organization is named, it can be difficult for staff who would be identified by it. I have often found that those who say 'by all means use my name', 'I am quite happy to stand up and be counted', are either anticipating 'good news', which will be helpful for image management of the organization, or are not fully aware of the possible repercussions from readers with different persuasions.

Secondly, identification may restrict what participants say. In the above situation, where the head was content for the school to be named, the teachers told me that they would not have spoken so openly had this been the case. However, the third and major reason for anonymizing people in case reports is that you cannot guarantee that those who read your case study will respond fairly and sensitively. This is something that we, as researchers, cannot control, especially in highly politicized contexts. However, by adhering consistently to ethical procedures, monitoring our judgements and actions, and engaging in dialogue with those in the field when dilemmas arise to seek joint resolutions, we can at least assure those within the case that we have treated them fairly and justly.

For all these reasons I think it is helpful to anonymize participants even when they have individually and collectively agreed to how they are represented in a case study. Further down the line when the research is published, it is some protection from unwarranted or unfair judgement from unexpected quarters and even agreed audiences. It can also be a protection from possible legal challenge. In a paper by Kushner published in Simons and Usher (2000), we respected and agreed with the author's intention to honour the perspectives of the persons portrayed, who wished to be named, for their identity to be retained and celebrated. However, the publisher, concerned about possible litigation, asked us to change the names or withdraw the paper.

With hindsight I am not at all sure that I and the author should have agreed to change the names (and I would think twice about it another time). It gave into a potential legal risk instead of respecting the wishes of the individuals. Withdrawing the paper would have meant that the individuals' stories were not told at all, but I am not sure, in retrospect, that this was an adequate justification for the decision we took. I remain uneasy. Whose interests did this course of action serve? The issue is a delicate one and had poignancy in the particular context. The individuals concerned were dying and had allowed, and indeed wished, to have their words celebrated. Anonymization is not necessarily always the best moral course of action. If we had had the written agreement of the individuals concerned and that of their relatives, to maintain their identity and celebrate their work posthumously, I wonder if the imperative from the publisher would have been so categorical, and whether we could have negotiated to maintain their names.

When children are involved in case study reports I would also anonymize for similar reasons to those stated above (with the exception of the example just cited). Children may be less able to defend their privacy or agree that information about them become public. This is especially the case with young children, say from the 3–5 age group, where video is used, and where, as in a study by Waters (2004), emotionally disturbed young children were involved. In such circumstances, anonymization is often not possible and permission has to be obtained from parents.

The case for non-anonymization
While I argue in the main for anonymization, there are several research contexts (apart from the situation where people are breaching the law) where anonymization is not the most appropriate procedure to adopt. First is the single institution or programme which is unique. Referring to staff in role is commonly used in such contexts in an attempt to anonymize individuals. However, this does not protect the identities of all; it would still be possible to identify senior people in an organization.

Second is the case of high-profile individuals or public figures who are either difficult to anonymize or should not be anonymized as they are publicly accountable. In such contexts, even if all is on the public record, it is still important to maintain trust by negotiating what data about them is part of the case study and possibly sharing the final case report with them before dissemination, though this might be seen as privileged access unless such a procedure is extended to all participants in the study.

Where it is not possible to anonymize, in a government policy case study, for example, and agreement on the final report of the research cannot be reached, you might wish to add a procedure to the effect that 'participants will have the right to indicate the points at which they disagree or make a short written response'. I have adopted this on more than one occasion. In the case reported in the previous chapter, where negotiation reached a stalemate over the insistence that I remove and even change data in a final report, the offer was not taken up, possibly because it might have been seen to reflect badly on the organization that a resolution could not be reached. In another case, the managers wrote a two-page account indicating where they disagreed and this was included in the final case report.

Third is the situation, say in participatory case study research, where you wish to acknowledge the contribution of individuals who have been, if not co-researchers, key participants. Fourth is where you are aspiring to an ethical practice and open research relationship with participants where data are progressively cleared and professional judgements and reports negotiated. In these last two contexts anonymizing individuals after working transparently and collaboratively with them throughout the research seems antithetical to the very process you are trying to establish within it.

Balancing principles – open to apology and renegotiation

Given that it is not possible to anticipate all difficult situations that might arise in case study research, it is a useful policy to include a procedure that allows you to re-establish 'good' field relationships should something unexpected happen. If a problem occurs which is an error of yours (or even if it is not) being direct – offering a simple apology – invariably allows you to get back on track. If the issue is more intractable and involves several people, confront it openly with one of the key participants/stakeholders and invite them to help you resolve it: 'what shall *we* do about this?' I included the last procedure on renegotiation in Case Study Memo 14 – 'where difficulties arise, all parties should be open to apology and be prepared to negotiate an agreed way forward' – to acknowledge this point. The following is an example of such renegotiation in action.

Example: Renegotiation of Procedure – Getting Back on Track

The opportunity to renegotiate arose in an external case study evaluation I was directing of a new curriculum in vocational education in a local education authority. In an interim report on the project, my co-researcher included a dialogue between a project manager and a project developer in which the developer voiced strong opinions about the manager. The issue seemed important to record, representing as it did a potential rift between these two key people in the case which was likely to affect the development of the new curriculum. Both had cleared their individual comments and the dialogue for public release. However, when other teachers in the project team read it, the manager became concerned about how he was perceived and wanted it retracted. He sought the advice of the Chief Education Officer (CEO), worried, he said, about the impact on the project as a whole. The CEO rang me to discuss the issue. I apologized and we agreed to meet to think of a strategy of damage limitation.

Though displeased that the report had raised an issue that was difficult for him internally, in the spirit of the last procedure in Case Study Memo 14 the CEO and I agreed a way forward that would ensure the project would continue with renewed goodwill on both sides. Issues that contributed to the resolution were the CEO's understanding of the reason for including the dialogue – to improve development of the project – and his realization that a conflict could easily have arisen between the protagonists. It was akin to a mismatch of styles. He then proposed that we organize a public meeting of all involved – teachers, heads of schools (there were six), the two protagonists and the evaluation team. The CEO, who chaired the meeting, acknowledged the important learning they had gained from the report, particularly through the dialogue which raised fundamental issues for development. He then persuaded the group to address the issues and in so doing diffused the problem the dialogue had presented. I agreed not to make the interim report public, only the final report.

I mention this incident to make three points. First, to highlight the importance of having a procedure that allows for renegotiation in the light of an unanticipated event which had unforeseen repercussions. Secondly, to underscore how important dialogue and good relationships are in interpreting and managing principles of procedure in action. In this case both the relationships and the procedures facilitated resolution of the incident. Thirdly, to illustrate the point raised at the beginning of this chapter that making ethical decisions entails not only negotiation and dialogue but balancing a conflict among principles or 'trading off one against another' (House, 1993: 168) in a concrete situation.

In this example, the principles that were in conflict were the protection of privacy of an individual (the project manager) and the responsibility to publicly report a situation that could, if handled appropriately, avert potential development failure. The trade-off was to retain the interim report within the local authority. It had served its purpose of informing decision-making at the point of need. The issue had been resolved internally. Not publishing the interim report was a compromise of the principle of public access I had negotiated at the outset but it was one I was prepared to take in the particular circumstances to ensure the project continued.

Complex Integrity

The principle of procedure in the above scenario was helpful in the resolution of the dispute, but it was not the only or even the most significant factor. It was the complex negotiation, reflection and judgement that took place between people in relation to it that led to the satisfactory agreed outcome. This is akin to Glen's (2000) concept of complex integrity.

In the context of practitioner action research in the health service, Glen draws a distinction between simple integrity, that undeniable belief and commitment to principles that tell us we are right, and complex integrity, which recognizes and needs to take into account the multifaceted and conflictual nature of much experience. Glen's essential thesis is that an adequate formulation of integrity as an ethical concept cannot be derived from ethical theory alone but needs to engage pragmatically with the researcher's reflective practice discourse.

Beyond being true to one's own principles and values, and those that circumscribe our professional moral practice, complex integrity, according to Glen (2000), means acknowledging and balancing mutually conflicting principles through reflection and dialogue in complex, particular moral situations (p. 15). This resonates with House's (1993) concept of ethical decision-making, with which this chapter began, and reminds us of its central theme – the relational and situated nature of ethics. It is only in and through relationships in the field, supported by procedures and negotiations over what is fair, relevant and just in the precise socio-political context, that we can *know* if we have acted ethically in relation to those who are part of our case.

Notes

1 For an overview of ethics in qualitative research in general, see Christians (2003); and Punch (1994); in quantitative research, Jones (2000) and Sammons (1989); and in evaluation research, Simons (2006).

2   See Simons, H. (1978–9) 'Mother Tongue and Culture, First External Evaluation Report EEC-Sponsored Pilot Project', Cambridge and London: Cambridge Institute of Education, University of London Institute of Education and copyright libraries in the UK.
3   In the initial characterizations of these different forms of evaluation the author noted that these were ideal types. In practice, in the socio-political contexts in which we conduct case study research, there may be elements of more than one type. For further details of the concept of the democratic model see MacDonald (1976) and for the model in action, Simons (1987).
4   This is an inference from the Kaupapa Maori framework (prescribed by Smith (1997) and cited by Mataira (2003)), the second precept of which is *Kanohi kitea* ('the seen face', a requirement to present yourself 'face to face').

Further Readings

Alderson, P. and Morrow, V. (2003) *Ethics, Social Research and Consulting with Young People*. London: Barnardo's.

An extensive discussion of ethics of research with children and young people raising a series of questions and dilemmas in relation to traditional ethics and legislation and ethical practice.

Burgess, R.G. (ed.) (1989) *The Ethics of Educational Research*. Lewes: The Falmer Press.

Explores ethical dimensions in different forms of educational research, including case study, action research, quantitative research and in different contexts. Several chapters outline specific principles and procedures to guide practical ethical decision-making.

Lee-Treweek, G. and Linkogle, S. (eds) (2000) *Danger in the Field: Risks and Ethics in Social Research*. London: Routledge.

Focuses through case examples on how researchers have faced danger in the field. Only one section refers to actual ethical danger (the others being physical, emotional and professional). Important for drawing our attention to the need to consider ethics for the researcher as well as for participants.

Oliver, P. (2003) *The Student's Guide to Research Ethics*. Maidenhead: Open University Press.

Explores ethical issues the research student may encounter at each stage of the research process from design to publication and dissemination. Ethical dilemmas and dialogues facilitate reflective thinking on the theoretical ethical positions outlined.

Simons, H. (2006) 'Ethics and evaluation', in I.F. Shaw, J.C. Greene and M.M. Mark (eds), *The International Handbook of Evaluation*, pp. 243–265. London: Sage.

An extensive review of the ethics involved in evaluation, including differences between ethical rules, principles, guidelines, theories; situated ethics and democratic ethics; re-interpretation of procedures of informed consent, anonymity and confidentiality, institutional reviews boards and ethical committees.

Simons, H. and Usher, R. (eds) (2000) *Situated Ethics in Educational Research*. London: Routledge/Falmer.

Makes the case for ethics as a situated practice in different research traditions and contexts – feminist, postmodern, evaluation, participatory, image-based. Each chapter is case-based, exploring the particular ethical issues that arose in unique socio-political settings, including those of race, post-colonialism and health care.

MID-TERM LETTER

Half way through the writing of the book I sent the early chapters to Laura and enquired how she was getting on with her research. This is her reply.

Dear Helen

Thank you for enquiring how my research is going. I think I am on track. I seem to have successfully negotiated my way into the study and established good field relationships. No difficult problems have arisen ... yet! though I am aware from your tales from the field that I need to be constantly vigilant. I reflected at the beginning on the values I hold in relation to my research topic. I keep a research journal noting critical incidents and how I feel about people and issues. I am mindful of the fact that I am an inevitable part of data gathering and interpretation so am documenting everything as closely as possible to examine how I am affecting the data and how it impinges upon me and my research.

What worries me now, or rather what worries my supervisor, is how I will collate all the data and make sense of it. I have practically finished data collection and will soon reach saturation point. There are three issues that I would welcome help with at this stage — how to analyse and/or interpret; whose theories or theoretical framework to draw upon in explaining the data; and what leeway I have in how I report my findings.

A slight confusion over the first issue stems from my reading and the extensive procedures outlined in many texts, Miles and Huberman (1994) for example, for the analysis of qualitative data. I am concerned about the rationality of this approach. I am afraid that my intuitive grasp of the understanding I am gaining will be lost or reduced. Other writers indicate interpretation is the prime 'making sense' process in qualitative research. Is there a difference? And, if there is, how do I justify choosing interpreting over analysing?

The second issue is theoretical frameworks. Much of what I read discusses analysing in a theoretical framework and my supervisor keeps asking what theoretical frameworks I intend to use. I can see there is a certain security in working within an existing theoretical framework, whether it is generated by me or by others, but this seems a little mechanical. I do not wish to pre-empt insights arising from deep immersion in the data. I am concerned that if I use a pre-existing framework, I may simply see in the data what fits the categories in the framework and fail to see what does not.

There is also the issue of grounded theory. Many texts advocate the use of grounded theory as the main way to generate theory in qualitative research and I assume this includes case study. Yet I also find this (and it may just be my reading of it) a rather overly rational approach. I would like to interpret and theorize from a more intuitive stance. Is it too outlandish to think that I might generate a theory of the case more intuitively? Is this OK? Or will I not then make the grade? Or be given a hard time in the viva?

The third issue is how much leeway I can have in how I report the case study. Do I have to formally present all the evidence, which I then explain? Or can I write an interpretative case study starting with, for example, a story of one of the key players, a critical incident in the setting, or a poem that captures the essence of the case? One of the ways in which I have tried to make sense of my research experience along the way has been to write in poetic and narrative form. Sometimes I have also made collages to make sense of seemingly disparate issues. Is it OK to use these forms of presentation? And is it also legitimate, assuming proper ethical procedures for clearance have been followed, to include visual and audio data (a CD or DVD) in my thesis?

I would really welcome support in thinking through these issues.

With many thanks

Laura

I responded to Laura's letter by reminding her of the themes of the next three chapters, which focus on analysis and interpretation, examples from practice and different forms of reporting case study research, indicating that I would also keep her specific issues in mind.

Section III
MAKING SENSE

7

BEGIN AT THE BEGINNING: ANALYSIS AND INTERPRETATION

Analysis and interpretation are perhaps the two aspects of case study research that are written about least. This is possibly for three reasons. Qualitative case study, and some forms of it in particular, depend heavily on the interpretative skills of the researcher. These are often personal and intuitive, reflect different experiences and differ widely from one researcher to another. Secondly, it is not easy to establish guidelines for analysis that are replicable or appropriate in all situations. Thirdly, it has taken some time to formulate ways of analysing case study data that are not simply an attempt to apply analytical tools more apposite for other kinds of inquiry.

Analysis

For the purpose of this chapter I take analysis to mean those procedures – like coding, categorizing, concept mapping, theme generation – which enable you to organize and make sense of the data in order to produce findings and an overall understanding (or theory) of the case. It is frequently a formal inductive process of breaking down data into segments or data sets which can then be categorized, ordered and examined for connections, patterns and propositions that seek to explain the data.

Interpretation

Interpretation I take to mean the understanding and insight you derive from a more holistic, intuitive grasp of the data and the insights they reveal. This may take into account understandings gained from formal analysis but more emphasis is placed on retaining the holistic nature of the data through intuitive and hermeneutic processes[1] than deductive or inductive analyses. Insights may be evoked through metaphors, imaging, reflective thinking, puzzling over incidents and observations, exploring alternative interpretations, angles of perception, seeing through different lenses, lateral thinking.

Interpretation is a highly skilled cognitive and intuitive process, often involving total immersion in the data, re-reading transcripts, field notes, observations and other forms of data in the data set, such as poems, vignettes, cameos or narratives. It is open to different senses of understanding, such as dancing with the data (Cancienne and

Snowber, 2003), visual imaging, drawing or painting (Spouse, 2000), poetic form (Richardson, 1997; Sparkes and Douglas, 2007), and writing and rewriting of narratives. It can incorporate contradictions, ambivalence of meaning and paradox.

For many authors in the social sciences interpretation is the key process for making sense of what has been learned. Denzin (1994) calls this *'the art of interpretation'* (p. 500). Wolcott (1994) talks about transforming qualitative data. Both concepts draw attention to the creative and personal skills required to make sense in this way. There are no set rules or procedures to follow. Each researcher will find her own particular way of interpreting the data, even if using well-known strategies.

Though it is possible to make this distinction between analysis and interpretation, it is also important to state that these are not discrete processes. Each may be present to different degrees at different stages; they are interactive and iterative throughout the research and in your thinking. Flashes of insight, images or metaphors may come as you engage in the formal categorization of data. Connecting themes identified through a specific analytic process may lead to a particular interpretation and so on. The process is one of moving backwards and forwards between the data, the understandings that you are gaining, the questions you are refining and the next field visit, set of observations or interviews.

Data Do Not Speak for Themselves

A word of caution before you begin. In the social sciences, says Denzin (1994), 'there is only interpretation. Nothing speaks for itself' (p. 500). Walker (1980) makes a similar point in noting how experimental biologists make sense of evidence: '("It does not tell a story. The researcher does") … Making sense is essentially a matter of selecting meaning' (p. 234). You will be aware from early data gathering that you have begun to select meaning with the choices you make about what to observe, question and record.

When you come to organize the data, you identify categories or ideas in the data, you look for themes and patterns, you decide which data to include as evidence for the story that is developing. It is clearly you who is making sense. Wolcott (1994) makes a telling observation on this point when he notes that 'Data that do not "speak" to the person who gathered and reported them are not likely to strike up a conversation with subsequent readers either' (pp. 13–14).

Simply presenting quotations from interviews or observations without any thematic structure, analysis or interpretation is unlikely to convey the meaning of the case. Even in a case study where the intent is to portray the verisimilitude of the setting or engage the reader vicariously with participants' experience, through using interview excerpts and observations, you need to select data that will tell an eventual story.

Start Analysis/Interpretation Early

How you approach analysing and interpreting data – the processes and criteria you choose to assure the quality of your interpretation – will partly depend upon the overall perspective you take to your research and how you see the social world, whether, for example, from a positivist, realist, constructivist, interpretativist or postmodern perspective. This is why I suggested in Chapter 1 that you think at the outset what kind of case study you wish to conduct for what purpose, and why, in Chapter 3, there is a specific design illustrating in one case how the researcher, Sue, chose certain methods in relation to the overall perspective of her research.

Begin at the beginning

Most texts on qualitative research include the imperative 'begin at the beginning'. From the moment you select your research questions and design your study you are foreshadowing issues or indicating frames for analysis. Once in the field, having interviewed and observed, you will have written field notes and summary memos on what you saw, heard and experienced. You may have made what Lou Smith has termed 'interpretative asides' in your field notes, which indicate what you found interesting, what struck you as significant, odd or puzzling and how different pieces of information relate to each other. You may have taken an interview transcript and started to search for meaning through identifying key categories or issues. You may also have made more direct interpretations in vignettes, cameos, critical incidents and short narratives you have written. These are the beginnings of data analysis and interpretation.

As you go from interview to interview and observe more situations in the field, you may change the questions, decide there are further issues to investigate, refine the 'interpretative asides'. At some point these early interpretations may become a little more formalized into what Cronbach has called 'working hypotheses'; that is, a statement of a general finding, often in propositional form, that is provisional and may be disconfirmed or confirmed as the study proceeds. These working hypotheses are just that, work in progress. They alert you to what seems worth pursuing at a point in time but they may not survive the whole journey. As data gathering continues they may become more focused or be replaced by others that reflect your developing understanding of what the data mean. This furthers your analysis and interpretation.

There is also a stage in the research, once you have completed a fair amount, if not all, of the data you intend to collect, where data analysis and interpretation is more intensive as you come to make sense of the whole. In the remainder of this chapter I concentrate on this stage, although many of the strategies and processes will also be relevant to how you make meaning throughout.

Strategies for Making Sense of the Data

Whatever strategies or processes you use to make sense, all involve sorting, refining, refocusing, interpreting, making analytic notes and finding themes in the data. Some, like coding, categorizing, thematic analysis and cognitive mapping, relate more to formal inductive analysis. Others, such as poetic reconstruction and narrative, rely more on direct interpretation, hermeneutic analysis and intuitive processing.

I do not indicate all the various ways you can analyse and interpret. In the past twenty-five years many excellent books have been written on the subject of qualitative analysis and several are noted in the Further Readings. Nor do I discuss particular methods, such as content analysis, documentary analysis, discourse analysis, or computer analysis of qualitative data, the growth of which has accelerated markedly since the mid-1980s (Kelle, 2004; Seale, 2000; Weitzman, 2003).[2] My focus is on processes that can be used in a range of case study applications and settings, whatever the particular methods used.

Perspectives to Consider

Reducing data

The classic text and perhaps the most widely quoted, if not the most widely used, on analysing qualitative data these past twenty-five years, has been Miles and Huberman's (1994) *Qualitative Data Analysis*. Miles and Huberman take a systematic approach to data analysis that centres on three interlinked processes which they term *data reduction, data display,* and *conclusion drawing and verification* (pp. 10–12).

Data reduction is the process of selecting, focusing and abstracting key data from interviews, observations and field notes. It will be guided by choice of questions, methods and conceptual frameworks and, once data are collected, through coding, writing memos, summaries, organizing data into categories, clusters and themes. Data thus reduced are displayed in a diagram or visual form – *data display* – in a matrix, chart or network, for example – which enables you to 'see' what is happening in the data and what action might be needed to further the analysis. *Data conclusion and verification* is the process through which emerging patterns, propositions and explanations are gradually confirmed and verified.

Miles and Huberman (1994) suggest a variety of tactics for generating meaning, including making contrasts and comparisons, noting patterns and themes, clustering, making metaphors, building a logical chain of evidence, making conceptual/theoretical coherence (pp. 245–262). They also propose a list for verifying conclusions, such as triangulation, checking the meaning of outliers, looking for negative evidence, checking out rival explanations, following up surprises, getting feedback from informants (pp. 262–277).

It is possible to read these three processes as analytic linear stages, but this would be a misreading. Miles and Huberman refer to them as streams to emphasize that they are interwoven and proceed in parallel throughout the whole research process – 'the three types of analysis activity and the activity of data collection itself form an interactive cyclical process' (p. 12). While the emphasis in this approach is on generating analytic categories and concepts to describe and explain the data, this can be done deductively or inductively (p. 65).

This approach to data analysis is ordered, sequential and easy to follow. It can also appear, in its thoroughness, to be overly rational and rather daunting. However, you do not need to follow every aspect in detail. Choose those tactics and strategies that best enable you to make valid sense of your data.

Transforming data

Quite a different approach to making sense of the data is that proposed by Wolcott (1994) in *Transforming Qualitative Data*. Reducing the data from a mass of transcripts, field notes and observations is still part of what needs to be done here. However, 'transforming' has a qualitatively different ring to it from 'reducing' data. To me, it is more open and expansive. People talk about their lives being transformed through one experience or another or certain events having the potential to transform the way you think or act. It also evokes the sense of movement – data analysis and interpretation can develop, change, move into another dimension. It is what leads me, in fact, to feel comfortable with 'dancing with the data' in a metaphorical and physical sense.

Wolcott (1994) has chosen to make distinctions between three ways of organizing and making sense of qualitative data – description, analysis and interpretation – to emphasize the myriad of different ways qualitative data can be transformed and to address different questions. *Description* addresses the question – what is going on here – staying close to the data as originally recorded. *Analysis* examines the question of how things work or why they don't, moving beyond the purely descriptive to systematically identify key factors and relationships, themes and patterns from the data. *Interpretation* focuses on the major question of meaning, 'What is to be made of it all'. The aspiration here is to go beyond 'what can be explained with the degree of certainty usually associated with analysis' (p. 11), to reach an understanding that 'transcends factual data and cautious analyses and begins to probe into what is to be made of them' (p. 36).

These three categories, Wolcott points out, are not mutually exclusive or discrete (p. 11). Nor are they necessarily sequential or to be applied in all cases. They are different ways of organizing and presenting data. Though it may make sense to build from description to analysis, it is also possible to move from description to interpretation. Or it may be that what suits your case is a blend of these approaches or an emphasis on one or another.

Processes to Explore

Coding and categorizing

Coding and categorizing are two processes commonly adopted in analysing as you begin to make sense of the data. Coding breaks down the data into segments, and assigns a name to each. Codes can be descriptive or more analytical and explanatory, whether you are working from a pre-existing theoretical framework or the perspective of grounded theory. These are compared with other segments of the data and refined or renamed if necessary to reflect a more accurate 'reading' of the initial code. You can then use the most frequent or significant codes to sort through large amounts of data and eventually categorize them to a more theoretical level.

Coding and categorizing is systematic, comprehensive (searching all the data until the categories are saturated) and cumulative, gradually building understanding or explanations. The dangers are that it becomes mechanical and formulaic, that it stays at a descriptive level and that codes remain fixed rather than open to change as more data are examined and understanding grows.

Opinions differ on whether it is useful to use a system of *precoding* (either content- or process-focused) or *subsequent coding* from the data. Precodes can be generated either from a theoretical or methodological framework or issues identified by the researcher. Those who prefer to generate codes and categories from the data often aspire to use the language and context of participants to emphasize that the categories are grounded in the data rather than stemming from the a priori preconceptions of the researcher.

There are difficulties with either route. While it is possible to argue, if precoding, that you should remain open to unanticipated categories, this is difficult in practice; if you change midstream you may lose part of the analysis and waste time. If generating codes from immersion in the data you need to be aware that however much you aspire to present data grounded in participants' constructs, what you think and value will inevitably affect what you select as significant. You can ameliorate this to some extent and counteract any undue dominance of your constructs over those of participants by taking a reflexive approach to exploring your values and reactions in the research.

Progressive focusing – issue and theme generation

Progressive focusing is another way of reducing and making sense of the data to generate issues, themes and patterns. As outlined by Parlett and Hamilton (1976), it has three phases – making initial sense of the data, reducing observational and interview data to issues, themes or areas for further exploration, and explanation. It begins early in refining research questions and issues in the light of early fieldwork and knowledge about the case in its 'real life' context.

It continues throughout in data gathering, in reframing foreshadowed issues and in redefining interview questions and the focus of observations. Yet there is a further stage of progressive focusing when issues are no longer foreshadowed or the status of 'working hypotheses' turns into propositions that can be justified with evidence from the case. Parlett and Hamilton (1976) use the term 'explanation' to refer to this third stage in the process. I prefer 'interpretation', to reflect the more intuitive side of data processing and making sense of the data.

Concept mapping

Concept maps are a means of representing knowledge visually and mapping links between related concepts in making sense of the data. Most often concept maps are used to organize and analyse theoretical constructs and ideas or individuals' perspectives and interpretations, that is, they are primarily cognitive, but they can also be used to map emotional states.

The central feature of cognitive mapping is modelling the data in visual form, first to code and categorize the data, second to identify themes, and third to map the interrelationships and patterns between them visually. Often the mapping is done from interviews (and field notes), with each interview first mapped on one sheet of paper and subsequently compared with the others to generate common themes and indicate relationships. These can then be represented on one large map to gain a holistic representation of the main categories, themes and findings.

The map can be constructed in different ways – from transcripts of interviews or directly from listening to audio-recordings. Working directly from audio-recordings avoids the tendency to view the transcript as a sacrosanct record to which one can return at a later date to analyse. It also avoids falling into the trap of assuming that transcripts carry all the meaning. But it does carry the risk referred to earlier of the researcher's categories taking precedence over those that stem from participants' data, and there is no opportunity for others to check the validity of the chosen categories.

There are other choices to make concerning what level of categories to map, what symbols to adopt to denote relationships between categories and themes, whether to include notes of the process and context of interviews (which offer important clues to meaning), and whether to note emerging theories, contradictions, ambivalent findings. The latter observations are important to ensure that you are staying close to the process and context in which the data were gathered and are not reaching unwarranted closure on emerging themes and patterns.

Cognitive mapping may be used in four different ways in making sense of the data. It is often associated with a grounded theory approach to research (for an example see Jones, 1985), but equally, it can be used to interpret from a pre-existing theoretical framework. It can prove helpful for engaging participants in interpretation of data by asking them to examine whether the map you produce adequately reflects an analysis of their perspectives in context. It can also be a heuristic device to help you make sense throughout the process.

With respect to the last of these, Sue, whose research design was considered in Chapter 3, used concept maps cognitively and affectively to capture visually what she was thinking and feeling at different points in the research process. She not only worked from interview data and field notes, but also poems or interpretative vignettes she had written and images that represented her feelings and emotions. Maps may be comprised of these different written data or alternatively presented as a collage of visual images, thoughts, emotions, feelings, interpretations (Duke, 2007).

In the context of case study research, unless you have huge resources, it may be that a variation of concept mapping as an analytic tool might be useful to begin to systematically identify categories and themes, but you may not wish to analyse every interview in this way. Cognitive mapping takes a lot of time, though one of my former students has noted that 'the process of transcription and coding as a combined action greatly reduces the time taken when using conventional methods' (Northcott, 1996: 459–460). For those who wish to explore this strategy, below is a practical example of how Nigel used cognitive mapping in his study of appraisal in nursing working directly from listening to audio-recordings.

> Example: Cognitive Mapping Guidelines
>
> 1. Ensure each 45 minutes of interview time is followed soon after by production of the map, for which at least three hours should be allowed.
> 2. Generate field notes at the end of each interview to report the interview process, and have these to hand when mapping.
> 3. Be prepared with a large (at least A3) sheet of paper, Sellotape and a black pen. (Use black and avoid colours to facilitate subsequent photocopying.)
> 4. Listen to the tape right through without stopping to write any comments, and rewind.
> 5. Start mapping. Start at the centre of the paper with a focal word from the research, or the respondent code. Run, rewind, run etc., to ensure data are obtained accurately from the tape.
> 6. Set out and consider the data 'cognitively'! This requires the researcher to formulate codes, make connections, and record non-verbal data, to produce a record that reflects the construction of the respondent. If necessary, take breaks to allow time for thought.
> 7. Keep verbatim quotes separately, indicating on the map where they arose.
> 8. Annotate the map to identify connections as well as respondent and researcher input.
> 9. Underline to emphasize, and use any personalized way of adding data, or for ensuring clarity.
> 10. Be dynamic, and be prepared to develop the technique to optimize the process of coding, categorizing, interpreting and transcribing all in one activity.
>
> (Northcott, 1996: 459)

Grounded theory

The grounded theory approach to analysis classically associated with Glaser and Strauss (1967) and later Strauss and Corbin (1990) aspires to understand, and eventually generate theory from, participants' perspectives and interpretations, from how they 'construct' their worlds. It is the 'most widely used qualitative interpretative framework in the social sciences today' (Denzin, 1994: 508), surviving three decades of broad-ranging critique (Thomas and James, 2006).

Its enduring appeal stems from the precise procedures it outlines. Yet, as Denzin (1994) points out, it has many dangers and criticisms when not fully understood. Three such dangers, he notes, are getting lost in category and coding schemes, lack of clarity about exactly what a theory is and the possible subordination of 'lived experience' and its interpretations to the grounded theorist's reading of the situation (pp. 508–509). These dangers resonate with my experience of supervising research theses that aspire to use classical grounded theory. I have seen few that actually produce adequate or 'grounded' theory to explain the case through the process of grounded theory as prescribed in classic texts.

Charmaz (2006) has recently provided another perspective on grounded theory, stemming from symbolic interactionism. In acknowledging the origin of the classic concept of grounded theory in the Glaser and Strauss (1967) classic text, Charmaz points out that the perspective she advocates was partly there. The two authors came from different traditions, Glaser from Columbia University positivism and Strauss from the Chicago school of pragmatism and field research (pp. 6–7). She summarizes the distinct contribution of each of the originators thus:

> Glaser imbued grounded theory with dispassionate empiricism, rigorous codified methods, emphasis on emergent discoveries, and its somewhat ambiguous specialized language that echoes quantitative methods ... Strauss brought notions of human agency, emergent processes, social and subjective meanings, problem-solving practices, and the open-ended study of action to grounded theory. (p. 7)

During the past forty years there have been many developments in grounded theory by these two authors and Strauss's collaboration with Corbin as well as, in the early twenty-first century, a move away from the positivism in both Glaser's and Strauss and Corbin's versions of the method (Charmaz, 2006: 8–9).

Charmaz's approach to grounded theory returns to the emphasis in the original statement on processes, actions and interpretation of subjective meanings. She views grounded theory methods as a set of principles and practices, not prescriptions, that researchers should use flexibly to generate meaning – that is, develop theories of – experiences and processes situated in time and context. It is a constructivist perspective. Unlike the initial concept which talks about 'discovering theory as emerging from data separate from the scientific observer' (p. 10), Charmaz assumes that neither data nor theories are discovered: 'We *construct* our grounded theories through our past and present involvements and interactions with people, perspectives, and research practices' (p. 10).

In my own case study research, I always work from an intention to reflect and accurately represent participants' meanings in the policy and practice contexts in which they work, that is, for these to be grounded in participants' perspectives. However, I have not followed the Glaser and Strauss (1967) classic approach. I am more concerned with theorizing throughout using a range of different processes and ending up with an interpretative theory of the case.

For me, the classical grounded theory approach is a step too far from the immediacy and 'lived experience' of the people in the cases I have studied. The extent of categorization and abstraction involved, in breaking down and systematically ordering and reordering the data, certainly offers a way of managing the data and making sense. Yet when connections are made and over-arching themes generated, for me, something is lost. Making sense, in this way at least, can mean losing meaning (Walker, 1980). It is not like analysing and interpreting a sonnet. Re-reading the whole sonnet, once you have interpreted each stanza and explored the images, thoughts and emotions each conveys, has a quite different 'feel' to it – the holistic nature of the meaning is retained and enriched, the whole is indeed more than the sum of its parts.

In deciding whether you will use a grounded theory approach, you may wish to explore the overview of the approach presented by Strauss and Corbin (1990, 1998), the reinterpretation in a constructivist perspective (Charmaz, 2006) and also the Thomas and James (2006) paper, which argues that

> far from providing the epistemic security promised by grounded theory, these notions ['theory', 'ground' and 'discovery'] – embodied in continuing reinventions of grounded theory – constrain and distort qualitative inquiry. (p. 767)

These authors recognize that grounded theory procedures do provide sign posts for qualitative inquirers but warn that the significance of interpretation, narrative and reflection can be undermined by such procedures.

The Interpretative Re-turn

I have outlined these different processes of analysis and interpretation to indicate that there are many options to consider in getting from data to an understanding of your case. In re-reading this chapter, I realize that the section on strategies for making sense of the data has a rather formal, rationalistic ring to it. This was not my intention. It is a feature, I think, of my aspiration to communicate what has sometimes been a hidden process in getting from data to a theory of the case. It also reflects the fact that the processes described above are easier to spell out than interpretative processes. But I may have gone too far.

So I want to end this section by re-emphasizing the important aspects of interpretation I raised at the beginning – the instinctive feelings or insights you have that certain issues are significant, the puzzles in the observations and data that do not fit emerging themes, the metaphors, images and other artistic ways in which you gain an intuitive grasp of what the data mean.

These processes are as important, and more so in some cases, than formal methods of analysis. For they retain the holistic nature of the data, detaching it neither from the context in which it arose nor the person who collected it and is now 'making sense'. Interpretation in all these ways is an art, an integrated knowing stemming from deep immersion in the data and drawing, in some indefinable way, on the whole range of data you have encountered. So do use your intuition and affective as well as cognitive ways of knowing in coming to an understanding of the case. The next chapter gives some examples of how these processes have been used in actual cases which may help you decide which may work for you and your case.

Case Study Memo 15 **Analysis and Interpretation**

- Decide what overall perspective you will adopt in making sense of the data. Will you choose a formal process of analysis – involving coding, categorizing and aggregation of data? Or will you opt for direct interpretation and transforming data more intuitively?
- Consider the range of processes available – concept mapping, progressive focusing, issue-theme generation.
- Think through which analytic or interpretative strategies best suit your research data, purpose, audience or your own predilections. But also consider going

- beyond your comfort zone. Try alternative ways of making sense and see where they lead.
- Remember, data do not speak for themselves. It is you who has to make sense of them. You have to interpret the data, identify themes, reveal insights, generate explanations.
- Recall the many ways in which you can interpret – through images, metaphors, puzzling through, staying with paradox, seeing through different lenses, using artistic forms.
- In making sense of the data use both cognitive and affective ways of knowing, your intellect, emotions and intuition.
- Think about how you might use theory in the analysis and interpretation of your case. Will you start with a theoretical framework, given categories and precoding, or choose to derive codes and categories from the data? Will you aspire to produce 'grounded theory'?
- Will you interrogate the data in terms of an existing theory or theories? Or will you evolve an interpretative theory of the case as you proceed?
- Do not leave all the analysis and interpretation to the end. Begin at the beginning and keep the process alive throughout, moving iteratively between the data and furthering understanding.
- Whichever strategies and processes you use to make sense, make sure you are developing a coherent story. You may have generated rich data but this alone does not convey meaning. Data need to be analysed and interpreted to reach a theory of the case.

Validity

The different ways of analysing and interpreting mentioned in this chapter appeal to different ways of knowing and different conceptions of validity for assuring the quality and adequacy of findings from the case. Validity is concerned with how you establish the warrant for your work; whether it is sound, defensible, coherent, well-grounded, appropriate to the case, 'worthy of recognition' (House, 1980: 250). You will have been mindful of this throughout as you checked the accuracy and relevance of participant perspectives, negotiated meanings, verified accounts. In some contexts the validity and credibility will be evident in a reading of the case. In others, and particularly for your thesis, you need to outline the criteria you applied. This section summarizes different ways in which validity has been conceived in qualitative inquiry to help you justify why readers can trust your findings.

Internal/external validity

Many of the conventional procedures for assuring quality and validity in educational research and social research, such as internal validity, external validity, reliability and objectivity, stem from traditional approaches to educational research (primarily quantitative and often termed positivist). With the exception of internal and external validity, these are less applicable to qualitative case study research. Attempts to apply these concepts to qualitative inquiry may simply be inapplicable or result in distorting the nature of qualitative inquiry – straining the data to meet the concept and losing the meaning in the process. In the context of discussing fieldwork, Wolcott (1995) goes further and argues against the use of the terms 'reliability' and 'validity' (in their original technical sense) in qualitative inquiry. However, fieldworkers, he says, do need to be able to justify the truth value of their accounts as 'more likely' or more 'credible' (p. 170).

Credibility

Credibility is also a major criterion in evaluation case study. Technical criteria are not the only criteria that matter. In this context, House (1980) has pointed out that validity claims differ according to whether you choose objectivist or subjectivist approaches. He critiques objectivist approaches for relying primarily on explicated methods for their claim to validity, emphasizing replication and reliability in measurement and focusing on the truth aspect of validity to the exclusion of the credibility and normative aspects.

Approaches he labels subjectivist (where he includes art criticism and case study) appeal to experience and the actual situation as the basis for validity rather than scientific method. Accuracy in reflecting the situation, relevance, timeliness and utility are important. To be adequate, the evaluation must be understandable and meaningful to participants and audiences. In evaluation of public programmes, there is a further criterion. At a minimum level it must be true, but evaluation – a public decision procedure – has obligations to the larger society: '…it is not enough for the evaluation to be true and credible; it must also be normatively correct' (p. 250). Fairness, justice and democratic process become important criteria in establishing the validity of the case.

Trustworthiness and authenticity

In the past twenty years, Guba and Lincoln have developed a range of validity criteria which they believe are more apposite to qualitative inquiry. In 1985 they introduced the concept of *trustworthiness* and suggested a parallel set of criteria to the traditional criteria of internal validity, external validity, reliability and objectivity. Respectively, these were credibility, transferability, dependability and confirmability. Though alternatives, they are primarily methodological criteria and, as Guba and Lincoln (1989) themselves later indicated, they have a positivist ring: 'there remains a feeling of constraint, a feeling of continuing to play "in the friendly confines" of the opposition's home court' (p. 245). The development of alternative criteria has moved on since then; this comment needs to be seen in the context of where the debate between qualitative and quantitative methods in evaluation was at the time.

In their 1989 book, these authors introduced a second set of criteria around the concept of *authenticity* (which includes fairness, respecting participants' perspectives and empowering them to act). This concept relates more closely to the process and quality of the evaluation and how the data come to be negotiated and understood, connecting more to the constructivist perspective that underpins their approach to qualitative inquiry. It also resonates strongly with the democratic criteria for establishing validity espoused by House above.

Intrinsically qualitative

Further criteria may still be needed for qualitative inquiry, as Denzin and Lincoln (1994: 480) point out, that are independent of previous traditions to reflect more the nature of the *qualitative* in qualitative inquiry, stressing subjectivity, emotionality and feeling, for example. Lincoln (1995) has also outlined a set of standards that reflect the interpersonal nature of qualitative inquiry and the political intent in some cases to improve people's lives. These include criteria such as giving voice to marginalized groups, critical subjectivity and reflexivity of the researcher, and reciprocity (cited by Finley, 2003: 282). These are close to the concerns of those who work in applied social settings in education, health and social care, and in community contexts, and offer a potentially more valid way to capture and acknowledge experiential understanding and interpretation.

Similar criteria to value the *qualitative* are also being explored in arts-based inquiry. Some relate to aesthetic merit and form, others, such as reflexivity and engagement, more to the process and impact. For further exploration of the way in which validity may be conceived in this field and discussion of possible criteria see Mullen (2003), Finley (2003), Mullen and Finley (2003), Lincoln (1995), Simons and McCormack (2007) and Sparkes and Douglas (2007).

Strategies for Validation

Two main strategies advocated in qualitative case study to validate accounts and experiences are *triangulation* and *respondent validation*. Triangulation – seeing things from different angles – stems more from concern with method; respondent validation with process. Neither ensures validity, though they do contribute to it. Other factors – reflexivity of the researcher, adequacy of sampling, appropriateness of methods for understanding the topic – also need to be taken into account. Even more critical are the relationships you create in the field, which enable you to gain 'quality' data that accurately represent the phenomena you are studying and negotiate meanings that are valid for the specific purpose in the particular context.

Triangulation

Early conceptions
Triangulation is a means of cross-checking the relevance and significance of issues or testing out arguments and perspectives from different angles to generate and strengthen evidence in support of key claims. Originally connected with an analogy

to surveying or navigation in which a position on a map is discovered by taking two points that intersect with the observer's position, the use of triangulation derives from discussions of measurement validity by quantitative methodologists such as Campbell and Fiske (1959). This has been noted by Seale (1999), Greene (2007) and Stake (1995). According to Seale (1999: 53), triangulation was first advocated and developed in *qualitative* research by Denzin (1970). In both traditions, one of the major reasons was to overcome the deficiency or bias of any one method.

Denzin (1978), in a second edition of the 1970 text, outlines four types of triangulation – data triangulation, investigator triangulation, theory triangulation and methodological triangulation. Methodological triangulation, exploring significant similarities between methods, and data triangulation, using different data sources to gain understanding of the issues, are common in case study research, adding richness to the description and providing verification of the significance of issues through different methods and sources. Investigator triangulation is useful in team research and theory triangulation can be used by teams or individuals in developing an understanding of the specific case.

Early conceptions of triangulation have been located within a realist agenda, where it is assumed that convergence and confirmation, by whichever concept of triangulation, is 'closer to the 'truth' of the reality (often a single reality) observed. Where different investigators are used, this has sometimes been termed inter-subjective reliability and assumed to contribute to the validity of the findings.

Relationship to mixed methods
Methodological triangulation is often advocated as a rationale for mixed methods research (Greene and Caracelli, 1997), though there is a different and broader argument to be made in mixed methods research for the integration of diverse paradigms, not merely the combination of different methods. Combining or mixing methods does not necessarily strengthen validity. Much depends upon how this is done. See Greene (2007) for an extensive discussion of this issue and of the early connection between mixed methods and triangulation.

Mason (1996) has also advised that researchers need to think strategically about how to integrate different methods and not simply piece them together in an *ad hoc* and eclectic way. To facilitate thinking about this issue she suggests researchers ask a series of questions, such as:

> What can each method yield in relation to my research questions? Which parts of the puzzle do they help me address? ... How do the different methods feed into each other? How do they integrate logistically as well as intellectually? ... How will I derive data from each method – literally, interpretively, reflexively? ... Can I feasibly do everything I want to do? (pp. 79–80)

Answering questions such as these will prevent you assuming too simplistic an approach to cross-checking issues from different methods or too closely and erroneously corroborating data from different methods when one is not confirming of the other, as it is generating a different kind of data.

Later developments

Over the past thirty years the concept of triangulation has broadened to take account of forms of social research, including case study, which acknowledge multiple perspectives and that these are socially constructed. Triangulation, in this concept of research, is less concerned with confirmation or convergence, whether through different data sources, methods, theories or researchers, but with exploring different perspectives and how they do or do not intersect in the particular context. How different perspectives came to be constructed and meaning attributed to them, and the extent to which they diverge (Mathison, 1988), may be just as significant in determining accuracy and meaning of interpretations as convergence.

Richardson's (1997) metaphor of a crystal reflects a similar aspiration. The crystal is a useful metaphor for validity in qualitative case study as it allows us to view the data from different angles and encapsulate the different ways we can interpret. The crystal is a solid object, yet it can be turned in many directions to reflect and refract light. We can see alternative meanings, subtleties (shades of meaning) and how elements of the data may have separate significant meanings yet retain a connection and integration to the whole.

These developments lend credence to the claim that triangulation can strengthen validity. However, the claim has a different basis from that often assumed in earlier forms through a 'flat' intersection of methods, sources or perspectives. Open to different ways of seeing, constructing meanings, acknowledging divergence and seeing from different angles, enables us to pursue interpretations further and deepen understanding to portray a valid picture.

Respondent validation

Respondent validation refers to checking the accuracy, adequacy and fairness of observations, representations and interpretations of experience with those whom they concern. These may be participants from whom you have sought data, stakeholders who have an interest in the programme, issues being investigated to see if they 'ring true', or beneficiaries and other audiences to check the credibility of the case and whether it persuades.

This may happen at different stages throughout the research and in relation to the final case. This process of validation is prominent in democratic case study and in evaluation case study where different interests and values need to be represented fairly in the programme and where the aspiration is to equalize the relationship of the researcher and the researched in the process of the research. It thus has political intent as well as being a strategy for ensuring accurate and adequate multiple validation of events and experiences.

Multiple and Diverse Paths to Validation

I have outlined these different ways in which validity can be conceived and several strategies you may use in the process to offer choices for how you justify the validity of your findings. There are strengths and weaknesses in each.

Using multiple methods, perspectives and sources may offset bias arising from any one, but you need to ensure that how you do this contributes to a collective understanding of the phenomena you are studying.

Looking from different angles and for divergence is likely to enhance the complexity of your understanding, but you may need some way of determining what is central and what is not, especially to inform particular audiences.

Respondent validation allows individuals to see if they have been represented accurately and fairly and allows audiences to decide whether the interpretation is credible, but you may still need to cross-check individual accounts from other sources and have criteria for deciding what different audience responses are worth.

In deciding which strategies to adopt, choose those that are most appropriate for the kind of case study you are conducting, the purpose of the study, the methods used and the audiences you seek to influence. Whoever they are – research sponsors, examiners, community stakeholders – readers of your case study need to be assured that your findings are accurate, credible, plausible and trustworthy given what you are trying to understand in the particular context of your case.

Case Study Memo 16   **Validity**

- Decide which criteria of validity you will use to assure and justify your findings.
- Remember that in analysing and interpreting you are likely to be integrating data from different sources gathered at different times. Stay aware of this difference and time dimension. Losing sight of this in the interpretation may pose a threat to validity.
- Interrogate the data for different interpretations until the 'significance' of the issue/finding is saturated, that is, no contrary findings are relevant or confirmed for the particular theory or interpretation that is developing.
- At the same time, do not dismiss negative instances when they appear not to add to your growing understanding. One negative instance may yield a powerful relevant insight.
- To ensure internal validity, check with participants that your reporting of their perspectives accords with their 'telling' and their meaning. This is sometimes referred to as respondent validation.
- To establish external validity, check with a range of stakeholders whether they find the case study credible and useful.
- Triangulation of data – cross-checking the significance of data from several sources, methods or perspectives – is often assumed to increase validity of accounts. It does not guarantee validity, though it can contribute to it and help ensure the credibility of findings.
- View triangulation as a process where different methods and perspectives intersect rather than a 'flat' confirmation of data from different sources and methods that assumes a 'truth' status in relation to a fixed point or a single reality.

- Do not assume that convergence of data is always closer to the truth in a particular setting. Triangulation can also be used to check divergence, which may be equally important in understanding the case.
- In team research, cross-corroborate each team member's interpretation of the findings.
- Recall the processes for monitoring subjectivity in Chapter 5 and the ethical procedures in Chapter 6; these are all part of the process of ensuring validity.
- Stay reflexive throughout. Note where an interpretation is a bias and where it is the 'intelligence' you have about the topic which can further the analysis.
- See the process of validation as a dynamic one of gradually refining and corroborating evidence that is 'true, credible and right'.
- In presenting what you have found, do not over-claim; stay close to the evidence and demonstrate how interpretations and findings were reached.

Notes

1 Hermeneutics refers to the nature and means of interpreting a text – coming to understand the meaning of the whole of a text by making sense of its parts and their interdependence with the whole (Schwandt, 2001).
2 Kelle (2004), for example, points out that there are now over twenty different software packages available to assist qualitative researchers, and some, such as NVivo and ATLAS/ti, are widely applied.

Further Readings

Atkinson, P. and Coffey, A. (1996) *Making Sense of Qualitative Data: Complementary Research Strategies*. Thousand Oaks, CA: Sage.
An excellent account of a variety of ways of making sense of qualitative data illustrating a range of processes and strategies through examples from an actual research project.

Charmaz, K. (2006) *Constructing Grounded Theory: A Practical Guide Through Qualitative Analysis*. Los Angeles, CA: Sage.
The process of how to do grounded theory from an interpretative, constructivist perspective. Includes how to code and categorize, use memo writing, sample theoretically, theorize and extend the analysis through writing drafts.

Cortazzi, M. (1993) *Narrative Analysis*. London: The Falmer Press.
A systematic introduction to a variety of different models of narrative analysis (sociological, psychological, literary, anthropological) and the role of narrative in the study of teaching.

Miles, M.B. and Huberman, A.M. (1994) *Qualitative Data Analysis: A Sourcebook of New Methods*, 2nd edn. Thousand Oaks, CA: Sage.
As its title suggests, an excellent sourcebook, not to be followed in every detail, but searched for relevant formal tools to aid analysis. There are useful sections on tactics and strategies for determining warrant in Chapter 13.

(Continued)

(Continued)

Richardson, L. (1997) *Fields of Play (Constructing an Academic Life)*. New Brunswick, NJ: Rutgers University Press.
Makes the case for writing as interpretation, exploring a range of artistic modes of interpreting and communicating qualitative experiences, including ethnographic drama, poetic representation and stories.

Ritchie, J. and Lewis, J. (2003) *Qualitative Research Practice: A Guide for Social Science Students and Researchers*. London: Sage.
Chapter 8 offers a useful account of the processes involved in analysis from data management to descriptive accounts to explanations. Chapter 9 explores various analytic processes through an example and a matrix-based analytic method which generates themes, concepts and emergent categories without losing sight of the 'raw data'.

Silverman, D. (ed.) (2000) *Doing Qualitative Research*. London: Sage.
A useful book for qualitative research in general. Part Three (Chapters 10 and 11 in particular) offers practical guidance both for 'kick starting' and developing analysis in relation to interviews, field notes, texts and transcripts.

Strauss, A.L. and Corbin, J. (1990) *Basics of Qualitative Research: Grounded Theory, Procedures and Techniques*. Newbury Park, CA: Sage.
A classic text exploring the procedure and processes of grounded theory.

Computer-assisted qualitative data analysis

Kelle, U. (2004) 'Computer-assisted qualitative data analysis', in C. Seale, G. Giampietro, J.F. Gubrium and D. Silverman (eds), *Qualitative Research Practice*, pp. 473–489. London: Sage.
Focuses on the coding and retrieving facilities of different CAQDAS (Computer-assisted Qualitative Data Analysis) packages and the role of the researcher's previous theoretical knowledge in the process.

Seale, C. (2000) 'Using computers to analyze qualitative data', in D. Silverman (ed.), *Doing Qualitative Research*, pp. 154–174. London: Sage.
Discusses the advantages and disadvantages of, and mainstream packages for, computer-assisted analysis of qualitative data.

Weitzman, E.A. (2003) 'Software and qualitative research', in N.K. Denzin and Y.S. Lincoln (eds), *Collecting and Interpreting Qualitative Materials*, 2nd edn, pp. 310–339. Thousand Oaks, CA: Sage.
Explores the early history of computers in qualitative research, what software can and cannot do and issues to consider in choosing which software package may be appropriate for what purpose.

8

FROM DATA TO STORY: EXAMPLES IN PRACTICE

The last chapter outlined a number of ways in which you could analyse and interpret the data to reach the case study story.[1] This chapter presents some specific examples. In relation to the distinction raised in the previous chapter, the first three focus more on analysis, the second three more on interpretation. The examples stem from different decades and represent different stages in the growth of case study research over forty years, particularly in evaluation, which needed to be responsive to what different audiences sought or accepted. This also applies to reporting, the subject of the following chapter. In the contexts in which we conduct case study research today, the need to meet audience expectation of particular forms of analysis and reporting stills prevails, though in some contexts there is scope for alternatives. For this reason, and to suggest options for how you analyse and interpret in your thesis, I have chosen a range of examples.

From Interviews to Story

On first and second readings

From one transcript – to categories or stories
There are many ways to analyse and interpret from interviews. The single interview transcript is often a useful starting point. From one transcript you can begin to identify categories that can be checked out in subsequent interviews through confirming or disconfirming the initial categories. Or you can read a transcript with a more intuitive eye, looking for the story the individual has chosen to tell in that context. If your choice for telling the story is through profiles or portrayals of individuals, you may prefer this approach. Most likely, it will not be the full story from one interview, especially at the beginning of the research. The exception is the 'life story' interview in which you can reach quite a deep understanding from a single in-depth interview.

From several transcripts – to themes
Staying essentially with interview data, another way in which the case study story can be built is from an analysis of many transcripts that have been searched for significant themes. This is often a three-stage process. The first is identifying and confirming categories. The second is examining the relationships and connections between them. The third is the generation of over-arching themes that tell a story or part of a story

of the case. Themes may be presented in narrative form or illustrated on a concept map with edited excerpts as evidence in support of the themes.

You can work inductively from the transcripts, highlighting issues participants raise, or search the transcripts for foreshadowed issues adding any necessary notes to contextualize meaning. When I have taken this route, once I am clear that the themes adequately represent my growing understanding of the data, I photocopy each annotated script, cut up the excerpts that contribute to each theme, place them in piles and examine their consistency or otherwise and any patterns that may be detected between them. From here I can begin to see the underlying structure of the case study story. It is clear from even this first example that both processes of analysing and interpreting are involved in 'making sense', even if one is predominant. Analysing data from transcripts can also be undertaken by computer-assisted qualitative analysis. References for how you might do this are noted in Further Readings in the previous chapter.

It is tempting to wait until all interviews are transcribed before analysing but examining transcripts months removed from the dates of interviews can risk losing meaning and make analysis more difficult. The longer transcripts are left before analysis or interpretation, the more difficult it can be to recall subtleties in the context that help determine what the data mean.

On second and third hearings

An alternative means of making sense of masses of interview data is through listening and re-listening to audio-recordings of the interviews, along with immersion in other field data. Words on a page do not contain all the meaning, as we noted in Chapter 3, and as Nisbet (2006) has recently reasserted. The transcript should not be treated as a separate rational construct disconnected from context or the process of the interview. Through listening and re-listening you can reconnect with the 'live' experience of the interview. Recalling social, emotional and behavioural cues helps to capture more of the meaning than is evident from words alone. You often pick up things you did not hear the first time around and, on re-hearing the tone of voice, can modify the meaning you first gained. You can also 'tune in' to the tacit understanding acquired on site, which will help ensure that any quotations and excerpts eventually selected as evidence in a thematic analysis represent as closely as possible the meanings participants aspired to convey.

One of the best examples I know of a thematic case study that used this process of re-reading transcripts and re-listening to audio-taped interviews is that by Denny (1977). This case study tells the story of science education in one high school in a district in Texas largely through edited excerpts from interviews skilfully woven with narrative. Writing about this process Denny said, 'Teachers filled about fifty hours of my cassette tapes. Since then I have read and listened to their words again and again. It is incredible what I hear the second or third time around' (pp. 1–2).

Re-listening helped ensure that the interview excerpts included in the written case were as close as possible (taking into account nuances of tone, language and context) to what the interviewee meant at the time. Their meaning and relevance for the story eventually told was also grounded in the many hours of fieldwork and assimilation of contextual details and subtle clues picked up on site.

From Interim Interpretation to Story

In the following example from a case study of a secondary school exploring the level of adoption of centrally developed curriculum projects, I deliberately used interim interpretations from a limited fieldwork period (of three days) both as a means of checking initial understanding and to collect further data. The case study was part of a larger project,[2] in which there were four case study schools, exploring a democratic model of research which aspired to redress the power balance between the researcher and the researched. A significant part of this aspiration was to engage the participants actively in contributing to an understanding of the case, and negotiation was a key process which ensured both accuracy and adequacy of interpretations.

On the basis of three intensive days' fieldwork in the school, I wrote a semi-interpretative report of each department's record of introducing and developing a specific centrally developed curriculum project. Each report had elements of direct interpretation, analysis of initial themes drawn from interview transcripts, direct observation and questions to elicit further understanding. I asked the teachers to discuss the report in their departments, on the criteria of accuracy, relevance and fairness, and return any comments to me.

I had three reasons for doing this. One was to engage the teachers in the research. The second was to check on the accuracy and fairness of my interpretations (I had spent little time in the field though I had amassed a great deal of data in the three days). The third was to extend the process of data collection through their involvement and give them an opportunity to explore the issues together in my absence. This latter point had the additional advantage of signalling that participants had part responsibility for getting the story 'right' and offering a check on my biases. Without me there, they could easily dismiss my interpretations if they chose.

In one of the reports I offered two different interpretations of the same set of events and experience. In another, I offered only one interpretation, but soon got another back! In a third, which offered only one interpretation, I received several challenges to my initial interpretation and nuances of meaning that were important to them in their context and history. Maybe I could have captured these nuances in a few days' fieldwork but I did not. So I was grateful for the challenge.

Remember the case of 'strawberries, strawberries' in Chapter 3, where knowledge of the context was crucial to an understanding of what took place in that classroom. In addition to the advantages above in terms of getting the research story right, the process had a further advantage. This was to engage the departments at one level and the whole school at another in taking a reflexive look at how they individually and collectively managed innovation and change. In other words, the process aspired to be developmental and educative for those in the case.

What I gained, besides the check on accuracy, was indeed a check on my biases. In my hurry to interpret in the short timescale allotted to this case study, I had imputed to the school some understandings I had gained from previous research examining curriculum reform. In other words, I failed to recognize the 'unique' context of this particular school's reform efforts. This was chastening. I apologized, and in further correspondence with the school, and with their assistance, I tried to shelve my biases and listen more attentively to their interpretations.

From Mixed-mode Analysis and Interpretation to Story

The process of analysis in this next example included several of the processes above for incorporating interview and observational data, but had two further levels of complexity to contextualize the case nationally. These were an analysis of the historical development of nurse education and training in Ireland to foreground the study and an analysis of focus groups across the country at the end to ascertain how the programme was proceeding nationally by the time we left the site. The first we planned at the outset. The second was a response to the changing political scene.

The overall case was the evaluation of a major curriculum innovation in nurse education and training in Ireland (Simons et al., 1998), marking a shift from an apprenticeship model to university-based nurse education and training. The central feature was an in-depth case study of one pilot site to see how this was working before the 'new' programme was rolled out to the rest of the population.

The decision to locate this case within a descriptive analysis of the history of nurse education and training in Ireland was partly political – to demonstrate that we knew and understood the cultural context – and partly analytical – to identify the issues and themes that had driven the development of nurse education and training to the point of change. This, once corroborated and validated through the literature and through discussions with key nurse educators and administrators in Ireland, provided a baseline from which we could 'safely' begin to build and analyse changes that were taking place in the new programme.

This case highlights four points about analysis and interpretation I raised in the previous chapter – the need to begin at the beginning, to interpret throughout, to progressively focus and refocus, and to be open to changing strategies as understanding develops or the context dictates. Once we had started, we had to refocus early on. For example, in the tender and in the design of the research there was an aspiration to compare the outcomes of the new programme with the previous apprenticeship programme through comparing samples of students from each. However, this could not happen as the apprenticeship model (and hence those trained under it) ceased to exist during the period of the evaluation. There was no direct apprentice-trained student population with which to compare.

We also had to refocus later in the study as the political context changed rapidly. The notion of the evaluation as a 'pilot', on which a decision would be taken whether or not to roll the programme out to other sites, was a misnomer. By the time the evaluation ended eleven other sites had started the new programme. The speed of innovation outstripped the design of the case study. We had to gather further data to account for these factors and refocus the analysis. Any attempt in this context to use precoding or a pre-existing theoretical frame would have failed to represent what was actually happening in the site. While we could always have recoded, of course, it made much more sense, given that we knew the context was highly political, to undertake more formal analysis when we had a groundswell of data.

In addition to this refocusing in response to political change, there was the more formal process of analysis we undertook of the implementation case study in one site. This took place regularly in team meetings held every two to three weeks, where we identified emerging issues and 'working hypotheses' which were progressively focused and refocused in the light of further evidence. Yet there was also a later stage where we re-examined the whole database for key analytical themes, patterns and relationships between them, triangulated significant themes from different data sources and perspectives, and selected evidence to support the main findings. This analysis took place in the phases described in Case Study Memo 17.

Case Study Memo 17   One Example of a Formal Stage of Analysis

- Interview data, field notes, observations and relevant documentation were read by all members of the team (four initially and six in the latter stages) and issues were identified as significant to an understanding of the programme in action.
- These were triangulated, that is, each issue was scrutinized to see if it was supported by data from other sources and methods, a range of stakeholders and other participants. The significance of an issue raised by one or two individuals was also considered where relevant to an understanding of the case.
- The issues were re-examined in the light of evidence arising from further site visits to see if they were temporal or constant. Issues were reframed if necessary to reflect a refined understanding of the case.
- The interrelationships between the issues were then explored to see what themes and patterns were beginning to emerge.
- The whole database was searched again for further evidence to support the themes and emerging patterns.
- Issues and themes that were identified consistently and had sufficient data to verify their significance in understanding the case were incorporated into major findings.
- Implications for policy development were drawn from the findings to provide an agenda for future action.

(Adapted from Clarke, Gobbi and Simons, 1999)

From Artistic Interpretation to Story

The case study described in the previous section took place just before the millennium. More recently, from the late 1990s onwards, I have begun to experiment with artistic forms of interpreting and understanding. This has been possible for a number of reasons. The contexts in which I work have changed – from large-scale nationally or internationally funded evaluation projects to smaller projects – with less of an imperative to match the expectations of some policy-makers who value more 'objectivist' forms of evidence. In some contexts also, in the health and social care professions, for example, there is growing support for the use of the creative arts in research. But perhaps the most dominant factor has been my own decision to integrate creative art forms into my teaching and research instead of seeing them as my creative saviour for the weekends!

Dancing with the data

Using one of the processes described above – from interview transcripts to story – I have often cut interview transcripts, once categorized, into illustrative excerpts and laid these on the floor, along with observations and field notes on 3 × 5 cards. I move around these data physically, standing on them, stepping between them, backward and forwards, positioning and repositioning them until they make a certain sense. I may start with one transcript and set of field notes and observations and gradually add others that connect.

Alternatively, I might lay them all out at the beginning and, through a similar process, see what connections exist that result in an emergent theme and how robust (data-saturated) it is. In dancing with the data in this way, I am not only reading and re-reading the data, but seeing them from different angles. Standing on the data gives me a different view, and looking down and across, an overview from which I begin to get a holistic impression of their meaning. In moving the data and cards around with my feet and dancing between them I can detect themes and patterns. This is not simply a cognitive process. I feel and sense the meaning they convey.

In working in this way, many of the usual processes engaged in analysis and interpretation – confirming, disconfirming, verifying, deciding on outliers – are at play. What the movement adds is another sense and a 'knowing' that is embodied. In the context above I am using movement at a specific interpretative stage. Cancienne and Snowber (2003), in their paper 'Writing rhythm: movement as method', go much further in outlining how they use dance and movement in the whole process of conducting and presenting research. Their argument is persuasive and, as they point out, not dissimilar to the processes we often go through in other ways of interpreting data:

> The choreographer/performer has long known that the choreographic process is one of sorting, sifting, editing, forming, making, and remaking; it's essentially an act of discovery. Combining dance, a kinesthetic form, and writing, a cognitive form, can forge relationships between body and mind, cognitive and affective knowing, and the intellect with physical vigour. (pp. 237–238)

Dancing with the data, as I have described above, could be construed as a form of concept mapping, moving the data around on a large sheet of paper pinned on the wall or on the floor, though without literally dancing on it. However, I see it more as an interpretative form of thematic analysis that gains depth, insight and holistic understanding through the movement. While the process has an affinity with movement as method, as outlined by Cancienne and Snowber (2003), it stops short of performance. I am only discussing the use of movement here in the process of interpreting data, not communicating the findings to others. Communication of findings through movement, often termed 'dancing *the* data' (Bagley and Cancienne, 2001), is a different use of movement and has a different purpose from 'dancing *with* the data', as outlined here.

Using poetic form

In the following example, Sue, whose work you were introduced to in Chapter 3, made sense of the case she was studying through a number of narrative processes, leading to the generation of interpretative stories that documented her analysis and findings. These she chose to report in poetic form, itself a further process of interpretation. Narrative in this sense was more than analysis. She used features of narrative both to help her interpret the data and to frame the structure and presentation of the findings.

Sources of data were sorted into *field stories* – which included a variety of narrative forms, critical incidents, observational notes and memos, reflective analyses of practice, poems, diagrams, collages, concept maps – and field *documents* – secondary data such as appointment diaries, email correspondence, minutes from meetings and policies. The analysis then proceeded in four interconnected phases.

The first phase – *field data to data sets* – collated data into coherent narrative data sets, each of which told a particular story or account of her practice. Each data set included both field stories and field documents relevant to that story. A filing system was created to facilitate sorting and referencing. A total of 157 data sets were constructed.

Phase two – *data sets to story lines* – consisted of re-reading all the data sets to gain an understanding of how each related to the whole experience the research was exploring. Key themes and plot lines were identified across all the sets, related to what each story line (overall finding) might be about. This process was iterative, moving from each data set to the whole and back again, and imaginative, using metaphors, images and visual forms to create and imagine the wholeness of the story. Five story lines were identified (later reduced to four when themes overlapped) and also several that did not fit. These were negative cases but they nevertheless had an impact on the overall, final value analysis of the study. A note was made of which data set related to each story line and those that related to more than one. All the prose field stories from each data set relating to a story line were combined into one file.

Phase three – *story lines to short story narratives* – involved analysing the data sets for each of the five story lines through formal narrative processes, both structural and hermeneutic,[3] to construct short stories. Through these processes the units of analysis or plot lines for each short story line were identified and a story board constructed, moving the plot lines around until they told a story that best fitted the data. (Identification of the main themes in each story line was also informed by a review of theoretical and research literature relevant to the story line.) These short story narratives were composed in poetic form, interweaving the analysis with examples from the field stories, also in poetic form, to retain the 'lived experience' of the case.

The fourth phase – *short stories to evaluation* – examined the short story narratives for the values and issues of worth they revealed in the experiential account of practice. The outcome of this evaluative analysis was a synthesis poem which was the basis for discussion addressing the research question.

See Figure 8.1 for a visual record of the stages of this process and Duke (2007) for a more detailed account of what was involved in each stage.

The advantage of a diagram like this is that it enables you to see at a glance the different stages involved in a complex analysis. The disadvantage is that it may appear more linear than the process actually was. Indeed, presented like this it may seem little different from other forms of qualitative analysis that generate themes and patterns in stages, such as that outlined in Case Study Memo 17. But it is quite different.

In each stage the process of selection and reduction of data to reach the themes and story lines was much more intuitive and interpretative than that in Memo 17. It involved engaging the emotions, trying to make sense of confusions and contradictions in the data, allowing space for unconscious thought, drawing sketches and maps at different stages of understanding.

It also involved expressing ideas and emotional reactions in poetry or collage, writing memos, stories of practice, rewriting and reinterpreting in story and poetic form, deepening understanding and interpretation with each rewrite. It was also, as Sue commented herself on the process, 'about being authentic with how I "internally" knew the data – how I had lived it – trying really hard to make sure that what I was writing and expressing was congruent with how I came to "know" this "lived-experience"'.[4]

Writing as interpretation

It will be evident from this example that writing and rewriting is an integral part of coming to an interpretation of the case. Some see it as the key interpretative process itself (see, for example, Richardson, 1994, 1997; van Manen, 1990). From start to finish, writing is the art and process through which we make sense – give order and meaning – to what we have found. We can do this in the several ways already mentioned in this chapter – identifying categories or stories in transcripts, deriving themes and patterns by progressive focusing of issues, generating themes through analytic processes and integrating/rearranging interview and other field data to create a narrative in story or poetic form. What I am drawing attention to here is the preference for writing *as* the main mode of interpretation.

Richardson (1997) makes a compelling case for writing as interpretation, examining how the specific cultural circumstances in which we write affect what we write and who we become (p. 1). In exploring the narrative of her academic life in *Fields of Play,* she experimented with a range of different textual forms to recreate, reframe and reinterpret her experience and alternative forms of re-presentation, such as drama and poetry, to communicate that experience to others. While she is writing in this book primarily about her own narrative, you may find the artistic forms she uses helpful in writing narratives of the lived experience of individuals in your case.

Kushner (2000), in exploring the personalization of self and those who people our cases, also uses writing *as* interpretation. His interpretations include not only rich narrative

FROM DATA TO STORY

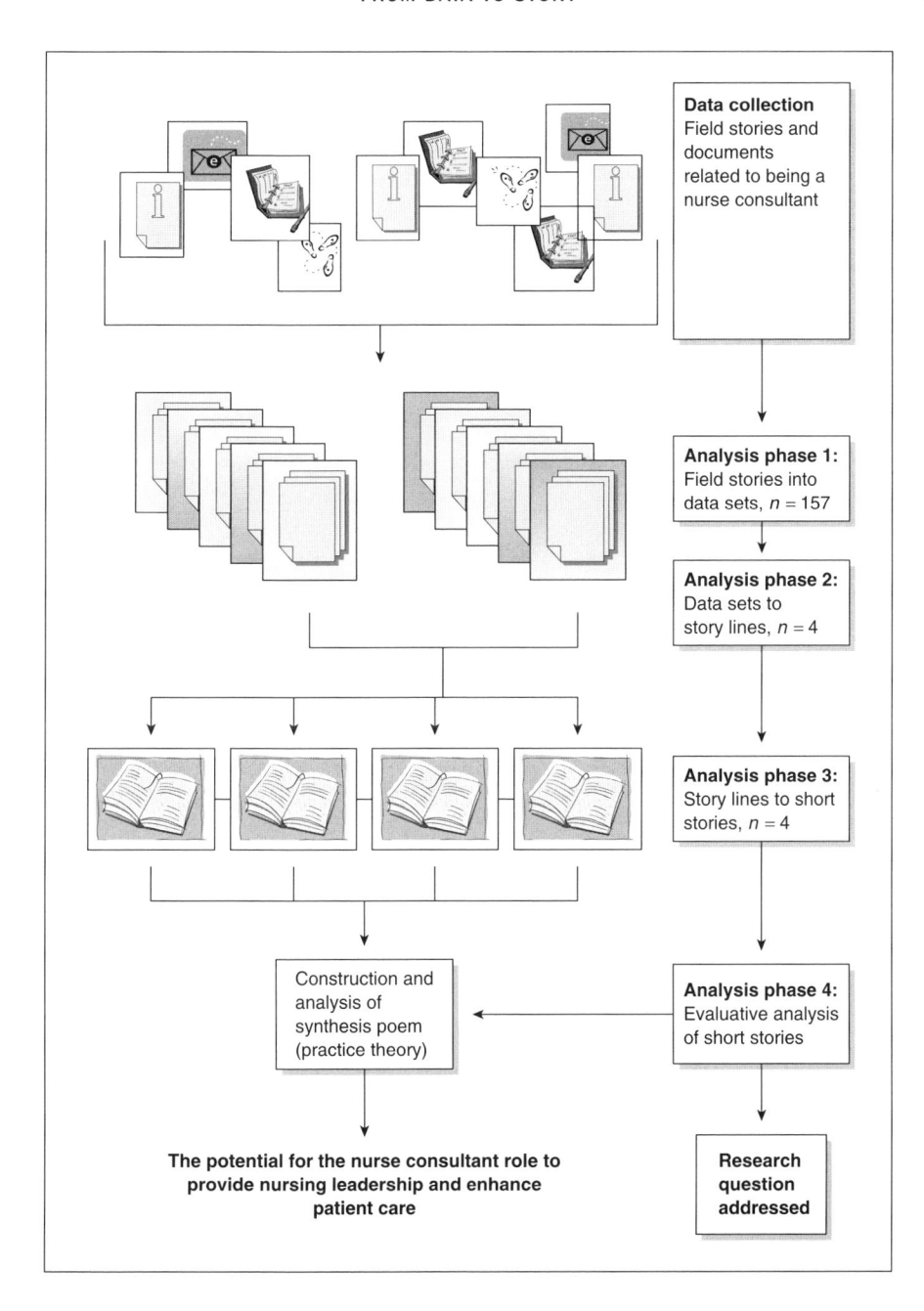

Figure 8.1 Four-phase analysis/interpretative process (from Duke (2007), reproduced with permission)

descriptions of events and incidents observed about the person's experience in the case but observations of what he is reading and thinking at the time, both personally and professionally. In this way he aspires to make transparent how he comes to make theoretical sense of the case through interaction between himself and others – to lay bare some of those factors that are sometimes hidden from the reader's view in closely interpreted accounts. I do not go further into writing as interpretation in this chapter. It will arise again in the next, where forms of presentation are discussed and where I outline some suggestions for the craft of writing itself.

Notes

1. In this chapter and the next I am using story in the sense raised in the introduction – the underlying argument or theory of the case that comes to be understood in the course of analysing and interpreting the data. See Chapter 9 for various ways in which the case study story may be told.
2. This was the Safari project (Success and Failure and Recent Innovation) referred to in Chapter 2, exploring the medium-term effects of innovation. The project was experimenting with the conduct of case studies in a short timescale – one week's 'condensed fieldwork' spread over a month with a year to analyse and write up. For further details of the exact procedures and process see MacDonald and Walker (1974, 1976), Norris (1977), and for an analysis of the procedures in action, Simons (1987).
3. Structural analysis refers to temporal elements, such as time and location, which maintain a connection with the particulars of the experience. Hermeneutic analysis is interpreting the meaning of the whole narrative, the interrelationship of the parts with the whole (see also note 1, Chapter 7). For further exploration of forms of narrative analysis see, for example, Reissman (1993), Ricoeur (1981), Polkinghorne (1995).
4. Personal communication, June 2007.

Further Readings

Richardson, L. (1994) 'Writing: A method of inquiry', in N.K. Denzin and Y.S. Lincoln (eds), *The Handbook of Qualitative Research*, pp. 516–529 Thousand Oaks, CA: Sage.
Presents an argument for writing as the key interpretative process and a series of exercises to practise your writing skills. See also Richardson (1997), Further Readings, in Chapter 7, which illustrates how data represented in poetic and dramatic form enhance communication and understanding of narratives.

Sparkes, A.C. and Douglas, K. (2007) 'Making the case for poetic representations: An example in action', *The Sport Psychologist*, 21: 170–190.
Explores the potential benefits of using poetic representations in interpretation and communication. Describes the process of constructing a poetic representation from interview data and suggests a range of criteria for judging poetic representation.

van Manen, M. (1990) *Researching Lived Experience: Human Science for an Action Sensitive Pedagogy*. New York: State University of New York.
An exploration of the case for lived experience and phenomenological writing.

Section IV
TELLING THE STORY

9
START AT ANY POINT: REPORTING AND WRITING

The title of this chapter reflects the advice of Mark Twain that a story can begin at any point. This is a helpful adage when faced with a daunting set of data that needs to be woven into a coherent story to communicate to outside audiences. You have listened long and hard to people. You have observed their transactions and reactions to events. You have made sense of what you observed and heard. So you have a story to tell, insights to communicate, wisdom to impart. In research language, we might call these findings, results, conclusions and knowledge perhaps, rather than wisdom, but I hope some of the latter as well. Now it is time to share that insight, knowledge and wisdom in the most persuasive way you can, while retaining the authenticity of the data.

I have used the word 'story' throughout to refer to the underlying, narrative structure by which we make sense of the case. This chapter explores different ways of communicating that central story. Yet it also includes a specific story form as one of these ways of telling. It is important to be clear that I am using story in these two senses in this chapter.

The main emphasis is on written text. Increasingly, it is recognized that texts can be created through other modalities, for example, movement (Cancienne and Snowber, 2003) and film (Jenny Elliot, 2008). Computer technology also opens up opportunities for reporting findings in visual and graphic form. For many purposes, however, the written text retains its prominence, which is why I focus on written forms of telling in this chapter.

Telling the Case Study Story

Scope and content

Whatever form of reporting you choose, the case study should have a clear focus, be data-rich, located in its socio-political context and fairly and accurately represent participants' judgements and perspectives. Above all, it should tell a story of the evolution, development and experience of the particular case. Potential data sources are observations (of classrooms, events, critical incidents, context), excerpts from interviews, analysis of policy documents, vignettes of issues, cameos of individuals. Further sources are graphs or charts, concept maps, products of a programme, paintings, drawings and photographs. Not all will be relevant to the story you have to tell. They are a repertoire of different kinds of evidence on which you can draw.

Making the database explicit

Having decided on your story line or argument, the evidence displayed should be sufficient to justify the conclusions or implications drawn within the scope of the database you have. This should be explicitly stated; for instance, who was interviewed and/or observed (in role or person depending upon the confidentiality agreements you have made), how many interviews/observations were conducted, and the number and scope of documents examined. It may also be helpful to indicate the total number of transcripts, field notes and observations amassed. Field notes, interviews, observations should all be dated. This is important when analysing and reporting – a reminder that data is neither context- nor time-free. The timescale allocated to the study should be noted, any constraints on the design in practice, and any other relevant details that signify the exact database of the case.

Ensuring data are adequately explored and appropriately represented

Alternative or contending perspectives and judgements need to be included where relevant and negative cases (those that do not fit the main story line) examined for their contribution to the overall meaning of the case. Sufficient evidence should be offered to enable readers to reach an independent judgement on the merit of the analysis and interpretation. In selecting evidence to support the findings and appropriate ways of reporting, you might consider how best to match the 'vocabulary of action'[1] and expectations of your audiences and the way in which they learn.[2] If the case is part of a broader study of many cases, ensure that you provide a rich database in each case for subsequent cross-case analysis. This can either be through common themes identified at the outset or subsequently through inductive analysis of unique cases.

Forms of Reporting

Formal

In many contexts in educational and social research, reporting more or less takes a linear form. Take a look at many a case study thesis or research text. It usually starts with an introduction describing the research, the case, question or problem to be investigated and then, chapter by chapter, outlines the nature of the project, its history and evolution, how it is located in a national or international policy context and the methodology adopted. Later chapters outline the findings or results, frequently with a theme or issue focus. The final chapter draws conclusions and discusses implications for action and policy. The story line here is historical and the data are organized chronologically. It has a beginning, middle and an end. It sometimes includes evidence from other studies that bear on or illuminate the case. It will be comprised of primary data and secondary data where relevant to an understanding of the case.

Portrayal

The purpose and central organizing principle in portrayal reporting is to engage the reader with the veracity and experience of the case through the organization or juxtaposition of data without too much interpretation.[3] Data is displayed rather than interpreted and discussed. The story is primarily data-led. It can start at any point – beginning, middle or end – and weave the tale to and fro. Excerpts from interviews and observations are frequent. Judgements or perspectives may be compared and contrasted. People will feature in the portrayal.

Portrayals can include vignettes of events, cameos of individuals, snapshots of classroom lessons, narrative descriptions, Socratic dialogue, collage of different voices. It may start with a critical incident or interview excerpt to engage the reader or a 'telling tale' or lesson from the field. The story could be told from different stakeholders' perspectives, through the eyes of protagonists, particular groups or those with different roles in the organization. You could retell the story several times from the point of view of different actors, much like the 'Rashomon effect' in the Japanese movie of that name, where the story is retold by several people revealing different attitudes to the main event.

More episodic than chronological, the inclusion of vignettes or snapshots and different voices may at times appear fragmentary. However, the underlying narrative coherence is still there. The essential elements of the story will be told (though the logic may differ depending upon where the story started), and conclusions will be evident from the interpretation displayed through the data.

Conclusion-led

In this approach the case researcher has analysed the data to tell a story that has definite conclusions to draw. It employs many of the elements of portrayal but the intent here is more analytic and explanatory. It may include interpreting data within a specific theory or theories to explain what happened in the case. More often than not, the theory is of the case itself. The coherence is transparent. There is usually a strong story line clearly argued and maintained. This does not necessarily imply starting at the beginning, though that is one possibility. An explanatory account can often be successfully told by a 'conclusion-led' approach (see Smith and Pohland (1974) for one example). In this approach you state the conclusion first and then proceed to tell the story, exemplified by excerpts from observations, field notes and interviews (all carefully dated) of how that conclusion was reached, repeating the process with each conclusion. Noting the time and date of field data is important in any form of reporting but it is particularly so where conclusions are stated first. The reader can see, through the telling of the story in reverse, as it were, how you reached your interpretation and what particular factors were important at what time.

Interpretative

This form of reporting weaves a story that is highly interpretative of the case from the outset.[4] The story can start at any point or chronicle how the researcher interpreted the case throughout, where the reader does not know the outcome until the end. It can be told through themes, issues, metaphors and images or whatever organizers you choose. It can involve controversies, contradictions, alternative interpretations and it may even, like a good detective story, leave some twists for the end. In reading this kind of case study we may see fewer data sources from which the interpretation is drawn, having to rely more on the credibility and coherence of the story and the integrity of the person telling the tale. Interpretative accounts are often tightly woven (less open to alternative interpretations of the evidence), but they have the power to persuade, conveying insights and meanings of the case in ways that readers can readily grasp.

Story-telling

Story-telling, as a form of reporting in case study, has its eye on the reader or listener as much as the writer, with an intent to engage the reader's feelings and emotions. Story-telling is an art that has a long history, much of it in an oral tradition. In traditional mythology, story-telling communicated insights, wisdom and heroes' journeys, and often served as the collective memory of communities. It is a mode of communication that has stood the test of time.

Story-telling today is experiencing a revival as individuals, groups and communities seek opportunities to see things differently, to cope with uncertainty, to experience an alternative view. It is the natural way, as Okri (1997) points out, that people learn. It engages both the intellect and emotion, enabling people readily to connect with the story being told. Sylvia Ashton-Warner (1963) epitomizes this point in the stories she wrote for and with her pupils to teach them to read, using 'an "organic key vocabulary" of love and fear words' (p. 8). In writing books for the Maori children, she tried to incorporate the instinctive living, the drama, the love, the violence that was part of their lifeworld in the natural dialogue that they spoke. This served as a transition from one culture to another, the European school classroom (pp. 69–71). Children could easily relate to the emotions in the stories and their language and learned to read.

Oral stories have a sense of immediacy. Much is communicated in the telling, aided by gesture, gaze, body language, tone of voice and live context. The listener is active in the process, identifying imaginatively with what is being told (Okri, 1997: 48). The same is true for written stories. The aim is to stimulate the creative imagination. However, the onus upon us is greater to recreate the setting and tell the experience without the benefit of clues to understanding in the 'live' context. This stretches our skills as writers and indeed as researchers. While we are not in case study research talking about story-telling in the mythical or fictional sense, we have much to learn from the skills and intent of story-telling to communicate insights and observations in a readable, accessible form.

Documentary film

In educational research and evaluation, parallels for crafting the case study story have often been drawn to the documentary film. Here the case writer carefully edits excerpts from interviews and observations to portray what was discovered in the case, much as a documentary film-maker edits hours of filming to tell a coherent story, leaving much of what was shot on the cutting room floor. This is a careful process of sifting, ordering and reordering frames and episodes until a story is constructed that makes coherent sense. It emerges from immersion in a mass of data involving both cognitive and intuitive ways of coming to know. It is a story the film-maker arrives at rather than begins with, as Wiseman has commented of his documentary films.

> you don't have to formalize it as a series of rational statements. It's more important that there be some kind of fusion between feeling it and thinking it, than to be able to state it. That's what the editing process is about too ... When I'm editing I try to work out a very elaborate theory which I set down as I talk to myself; for example, 'Well this fits that way, and that fits that way', but in the way I finally get to it I can see that the rationalization frequently comes after the connection exists. (Quoted in Graham, 1971: 44)

A good example of this type of case study reporting is the case study of science education referred to in Chapter 8, where the case researcher chose to portray the story primarily through the editing of excerpts from interviews. From about fifty hours of audio-recording, Denny crafted a story largely with the teachers' words into a script of 125 pages (1977: 1–2). Like a documentary film-maker, he also observed of course, and selection of these excerpts was situated in and influenced by the many observations and an intuitive sense of the whole gained from being on site for two months.

Artistic forms

The use of artistic forms for interpreting data was explored to some extent in Chapter 8. These are also effective as modes of reporting and communicating the case. While there is still more work to be done on how best to establish their validity as forms of reporting, in some contexts – arts and health, academia, community studies and the applied professions – increasingly there are spaces for reporting and communicating findings in artistic forms.

In my own work with colleagues in this field I have presented the findings of a case study using music, painting and poetry (Gibbons and Simons, 2002) and music and dramatic enactment (Hicks and Simons, 2006). Bagley and Cancienne (2001) have explored the presentation of research findings through dance. Richardson (1997) has used poetic and dramatic form. Her narrative poem 'Louisa May's Story of Her Life', in which she transformed an in-depth interview with Louisa May using her words, syntax and grammar into poetic form, illustrates the power of this mode of communication to tell the story. Sparkes (2002) has outlined the opportunities ethno-poetics and ethno-drama present compared with 'realist tales'.

In PhD research in recent years, artistic modes of reporting have also been accepted as part of the presentation of a case study thesis, sometimes along with videos, DVDs and CDs. See Rugang (2006) for a narrative analysis using photographs, poetry and a CD; Duke (2007) for a narrative analysis in poetic form; and Jenny Elliott (2008) for the integration of photographs, reflective drawings and a film of dance, which was the major medium through which she conducted her research.

Appropriateness for Purpose

These different approaches to organizing and reporting data in case study research are not necessarily discrete forms. In practice there may well be combinations and variations. The form you choose will partly depend upon the predilection you have for a particular style and whether the data were generated with this in mind. It is often useful to have some idea of how you intend to present the case when you begin so you can think about the crafting of it as you proceed. I do not mean here that you should deliberately seek vignettes and cameos that might enrich the account in an overly rational way or that you filter the text with poetic fragments or dramatic tales to embellish the reading of the case. It is more a question of staying open to the prospect of how the findings are best communicated and where content and image converge in form.

Finally, of course, the form in which the case study is presented will be influenced by the major purpose for which it was conducted. If it was a one-off study conducted entirely for your intrinsic interest, a personal, interpretative narrative approach might appeal. If it was a funded policy study, a more formal mode of reporting may be appropriate. If the purpose was to generate first-order data cases to enable others to conduct a cross-case analysis, a variant of traditional and portrayal approaches is likely to be helpful. You will need to decide. Like the process of research itself, in the final analysis, the choice is personal and political in the context of the purpose of the study.

Case Study Memo 18 Constructing and Writing the Case Study Story

- Think about what would be the most appropriate mode of reporting for your purpose and audience.
- Sketch an outline of what you think the structure might be, but do not be surprised if another emerges in the writing. As analysis and interpretation deepen, a different structure and a different form of telling the story may seem more appropriate.
- Start with whatever section or chapter you find most interesting to write. If it runs dry do not force yourself to complete it. Move to another and if the same thing happens shift again. Moving backward and forwards can also strengthen connections between sections.
- An alternative is to start at the beginning and work logically through, although this assumes that your initial structure is the most appropriate one.

- If thoughts or quotations relevant to the case as a whole occur, but are not pertinent for the particular section you are writing, make notes, record the reference, indicate its significance and even write a paragraph or two. This will prove useful when you come to write the section where it is apt and help you see what points are relevant for one section in relation to others.
- Establish a good recording and retrieval system of data, vignettes, quotations. Nothing is more wasteful than trying to remember where you read a critical point, phrase or quotation. If it is written down and referenced you only have to read through your notes.
- Set timetables for the ordering and completion of sections. Invariably these shift, but they help you see what progress you are making, how much time you have left and when you may be spending disproportionate time on any one section in relation to the whole.
- Metaphors are often useful in crafting a coherent narrative. If they are apt they provide a unifying theme that contributes to the telling of your story; if they strain or are overused they detract. Reflect on whether they help tell the story or get in the way of the telling.
- Use your imagination in deciding how to construct the story of the case but always keep your readers in mind – what will communicate, what will they tolerate, and from what might they learn.
- In ending your case study story you do not have to come to formal conclusions, though you may wish to draw implications, pose an agenda for development, suggest alternatives for policy-makers to consider or highlight the significance of findings for theory and practice.
- Try to avoid recommending what should happen. Rarely are you in a position (with the political knowledge and awareness of available resources) to make prescriptive statements.
- There is no need, and it is often not wise, to leave all interpretation to the end. The reader needs signposts early on and wants to be stimulated to read on.
- Make sure you offer evidence for the views, judgements and propositions claimed. Though you have to maintain a narrative structure, you do not have the licence of a fiction writer.
- Do not forget that the story should have a good ending – the most difficult part of all – and one frequently neglected in thesis writing. Provide signs throughout but leave a few punch lines (significant findings) for the end.

Inspirations for Improving Writing

To have the impact on our readers we desire, vignettes, cameos and narratives need to be well written. Students often tell me that they have difficulty in writing rich description and they worry about whether they have the skills to write in story form or use artistic modes of presentation. So in this section of the chapter I focus directly on the skill of writing and some of the techniques that may help you craft the case study story. There are many inspirations we can draw upon to develop our writing skills – literary, dramatic and poetic traditions, journalism and biography.

From a literary tradition

From a literary tradition we can learn the art of rich description, through creating scenes located in place and time, skill in portraying character, and elements, such as plot and dramatic tension, that help weave the story and engage the reader. In constructing a narrative, paying attention to the structural elements of time, space and scene (Clandinin and Connelly, 1994; Polkinghorne, 1995) will help retain the particularity of events and experience. Dramatic structure (plot, character) will help create a framework for the telling of the tale. Image and metaphor can signify themes and provide a unifying thread and coherence to the interpretative meaning (Simons and McCormack, 2007).

From journalism

From 'good' journalism, and particularly investigative journalism, we can learn how to write to communicate succinctly – one idea a paragraph, for instance, writing to space constraints, and how to create and maintain interest. From good investigative journalism we can also learn how to use both documentary and live sources to tell an authentic story. And from the 'new' journalism (Wolfe, 1973) we gain four specific techniques: scene-by-scene construction, the use of extensive realistic dialogue, use of the third-person point of view, and the inclusion of descriptive, symbolic details that give the reader access to what Wolfe calls the 'status life' of the subject (Denzin, 1997: 134–135; MacDonald, 1977: 52). The new journalism, according to Caulley (2008: 424), was the beginning of 'creative nonfiction', which he notes has exploded in the publishing and academic worlds since the early 1990s.[5] I will refer to this again later in discussing the issue of whether or not, or in what contexts, it may be appropriate to fictionalize in case study reporting. For the moment I wish to stay with what we can learn about writing from journalism itself.

For an excellent account of the parallel with case study research and what we can learn from journalism to improve our reporting and writing skills see Harrington (2003). In this paper you will find that many of the basic ways in which journalists are trained to observe, interview and report are equally applicable to case study research, as are the observations the author makes about the tacit knowledge we acquire through experience of the craft, which adds depth and insight to what and how we report. But it is the three particular points on writing that Harrington makes that I wish to emphasize here: first, about language and style; secondly, the inseparability of writing and reporting; and thirdly, the use of documentary detail.

Harrington argues for plain, precise, direct language, whatever the complexity of the ideas we are putting across. It is, he says, a craft hard-won. This not only refers to the technical study of grammar, punctuation and style essential to making meaning clear, but also to the quality of the writing itself.

> [This goes] beyond constructing sentences well to rendering scenes, capturing action, selecting telling details, avoiding melodrama, shaping material without distorting it, not being too obvious, not being too obtuse, aptly balancing the particular and the universal,

imposing themes that rightfully emerge from your reporting, structuring stories so insight emerges, action concludes, characters change, and tension is relieved. (p. 97)

These writing challenges, he says, have great implications for reporting, partly because there is no clear boundary between reporting and writing: 'You can't think of the two as separate.' He talks about the need to 'first "see" finished stories in your head', so you will know what to report to build your particular story (p. 97). He was referring here to documentary literary journalism, and you may not aspire to such a literary approach in your case study reporting. Nevertheless, the point he is making is that you need to have some idea of the finished story in order to choose what evidence and argument best enables you to tell it.

The third point concerns the use of documentary detail. We encountered this in Chapter 4 in relation to the portrayal of a principal in a school. We need to *observe* the detail to gain an accurate, in-depth sense of the person or event, but do not need to include it all in the portrayal. Documentary detail is also critical to good journalism and often takes hours of observation. Yet in writing, says Harrington, 'the substructure of inquiry is hidden from view in service to the story at hand … For a story to read easy, the hard work is hidden' (p. 98). While it is necessary to gather meaningful documentary detail, it is 'the interplay between detail and meaning' (p. 99) that gives the story its impact. It is not sufficient to describe an event or scene, however well you do this. Asking what it means is critical to convey its dramatic and subjective meaning.

The parallel with journalism, like many parallels, is not exact, of course. As Wilby (1980) has argued, in journalism the main motivation is to create news, and journalists write for popular audiences. Making news is not the prime motivation for case study research. The aspiration of research is to create knowledge and of evaluation to inform decision-making. Whether it is news is a secondary matter.

One consequence of the 'making news' motivation is that sometimes journalism goes beyond the data. Wilby (1980: 220) observes that *All the President's Men* (Woodward and Bernstein, 1974) is a good example of investigative journalism, something that cannot be said for its sequel, *The Final Days*. House (1980: 106–107) offers an analysis of how the intent to create a dramatic narrative of Nixon's final days, in the novel of this name, went beyond the telling of the facts of the case to weaving a tale – and portrayal of Nixon as a disintegrated man – the truth of which was questioned. This was a step too far. While dramatic forms can enhance the text, they can also misconstrue and be unfair.

From biography

Biographers go into much more detail of a person than portrayal of persons in case study research. Telling the in-depth story of a person is their art. However, they often present short vignettes within their biographies from which we have much to learn about how to craft a cameo of a person and also how to write. One biographer from whom I learned a great deal in this respect is Judith Thurman. A cameo of Karen Blixen from Thurman's (1984) biography of Isak Dinesen (the pseudonym under which Karen Blixen wrote) was presented in Chapter 4. A reminder of the cameo is presented here, and see below for a short analysis of the writing techniques Thurman employed, which may be useful in cameos or vignettes we might write in our case study work.

Example: A Cameo

There are certain irreducibles in the character of Isak Dinesen, as in the character of each of us. Some children have a depth to their nature, from birth – a passionate curiosity – while others are cautious, passive, or serene. While almost anything can happen to those original qualities – in particular they can easily be discouraged – they also define a mysterious ground of one's being that defies analysis. Tanne [Karen] was a proud, deeply feeling, touchy, and vital child. She was a dreamer from the beginning, and it was her fate to have that quality within her recognized and nourished by her father, who took his second-born as his favorite and gave her time the others did not share. In a sense she led a double life as a child – as one of three, and as herself, only. (1984: 45)

Later on the same page, Thurman makes a connection to Dinesen's work, capturing its essence as follows:

There is in Dinesen's work and thinking a frontier – more of a fixed circle, like an embroidery hoop – that separates the wild from the domestic. Within it there is firelight and women's voices, the steam of kettles, the clockwork of women's lives. Beyond it there are passions, spaces, grandeurs; there lie the wildernesses and the battlefields. Wilhelm led his daughter out of the domestic limbo and into the 'wild'. He took her for long walks in the woods or by the Sound; he willed her his great love of nature; he taught her to become observant, to distinguish among the wild flowers and the bird songs, to watch for the new moon, to name the grasses. He exercised her senses, made her conscious of them the way a hunter is, in imitation of his prey. This was a kind of second literacy that she says she acquired at about the same time she learned to read, and its discipline and pleasure were at least as important in her life as those of books. (1984: 45)

The biographer in these two short paragraphs has used a number of literary devices to distil the essence of the kind of child Karen Blixen was and portray how her childhood experiences influenced her work. In the first paragraph, carefully chosen adjectives describe the essential qualities of this particular child, the device of comparison being used to highlight her uniqueness. A chronological fact – 'his second-born' – links her with her father and the special time he gave to her as his 'favorite', which leads into the interpretation that concludes the paragraph – 'she led a double life as a child – as one of three, and as herself, only'.

In the second paragraph, a simile – 'like an embroidery hoop' – is used to convey the essential 'frontier' character of Dinesen's work that separates the wild from the domestic. This sets the scene for a series of descriptions of what is in and beyond the frontier. Juxtaposition of such comparisons between the domestic and the wild creates a feeling of the space and scope of her work. Explanation for this view is given through introducing the connection with her father again, detailing precisely how and what he taught her.

This language of description includes both the purely factual and physical – 'he took her for long walks in the woods', and the emotional force of his interest – 'he willed her his great love of nature', culminating in an almost physical description of the impact this had. This is heightened by a concluding metaphor – 'He exercised her senses, made her conscious of them the way a hunter is, in imitation of his prey.' This paragraph, like the first one commented on above, concludes with an interpretation – 'of second literacy' – a concept, introduced this time through a report of what the subject of the biography had said and what its importance to her was.

In summary, these two paragraphs, which have the density and sense of completeness that characterize the essence of a cameo – a brief picture of a life – have used the devices of chronological fact, comparison, direct reported fact, series of descriptive adjectives, metaphor and simile to convey the factual details of Dinesen's life.

We can also see the creative use of language, attribution of what another said, juxtaposition of comparison, reconnections of theme, explanation and interpretation through concepts that sum up the character of the person and the influence on her work. Not all of these devices may be needed for any cameo you portray in your case study. I leave it to you to determine how useful they are. For me, from reading this cameo I gained an immediate sense both of the person and the essential features of her work, a direct insight that seemed well-researched, authentic, and which compelled me to read on.

Representing or Fictionalizing

In suggesting the use of artistic forms or aspects of them in telling the case study story, I am not saying that we should aspire to be novelists, poets or dramatists. We should leave the writing of fiction, poetry and plays to the novelists, poets and dramatists themselves. However, as the above illustrates, we can learn something from their craft to help us structure and write the case study story. Whether we should fictionalize or write part of our cases as fiction is an issue that has arisen in this context.

Several reasons can be proposed for using fiction. First, it can help us understand and feel – gain a vicarious experience – of different lives and experiences. Secondly, it can tell more of the story, convey more of the complex reality and meaning than is possible when having to clear information with individuals whose words and observations are directly portrayed in an actual case. Thirdly, it helps overcome the difficulty of identifying individuals in a case, offering them some protection of privacy. Making a composite case is sometimes advanced as a solution to this difficulty of anonymizing individuals: that is, on the basis of observations and interviews with several individuals, write up and tell the story as though it were one person. Finally, fiction can enhance readability, an important aspiration in communicating effectively with audiences of our case studies.

While it is true that using metaphor, image, dramatic structure and other literary devices employed in fictional accounts can enhance the readability of our cases, and powerfully persuade, I remain a little uneasy about a drift into fiction. Case study research and evaluation is not fiction. It is about real people in real-life contexts. It has to be authentic. So while we may use dramatic and literary forms to enhance readability and convey complex meaning, we need to retain connection with real-life events and people. House (1980) puts the point well in the context of evaluation when he says, 'The dicta that apply to art, even documentary art, are not necessarily those that shape evaluation. One expects more veracity from an evaluation report than from a novel or a film' (p. 114).

With skill and practice in using artistic forms, I think we can learn to depict experience in real-life cases with such veracity that others will have vicarious experience. The 'new' art of creative nonfiction could be helpful in offering techniques to re-create such experience in ways that will engage the reader. The use of composites may also be a legitimate route if the authenticity of the data is retained and permission is given by those whose experience it is.

What concerns me most are three issues. The first is where the dramatic structure takes over and goes beyond the data, or where the coherence of the story is diminished or misconstrued. Whatever dramatic structure is used, the basic programme story should not significantly change (House, 1980: 116). It needs to be grounded in authentic evidence and analysis of the actual case.

The second is the unconscious slide into fiction, where the reader cannot discern what is based on 'real' life and context and what is fiction. The resolution here, I suggest, if you wish to use fictional elements in writing up your case study, is to make it clear which is which. A good example of the clarity with which an author outlines what is fiction and what is not comes from a fiction writer, Sebastian Faulks (2005), in *Human Traces*. In order to ensure factual accuracy with regard to real people and dates in this novel of two psychiatrists set in the nineteenth century, Faulks draws on actual letters and lectures and documents from real doctors drawn from documentary sources about the time when the novel is set. He makes it quite clear which sources he has used, where people existed as described, and where he reproduces a factual letter. He indicates when words in lectures given in the text were invented but intended to reflect accurately what was taught, based on the content of published lectures, the person's renown, style of lecturing and his audience. Finally, he notes that the major hospital depicted was as close to the reality as he could make it from the sources he consulted (p. 611).

The third concern is ethical. Those who people our research case studies are real people and we have an obligation to be fair in our portrayal of them. To me this means recognizing that they are living beings situated in context and community. It also means telling their story well. Literary, dramatic and poetic forms help to create artistic structure, but these should not be used at the expense of honouring actual experience. Sensitively crafted, they enhance communication and understanding. However, the power of language and metaphor can also over-persuade. There is a danger that in telling the story, the artistic meaning can take over and reduce the authenticity of the person's experience. To ensure this does not happen, I suggest we ask a number of questions.

- Is the language used over-emotive?
- Is the story 'true' to those from whom we gained the data?
- Where dramatic form has been used, have we allowed the performance to take over the re-presentation of experience?

And the acid test?

- If participants read your account or witnessed a dramatic construction of the data would they recognize themselves and feel that they were being honoured in your portrayal?
- If they did not recognize themselves, what does this say? Have you simply re-interpreted them? Or have you misrepresented them?

You might also ask the question that has sometimes been put to me: Does it matter if the audience learns from the telling of the story? Yes, ethically it does.

Case Study Memo 19 **Improving Your Writing**

- Write every day, even if you discard what you write afterwards. The chances are you are more likely to rewrite and are further on the way than not having written anything at all.
- Make quotations work for their inclusion. It is tempting to quote sometimes rather than rephrase in your own narrative but unless the quotation is particularly trenchant, makes the point eloquently, or no one has said it before, resist this temptation.
- Too many non-apt quotations may weaken the narrative, if not lose track of it. The exception is where you comprise a 'documentary' case study almost entirely from edited excerpts from interview.
- If you feel you have captured a lovely phrase or written a good paragraph read it once or twice perhaps, but do not dwell on it. There are more like that to be written.
- If you note that you have too many paragraphs that are each one long sentence, full of caveats, qualifying clauses, lists of points, the paragraph may be too long. Make an effort to write in short sentences. Be liberal with full stops.
- If you find that you have too many thuses and therefores, try cutting them out. More often than not they are not needed.
- If you get stuck, find the words trite, sentences repetitive, paragraphs too general, no focus, or nothing flowing at all, stop. Read for a while. Look for stimulus in your data, a relevant text you have found useful, or a novel that has the flair for language you admire. Assume you will become excited again. Do not sit around waiting for inspiration.

(Continued)

(Continued)

- Read good writing. Some of my favourites are Virginia Woolf, Niall Brennan, Jean Rhys, Ernest Hemingway, Ben Okri.
- Practise writing. Create cameos or vignettes from a selection of data as you proceed.
- Establish a writing circle with fellow students to share and critique examples of your writing
- Try out some of the writing exercises advocated by Richardson (1994) and Janesick (2004).
- You might also like to dip into any of the books by Natalie Goldberg that offer guidance on how to write, especially *Writing Down the Bones* (1986) and *Wild Mind* (1991). While these refer to writing fiction, many of the ideas they contain are useful for crafting vignettes and freeing up your writing skills.

Notes

1. 'Vocabulary of action' is a term introduced by House (1973) to signal that we need to use language that matches that of the audiences we hope to influence if we wish them to learn from our reports.
2. See Rogers and Williams (2006) for a discussion of the importance of linking evaluation findings and evidence to the theories of how people and organizations learn.
3. In indicating that the portrayal is data-led and primarily descriptive, I am not suggesting that it is not also interpretative. Interpretation is always involved in the selection and organization of data. It is a question of emphasis.
4. Interpretation is involved in how we make sense of the data throughout. What I am discussing here is an overt intent to produce an interpretative account as distinct from one that portrays the story of the case more indirectly.
5. Creative nonfiction is writing non-fiction using fiction techniques. According to Caulley (2008), it grew out of 'the new journalism' in the 1960s and 1970s, though the origin of the term 'creative nonfiction' and when exactly it became popular is unknown (p. 426). The journal of its name, *Creative Nonfiction*, was established in 1993. For further reading on the forms and techniques of creative non-fiction see Gutkind (1997) and Cheney (2001).

Further Readings

Denzin, N.K. (1997) *Interpretive Ethnography: Ethnographic Practices for the 21st Century*. Thousand Oaks, CA: Sage.
An extensive discussion of forms of ethnographic, interpretative writing in the twenty-first century, taking account of cultural and global changes that affect how we and those we study see the world. Includes exploration of experiential texts inspired by the new journalism, fiction, ethno-poetics and narratives of the self.

Ely, M., Vinz, R., Downing, M. and Anzul, M. (1997) *On Writing Qualitative Research: Living by Words*. London: The Falmer Press.
An inquiry into the art of writing qualitative research with extensive examples of how to construct meaning through different forms of narrative, metaphor, drama and poetry.

Chapters 4 and 5 examine respectively working in analytic and interpretative modes, and Chapter 7 considers the effect of writing on ourselves and others.

House, E.R. (1980) 'Coherence and credibility: the aesthetics', in *Evaluating with Validity*, pp. 97–117. London: Sage.
Discusses the merits of using artistic, narrative and dramatic forms in the telling of the programme story, indicating where the balance between aesthetics, truth and justice should lie.

Janesick, V.J. (2004) *'Stretching' EXERCISES for Qualitative Researchers*, 2nd edn. London: Sage.
An excellent sourcebook for practising your writing skills, interviewing techniques, powers of observation and role as researcher. Short exercises are offered for all these methods as well as the use of art forms to construct cameos and interpret text.

Richardson, L. (1990) *Writing Strategies: Reaching Diverse Audiences*. Qualitative Research Methods, 21. Newbury Park, CA: Sage.
Explores the diverse ways in which we can write up qualitative research, including the use of metaphor and narrative, with helpful sections on how to use quotations short and long and thematic biographical narratives. See also Richardson (1994, 1997).

Van Maanen, J. (1988) T*ales of the Field: On Writing Ethnography*. Chicago, IL: University of Chicago Press.
Addressed primarily to fieldworkers of an ethnographic persuasion, distinguishes between realist, confessional and impressionist tales and how to produce each.

Wolcott, H. (2001) *Writing Up Qualitative Research*, 2nd edn. Thousand Oaks, CA: Sage.
Offers practical guidance on how to begin writing up, maintain momentum, keep track, link to theory, tighten up and finally get to completion. Very accessible with useful checklists at different stages and helpful advice.

Woods, P. (2006) *Successful Writing for Qualitative Researchers*, 2nd edn. London: Routledge.
An exploration of the art of writing from getting started to editing and writing for publication. Includes chapters on how to structure a text, different forms of representation and styles of writing.

10

DISPELLING MYTHS IN CASE STUDY RESEARCH

In this final chapter I address the issues of subjectivity, generalization, theorizing and case studies in policy-making that Laura raised in her initial letter by exploring frequently held myths about case study research. These have been variously stated, often dismissively, as 'case studies are "too subjective"'; 'you cannot generalize from a case study'; 'you cannot generate theory in case study research'; 'case studies are not useful in policy-making'. Sometimes such judgements stem from an attempt to justify the case study approach on criteria more appropriate for inquiries in a positivist tradition. Other times they result from a misunderstanding of the central precepts of case study research.[1]

Stated in the negative, these issues are misrepresented of course. There are strengths and weakness in most research approaches and case study research is no exception. Subjectivity, uncertainty, complexity can be troublesome and the ethical risks and danger of becoming personally involved are potential threats. Managing diverse data sets and communicating unique cases to maximize understanding and use are further challenges to the researcher's skills. From some perspectives, these may be seen as weaknesses, from others, strengths. I recognize these different perceptions, but as you will have noted from preceding chapters, I err on the side of the strengths. I have chosen to address the issues in this chapter from the statements above as this is how students have presented their concerns to me; and my aim throughout has been to provide support to strengthen their argument for case study should they choose to use this research approach.

'Case Studies are "Too Subjective"'

Phrased in this way, 'too subjective' is value-laden. It suggests subjectivity is something negative that we should try to erase from the research process. From the early chapters in particular, it will be clear that subjective understandings are part of the strength of qualitative case study research. I will comment on this strength first and then explore the worry I think may lie behind the 'too subjective' criticism – that it may lead to a biased account.

For the most part in qualitative inquiry (including case study), we are exploring phenomena experienced subjectively. To dismiss such inquiries as 'too subjective' is inappropriate. They simply are what they are – studies documenting and analysing phenomena appealing to subjective ways of knowing to gain insight and understanding. Subjectivity is not something we can avoid whatever methods we adopt, though it is more visible in qualitative inquiry, where people, including the researcher, are an inherent part of the case. In certain contexts it is the most appropriate approach and you should not have to justify it *vis-à-vis* any other, but only in its own terms for the relevance it has for the specific topic of your research.

Take, for instance, the study conducted by Flewitt (2003, 2005a, 2005b) to explore communicative behaviours of three-year-old children in two different settings, home and playgroup. In order to document and understand the strategies the children adopted to communicate, Flewitt used a variety of qualitative methods to observe. These included compact digital video-recordings of playgroup and home interactions, audio-recordings, field notes, a research diary and semi-structured and informal interviews with staff and parents. These methods tried to capture, as unobtrusively as possible, the multi-modal communicative practices the children adopted with their mothers and their peers. It was indeed subjective. But was it 'too subjective'? I think not. It was a meticulous attempt to document and analyse naturally occurring phenomena in a context that could not have been studied by other methods, at least without a degree of distortion.

The 'too subjective' criticism can also lead to a false attempt to secure objectivity. I have often found students trying to demonstrate how they have eliminated their subjectivity, also sometimes referred to as bias. This is manifest in method in a 'rush to the questionnaire' or attempts to ask pre-structured questions in precisely the same sequence in each interview on the assumption that objectivity will be enhanced. In fieldwork it results in a denial of their own presence and social impact in the research. Each of these strategies is a false trail.

Eliminating subjectivity is not achievable in any event. It is inherent in the judgements we make, the views we express. Whether such judgements and views are biases is a separate question. Attempts to eliminate subjectivity as if it were bias arises, I suspect, from an assumption that 'objective *method*' holds the key to sound inquiry (Schwandt, 2001: 15–16). Bias in this understanding of method 'is always defined negatively as something that interferes with, prevents, or inhibits having true, genuine knowledge' (p. 16).

This view has been criticized by many qualitative inquirers (Denzin, 1989; Guba and Lincoln, 1989; Schwandt, 2001), who indicate that the more relevant approach to adopt in qualitative inquiry is to acknowledge its inherent subjectivity and concentrate on demonstrating how your values, predispositions and feelings impact upon the research. This is different from saying we can eliminate them. The aim, then, is not to try to erase subjectivity but to recognize, as noted in Chapter 5, when it contributes to insight and understanding and when it might become a potential bias. Where the latter is the case, document the procedures you adopted to prevent any biases distorting findings.

In the example cited above, conscious that she was part of the setting she was studying, Flewitt adopted a reflexive stance throughout the research, identifying her own social, political and personal values and monitoring her reactions and interpretations. To balance any potentially overly subjective findings – her bias – she also collaborated with adult participants (playgroup staff and mothers) in developing emerging issues and in examining conflicting perceptions of how they viewed children's different communicative strategies in playgroup and at home (Flewitt, 2005b).

'You Cannot Generalize from a Case Study'

I cannot recall the number of times over the years students have told me the case study approach is ideal for the topic they wish to research but they cannot generalize from it. Their response has often been to adopt an entirely quantitative approach, or introduce a questionnaire survey (sometimes even when it does not fit the topic they are researching) into the case approach thinking that it will boost the generalizability of the case. Those who stay with the case in all its uniqueness still worry that they may not be able to convince examiners of the validity or usefulness of their findings. As I noted in the introduction, the issue here is not whether one kind of data provides greater generalizability than another. It is how inferences are drawn from the data in different kinds of studies and to what validity claims they appeal.

In many contexts where we conduct case study research we have an obligation not necessarily to generalize but to demonstrate how and in what ways our findings may be transferable to other contexts or used by others. It is within this understanding of usability of findings that I suggest six different ways of generalizing in or from case study research.[2] I have chosen to stay with the word 'generalization' as it is commonly in use. The first five are: cross-case generalization, naturalistic generalization, concept generalization, process generalization, situated generalization. The sixth is not so much a generalization – moving out from the specifics of the case to other cases – but more a universal understanding or insight arrived at through intense, in-depth particularization.

All these forms of generalizing are not dependent upon generalizing in a propositional sense that is customary in positivist research. Formal generalizations appealing to propositional knowledge would assume that the case was typical of a wider population, and hence the findings, if rigorously conducted and analysed, would have some predictive power and could safely be generalized to that population.

This is not the situation in case study research. The cases we study are not typical. One case may have similarities to other cases. However, the way in which we can draw implications from one case to another differs. These are not abstractions independent of place and context. They depend for their meaning on maintaining a connectedness with the particulars of the concrete case in context. This resonates with Flyvbjerg's (2006) observation and argument that, in the study of human affairs, 'there appears to exist only context-dependent knowledge' (p. 221).

Cross-case generalization

Cross-case generalization is commonly adopted in a collective case study. Here you will have studied several cases and, through a process of cross-case analysis, identified common issues in each case and interconnecting themes between them. You may have started with one and as you moved from case to case re-examined the themes in different contexts to see what aspects of the analysis hold true from case to case and what might be different. From this analysis you may derive general propositions across the number of cases studied. While this is a degree of abstraction, it is not a formal propositional generalization to a wider population. Its meaning is grounded in these particular cases.

Naturalistic generalization

Naturalistic generalization, proposed by Stake (1980), is a form of generalization arrived at by recognizing similarities and differences to cases or situations with which readers are familiar. It appeals much more to tacit knowledge than propositional knowledge, to understanding rather than explanation. As Stake (1980) puts it:

> Naturalistic generalizations develop within a person as a result of experience. They form from the tacit knowledge of how things are, why they are, how people feel about them, and how these things are likely to be later or in other places with which this person is familiar. They seldom take the form of predictions but lead regularly to expectation ... (p. 69)

Given sufficient detail and rich description, a reader can discern which aspects of the case they can generalize to their own context and which they cannot. To assist the reader to generalize in this way, Stake (1995) says that we need to provide vicarious experience:

> Our accounts need to be personal, describing the things of our sensory experience, not failing to attend to the matters that personal curiosity dictates. A narrative account, a story, a chronological presentation, personalistic description, emphasis on time and place provide rich ingredients for vicarious experience. Emphasizing time, place, and person are the first three major steps. (pp. 86–87)

This way of learning from the case is applicable in many policy and practice contexts. It is particularly useful in professional practice to encourage professionals to take action in relation to the findings of the case or to research their own situations. As Flyvbjerg (2006) has recently argued from research on learning, working from cases and context-dependent knowledge is the way in which novices or rule-base beginners become experts (pp. 221–223). It can also be educative in policy contexts to give those involved in policy-making access to the vicarious experience of the case to inform their judgements.

Naturalistic generalization is persuasive to me. However, your supervisor may wish to see more evidence of what general propositions *you* have drawn from the data, rather than leaving readers to discern what is or is not relevant to them and their context. You may be required to undertake a second-order analysis in which you draw more conclusive statements or generate over-arching concepts from the case. Here I suggest that you consider developing either *concept* or *process* generalizations from your data.

Concept generalization

The best example I have come across of *concept generalization* that students have found helpful in their own work stems from an early illuminative study of the examination strategies of first-year university undergraduate honours geography students. In this study, Miller and Parlett (1974) found that students' examination strategies fell into three groups. Some were *'cue-conscious'*, that is, students were perceptive and attentive to cues sent out by staff about the examinations. Others were *'cue seekers'*, students who were not simply, content to pick up hints, but who were actively seeking information about exam questions or the external examiner and pursuing the tutor for cues. A third group were *'cue deaf'*, that is, neither particularly attentive to picking up cues nor actively seeking them. The study was of one student year group in one subject only. However, the concept of *'cue consciousness'* is one that is potentially applicable to examinations in other subjects and across different year groups. In other words, the *concept* generalizes even when the specific instance is different.

Process generalization

Process generalization is similar in that it is the process, stemming from the analysis of a case or cases, which is transferable even when the cases may be different in content and context. Take the following example from research into school self-evaluation. Through an analysis of case study evaluations conducted by schools over a period of time and in several countries, I generated a process of school development which had a built-in strategy of change and was sustainable over time. This process was collaborative at every stage of conducting case study in schools; in sharing the aims, planning and design, risks, data collection, analysis, reporting and action. Schools that were successful in maintaining a self-evaluation process all demonstrated these collaborative characteristics (Simons, 2002). It was not the content, nor the context here, that needed to be similar in order to generalize. It was the *process* of change that was applicable to many organizations.

Situated genererlization

Situated generalization, as the name suggests, is a concept that relies for its generality on retaining a connectedness to the situation in which the understanding first evolved. This concept was generated in a case study evaluation I co-directed of teacher research[3] to explain how professional practitioners transferred and used research knowledge. The programme, which was the focus of the evaluation, involved teams of teachers conducting research in their own contexts supported by higher education institutions and local education authority personnel. It took place in the late 1990s in England in the contemporary evidence-based practice movement to encourage and explore how teachers used research to improve practice.

Evidence from this study indicated that teachers were more likely to adopt research findings (that is, to recognize the significance of generalizations) for their own practice if two conditions were present: first, 'if there was a visble connection with the situation in which the improved practice arose' (Simons et al. 2003: 359); and secondly, if there was a climate of trust and confidence in a shared research experience. For a generalization to be usable both were needed. Validity in this context is not only technical, methodological competence. 'It is also grounded in professional agreement as to the usefulness or significance of particular insights, and in the trust and confidence that may be placed in colleagues offering them' (Simons et al., 2003: 359).

This concept of situated generalization is similar to Stake's concept of naturalistic generalization in the sense that from a context richly described and interpreted, individual teachers could generalize on the basis of recognition of similarities and differences to their own experience. However, there is a further dimension. Seeing the relevance of the research for teachers' own use was dependent on a shared understanding of the issues and problems the research explored and the collective experience (in some cases) of designing, conducting and analysing the research. Teachers had confidence in the findings because they trusted their peers and the transparent process through which the research was validated.

In the context of action research, John Elliott (2008) has recently drawn attention to a similar process of generalization in describing how teachers come to use knowledge that is situated and based upon collective judgements of practitioners:

The greater the particularization of descriptions of situations, the more they take the complexities of making wise judgements and decisions into account. Yet at the same time, I would contend, such situational understandings can also be of universal significance by throwing light on possibilities for action in other situations. (pp. 12–13)

In-depth particularization – universal understanding
The above forms of generalizations are helpful in extending the use of findings from a single case to other situations. Yet the strongest justification for gaining a general understanding from case study research remains, for me, in the insights developed through the in-depth exploration of the particular. This takes us right back to the arguments for the case study approach raised in Chapter 1 in exploring the case in-depth. If this is studied in all its particularity, there is potential both for discovering something unique and for recognizing a universal 'truth'.

The aim here is not to search for generality in the case, as in the examples above, but rather to try to capture the essence of the particular in a way we all recognize. This is something of a paradox, which I have written about elsewhere (Simons, 1996) in the context of examining how policy needs in education in the mid-1990s were tending to overlook the potential of case study in favour of large-scale survey or experimental modes of inquiry (p. 277).

The paradox is significant in three senses. The first is referred to above – by studying the uniqueness of the case in-depth, in all its particularity, we come to understand the universal. Secondly, in the context of policy-making, which often seeks certainty, comparison and conclusiveness, case study research is important precisely because it studies the particular in depth, and often yields outcomes that are inconclusive. While this renders policy-making uncertain, therein lies its strength for policy-making. Case study research, which presents multiple perspectives, interpretations in context, and aspires to directly encounter and re-present the phenomenon it is trying to understand, offers policy-makers opportunities to increase their understanding of complex social settings and programmes in order to inform the policy judgements they need to make.

The third sense of paradox is in the process of how we arrive at universal insights and understandings in case study research. Here I suggest we approximate the 'way of the artist' in making sense of data. When you think about how we gain insights from artists, poets, novelists, it is when we recognize something in what they have said or portrayed which communicates an essential 'truth' about the human condition or social context of the times.

In trying to capture that essence, insight or understanding, I argue that we should engage with the paradox within the case, the tension between the universal and the particular, and the ambiguity or conflict it presents. By holding the paradox open to disbelief and re-examination, we eventually come to realize both the significance of the unique instance or circumstance and the universal understanding (that insight we all recognize). This means staying with the particularity of the case, in all its contradictions and ambiguity, living with the paradox in fact until we reach that understanding. 'The tension between the study of the *unique* and the need to generalise is necessary to reveal both the *unique* and the *universal* and the *unity* of that understanding' (Simons, 1996: 239).

'You Cannot Generate Theory in Case Study Research'

The dictum that you cannot generalize theory in case study may have stemmed from several sources: from adopting a perspective on theorizing similar to that in positivist research – testing empirical generalizations, seeking casual explanations, for instance; from particular disciplines or orientations within them; from a concern to build cumulative knowledge of a specific topic where one case is not thought to be sufficient. I do not wish to contest these different ways of generating theory; each may well be appropriate within the logic of the specific discipline or research approach. My interest is in examining how theory, is generated in case study research. The issue is not whether we can generate theory, or indeed use theory in the case, but how this can be done.[4]

Theory is elusive to define and is much discussed in the literature (Punch, 1998), but at a broad level, following Punch, I take it to mean 'the attempt to explain whatever is being studied with the explanation being couched in more abstract terms than the terms used to describe it'(p. 16). Punch notes the major distinction between theory-verification and theory-generation studies, the first setting out to test theory, the second to build it (and the historical connection linking the first with quantitative and the second with qualitative studies), though he indicates that there is no necessary connection between purpose and approach.

The most widely adopted approach to generating theory in case study research (and certainly qualitative research more generally) is grounded theory (Denzin, 1994; Punch, 1998), different perspectives on which were discussed in Chapter 7. Grounded theory is essentially built, as the concept implies, from the ground up, from the data. The constructs and perspectives of participants in the case provide initial data, though it is you, of course, who code and categorize the data, make the connections, generate concepts and build the theory, as in any other type of theory-building.

You can also generate theory through cross-case analysis of a number of cases. In a collective case study, generating theory may be part of the intent as you move from case to case identifying themes, exploring patterns and interconnections that may ultimately result in a theory of the phenomenon you are researching. You might choose to develop the theory by using a grounded approach. Alternatively, you could examine the cases through a pre-existing theoretical framework, to examine whether this provides a basis for explaining the data or whether it needs refining to more adequately explain common understandings across cases.

A third approach is the generation of a theory of the single case as you make sense of the data to tell a coherent story. This form of theorizing is practically inevitable in the interpretative process. The theory would not be a theory abstracted from the case but rather a theory of the case itself that explains or interprets it. It will have evolved as you work iteratively with the data to identify the underlying narrative structure of the case.

A good example of this form of theorizing is that outlined by the documentary film-maker Frederick Wiseman (referred to in Chapter 9) in describing the editing process of making a film. This is an intuitive as much as a rational process. In deciding what scenes fit with what and where, Wiseman explains how he works out a theory of the film, but as he says, 'in the way I finally get to it I can see that the rationalization frequently comes after the connection exists' (Graham, 1971: 44). In other words, the theory is something that is arrived at through deep immersion in the data and an intuitive grasp of the connections between ideas or scenes.

In the process of conducting your case, you may also use theory in other ways. For example, you may use existing theories to inform how you select and make sense of the data. Or, if you are conducting an evaluation case study, you might start with an underlying theory of change of the programme you are evaluating, and seek to confirm or disconfirm whether this is indeed the theory of the programme in action. If undertaking a case study in social science more broadly, you may explore how a particular social or substantive theory applies to a case. (See also the discussion in Gomm et al. (2004) on how case study and theory has been conceived and used in political science, sociology and anthropology.) These are different uses of theory than the three processes described above for generating theory in case study research – grounded theory, building cumulative theory from cases or generating a theory of the case itself.

'Case Studies are not Useful in Policy-making'

This observation in relation to case studies is often voiced by those who do not believe that it is possible to evolve policy from a single case or those who, while agreeing that it might be possible for a case to inform decision-making, think it is an insufficient basis on which to determine or justify policy. Many policy contexts in the early twenty-first century are increasingly receptive to modes of inquiry that derive scientific legitimacy from large sample studies, often of experimental designs, that promise to provide evidence that is conclusive. The search is for certainty or at least a 'safe' basis on which to make decisions that involve financial resources and have human consequences. I respect and understand why some policy-makers may have this goal, especially those with responsibility for determining and justifying policy decisions. Confirmation of findings from large samples (and from certain methodologies) may seem to give a stronger justification for policy decisions. However, this is not the only criterion in determining policy. Many factors – social, political, economic – are involved and there are other bases and contexts from which people can learn to influence policy decisions. I do not discuss these differences and complexities further here. My emphasis is to examine what we can learn from a case study approach to illuminate and support policy decision-making.

First, even if findings from large sample studies appealing to objectivist ways of knowing are preferred, case studies provide an understanding of the process and context. This may in fact be needed to accurately interpret the meaning of findings gained through other methodologies. Secondly, a series of case studies, through cross-case analysis, can generate patterns and themes that have relevance in many contexts of a similar nature. Thirdly, and especially with the rise of computer-based technology, it is possible to collect and analyse large-scale data sets (quantitative and qualitative), including those obtained from case studies (Elliott, 2000; Schostak, 2002). This furthers collective understanding while retaining the essential connectedness with the contexts in which the data were derived, which is characteristic of the case study approach.

Fourthly, there is virtue in a close-up reading and immersion in the single case itself to inform policy decision-making, a point raised in the section exploring in-depth particularization. The case that is frequently cited in this connection is the film *Cathy Come Home* by Ken Loach, which reputedly led to a policy change in the mid-1970s in the way that homelessness was addressed in the UK. More recently is the case of Victoria Climbié, a child who died after years of mistreatment and abuse, through neglect of carers and lack of communication between agencies. *Every Child Matters* (2003) is a policy response to the inquiry into this case. It is a major restructuring of all the services relating to children, requiring integration of multi-agency services and a common assessment framework to ensure that such a tragedy does not happen again.[5] These are both prominent cases, but less dramatic examples do exist. One is the policy case study of nurse education and training referred to in Chapter 8. The Minister for Health and Children, in announcing a 'new' curriculum for a nursing degree, recommended that this study be taken into account in generating the 'new' curriculum.

Not all single case studies inform a specific policy. However, in a 'telling' way, through the presentation of complex, multiple realities and experience, they provide opportunities for policy-makers to increase their understanding of particular situations, which may contribute to policy-making in the longer term. While this may seem to make policy-making less certain in the short term, paradoxically, through the understanding gained of the complexity of social situations and experience, it can inform and improve the soundness of future policy decisions (Simons, 1996: 230).

Once again you have choices to make here about how which argument might be most appropriate for how you generalize or theorize in case study research and how you might defend the usefulness or transferability of your findings for policy-making and practice. Whichever you choose, it is the quality of the data, the understandings you present and how you justify your interpretations that will ultimately persuade.

Notes

1 See Flyvbjerg (2006) for an account of five particular misunderstandings about case study research and how these can each be restated to correct the misunderstanding.
2 See also the section on case study and generalizability in Gomm et al. (2004), which discusses a range of ways in which different authors argue for generalizability and issues on which they differ.
3 This was the Independent External Evaluation of the School-based Research Consortium Initiative funded by the Teacher Training Agency (TTA), a UK government agency, and the Centre for British Teachers (CfBT), a private, not-for-profit company. The evaluation was co-directed by Helen Simons and Saville Kushner and the team included David James and Keith Jones. I am indebted to my colleagues for the shared understanding we gained of this concept of situated generalization in this programme. This is described further in Simons et al. (2003).
4 For further exploration of the role of theory in case study research see Gomm et al. (2004: 117–258).
5 See DfES document *Every Child Matters: Change for Children* (2003) (www.everychildmatters.gov.uk) for the national framework for local change programmes to underpin this policy.

EPILOGUE

Dear Laura,

Here we are at the end. This has probably been a longer reply than you sought when you first wrote to me. I hope you found the last few chapters useful as you made sense of your data and that the arguments proposed in the final chapter will strengthen how you justify the case study approach in the final writing up.

I thought it might be helpful, as you are about to complete, to offer a short comment on the viva, as this can seem a daunting prospect. The overriding point to remember is that you are there to defend your research. Have confidence in the approach you have chosen. Indicate your awareness of other designs, where relevant, and complexities in the case approach itself. But above all, argue for its strength in relation to the purpose of your research, demonstrate how the findings are justly drawn from the data, and communicate in ways that will persuade.

In conclusion, let me broaden this letter with the following summary memo to share with your fellow students:

Case Study Memo 20   **Summary of the Case Study Process**

When you are conducting a case study for your research remember to:

- Consider which type of case study you wish to conduct. Keep your audience in mind and what would also be of use to them.
- Delineate the case clearly but stay alert to the possibility of the boundaries shifting.
- Identify research questions/subquestions or foreshadowed issues, though be responsive to other issues arising as the study proceeds.
- Plan and design the case carefully, choosing methods that will generate data to inform the questions you are asking.
- Be open to multiple means of data gathering (qualitative or quantitative) to provide a 'rich' data base from which to tell the story of the case.
- Cross-check the significance of issues through different methods, perspectives, participants, but also allow for insights that stem from a single person or event.
- Immerse yourself in the analysis process: dance with the data and see where it leads, draw cognitive or affective maps, generate logical pathways, write *haikus*, imagine before you write and see what metaphors might capture the meaning.

(Continued)

(Continued)

- In your analysis and interpretation, be attuned to the various ways you can make sense of the data and the potential for theory-building and generalizing.
- Ensure that your findings are drawn from the data. Do not over-claim.
- Think imaginatively about how to present your case study – in narrative, ethnographic, documentary, photographic, dramatic/poetic form.
- Consider whether a CD or DVD would facilitate understanding.
- Experiment at every stage. Find what is your preference and within your competence (and stretch it through your research training). Above all, enjoy the process. Know in those hours of wondering whether you will ever make sense of all the data that when you do, you will be elated, having learned so much along the way.

It is time for me to leave off and for you to complete. I wish you every success in the final writing up of your case study and … good luck with the viva.

Regards
Helen

BIBLIOGRAPHY

Abma, T.A. (1999) 'Introduction: Narrative perspectives on program evaluation', in T.A. Abma (ed.), *Telling Tales: On Evaluation and Narrative. Advances in Program Evaluation*, Volume 6, pp. 1–27. Greenwich, CT: JAI.

Adelman, C. (ed.) (1981) *Uttering Muttering*. London: Grant McIntyre.

Adelman, C., Kemmis, S. and Jenkins, D. (eds), (1980) 'Rethinking case study: Notes from the second Cambridge conference', in H. Simons (ed.), *Towards a Science of the Singular: Essays about Case Study in Educational Research and Evaluation*. pp. 47–61. Occasional Publications, No. 10, Norwich: University of East Anglia, Centre for Applied Research in Education. First published in *Cambridge Journal of Education* (1976), 6 (3): 139–150.

Adler, P.A. and Adler, P. (1994) 'Observational techniques', in N.K. Denzin and Y.S. Lincoln (eds), *Handbook of Qualitative Research*, pp. 377–392. Thousand Oaks, CA: Sage.

Alderson, P. and Morrow, V. (2003) *Ethics, Social Research and Consulting with Young People*. London: Barnardo's.

Ashton-Warner, S. (1963) *Teacher*. New York: Simon and Schuster.

Atkinson, P. and Coffey, A. (1996) *Making Sense of Qualitative Data: Complementary Research Strategies*. Thousand Oaks, CA: Sage.

Bagley, C. and Cancienne, M.B. (2001) 'Educational research and intertextual forms of (re) presentation: The case for dancing the data', *Qualitative Inquiry*, 7 (2): 221–237.

Ball, S.J. (1987) *The Micro-Politics of the School: Towards a Theory of School Organization*. London: Methuen.

Bassey, M. (1999) *Case Study Research in Educational Settings*. Buckingham: Open University Press.

Bellah, R.N., Madsen, R., Sullivan, W.M., Swidler, A. and Tipton, S.M. (1985) *Habits of the Heart*. London: Harper & Row.

Bentz, V.M. and Shapiro, J.J. (1996) *Mindful Inquiry in Social Research*. Thousand Oaks, CA: Sage.

Berger, J. and Mohr, J. (1967) *A Fortunate Man: The Story of a Country Doctor*. London: Writers and Readers Publishing Co-operative.

Black, P. and Atkin, J. Myron (1996) *Changing the Subject: Innovations in Science, Mathematics and Technology Education*. London: Routledge in association with OECD.

Bochner, A.P. (1997) 'It's about time: Narrative and the divided self', *Qualitative Inquiry*, 3 (4): 418–438.

Burgess, R.G. (1984) 'Methods of field research 2: Interviews as conversations', in R.G. Burgess (ed.), *In the Field: An Introduction to Field Research*, pp. 101–122. London: Allen & Unwin.

Burgess, R.G. (ed.) (1989) *The Ethics of Educational Research*. Lewes: The Falmer Press.

Campbell, D.T. (1975) 'Degrees of freedom and the case study', *Comparative Political Studies*, 8 (1): pp. 178–193.

Campbell, D.T. (1976) *Assessing the Impact of Planned Social Change*. Occasional Paper 8. Kalamazoo, MI: The Evaluation Centre, College of Education, Western Michigan University. (Originally published in 1975.)

Campbell, D.T. (1979) '"Degrees of freedom" and the case study', in T.D. Cook and C.S. Reichardt (eds), *Qualitative and Quantitative Methods in Evaluation Research*, pp. 49–67. Thousand Oaks, CA: Sage.

Campbell, D.T. and Fiske, D.W. (1959) 'Convergent and discriminant validation by the multi-trait-multi-method matrix', *Psychological Bulletin*, 56 (2): 81–105.

Campbell, D.T. and Stanley, J.C. (1966) *Experimental and Quasi-experimental Designs for Research*. Chicago, IL: Rand McNally.

Cancienne, M.B. and Snowber, C.N. (2003) 'Writing rhythm: Movement as method', *Qualitative Inquiry*, 9 (2): 237–253.

Caulley, D.N. (2008) 'Making qualitative research reports less boring: The techniques of writing creative nonfiction', *Qualitative Inquiry,* 14 (3): 424–449.

Charmaz, K. (2006) *Constructing Grounded Theory: A Practical Guide Through Qualitative Analysis.* London: Sage.

Chelimsky, E. (2006) 'The purposes of evaluation in a democratic society', in I.F. Shaw, J.C. Greene and M. Mark (eds), *The Sage Handbook of Evaluation,* pp. 33–55. London: Sage.

Cheney, R.A.R. (2001) *Writing Creative Nonfiction: Fiction Techniques for Crafting Great Nonfiction.* Berkeley, CA: The Speed Press.

Christians, C.G. (2003) 'Ethics and politics in qualitative research', in N.K. Denzin and Y.S. Lincoln (eds), *The Landscape of Qualitative Research: Theories and Issues,* 2nd edn, pp. 208–243. Thousand Oaks, CA: Sage.

Clandinin, D.J. and Connelly, M.F. (1994) 'Personal experience methods', in N.K. Denzin and Y.S. Lincoln (eds), *The Handbook of Qualitative Research,* pp. 413–427. Thousand Oaks; CA: Sage.

Clarke, J. (2007) 'Case profiles', in H. Simons (ed.), 'Cases and Contexts: Representing Context in a Research Archive of Educational Evaluation studies', in 'Education Evaluations' Qualitative Archive Demonstrator Scheme (QUADS) funded by the Economic and Social Research Council, 2006–2007. http://quads.esds.ac.uk.

Clarke, J., Gobbi, M. and Simons, H. (1999) 'Evaluation case study of the Registration/Diploma in Nursing Programme', in M.P. Treacy and A. Hyde (eds), *Nursing Research: Design and Practice,* pp. 207–224. Dublin: University College, Dublin Press.

Clarkson, P. (1989) *Gestalt Counselling in Action.* London: Sage.

Coffey, A. (1999) *The Ethnographic Self: Fieldwork and the Representation of Identity.* London: Sage.

Collier, J. Jr. (1967) *Visual Anthropology: Photography as a Research Method.* New York: Holt, Reinhart & Winston.

Cortazzi, M. (1993) *Narrative Analysis,* London: The Falmer Press.

Cronbach, L.J. (1975) 'Beyond the two disciplines of scientific psychology', *American Psychologist,* 30: 116–127.

Denny, T. (1977) *Some Still Do: River Acres, Texas.* Case Studies in Science Education (Booklet No. 1). Champaign, IL: University of Illinois at Urbana-Champaign.

Denny, T. (1978) 'Story telling and educational understanding', Occasional Paper Series No. 12, November. Kalamazoo, MI: Evaluation Center, College of Education, Western Michigan University.

Denzin, N.K. (1978) *The Research Act: A Theoretical Introduction to Sociological Methods,* 2nd edn. New York: McGraw-Hill (1st edn London: Butterworth, 1970).

Denzin, N.K. (1989) *Interpretive Biography.* Newbury Park, CA: Sage.

Denzin, N.K. (1994) 'The art and politics of interpretation', in N.K. Denzin and Y.S. Lincoln (eds), *The Handbook of Qualitative Research,* pp. 500–515. Thousand Oaks, CA: Sage.

Denzin, N.K. (1997) *Interpretive Ethnography: Ethnographic Practices for the 21st Century.* Thousand Oaks, CA: Sage.

Denzin, N.K. and Lincoln, Y.S. (eds) (1994) *The Handbook of Qualitative Research.* Thousand Oaks, CA: Sage.

Dowell, J., Huby, G. and Smith, C. (eds) (1995) *Scottish Consensus Statement on Qualitative Research in Primary Health Care.* Dundee: Tayside Centre for General Practice, University of Dundee.

Duke, S. (2007) 'A narrative case study evaluation of the role of the Nurse Consultant in palliative care'. PhD thesis, University of Southampton, England.

Elliott, Jenny (2008) 'Dance mirrors: Embodying, actualizing and operationalizing a dance experience in a healthcare context'. PhD thesis, University of Ulster, Belfast.

Elliott, John (2000) 'How do teachers define what counts as "credible evidence"? Some reflections based upon interviews with teachers involved in the Norwich Area Research Consortium'. Paper presented at the British Educational Research Association's Annual Conference, Cardiff, Wales, 7–9 September.

Elliott, John (2009) 'Building educational theory through action research', in S. Noffke and B. Somekh (eds), *The SAGE Handbook of Educational Action Research.* Thousand Oaks, CA: Sage.

Elliot, John and Kushner, S. (2007) 'The need for a manifesto of educational programme evaluation', *Cambridge Journal of Education,* 37 (3): 321–336.

Ellingson, L.L. (1998) 'Then you know how I feel: Empathy, identification, and reflexivity in fieldwork', *Qualitative Inquiry,* 4 (4): 492–514.

BIBLIOGRAPHY

Ellis, C. (1996) 'Evocative autoethnography: Writing emotionally about our lives', in Y.S. Lincoln and W.G. Tierney (eds), *Representation and the Text: Reframing the Narrative Voice*, pp. 115–142. Albany, NY: State University of New York Press.

Ellis, C. (2007) 'Telling secrets, revealing lives: Relational ethics in research with intimate others', *Qualitative Inquiry*, 13 (1): 3–29.

Ely, M., Vinz, R., Downing, M. and Anzul, M. (1997) *On Writing Qualitative Research: Living by Words.* London: The Falmer Press.

Erben, M. (ed.) (1998) *Biography and Education: A Reader.* London: The Falmer Press.

Etherington, K. (2007) 'Ethical research in reflexive relationships', *Qualitative Inquiry*, 13 (5): 599–615.

Every Child Matters (2003) Cm. 5860. London: The Stationery Office.

Faulks, S. (2005) *Human Traces.* London: Hutchinson (Hardback edition).

Fine, M. (1994) 'Working the hyphens: Reinventing self and other in qualitative research', in N.K. Denzin and Y.S. Lincoln (eds), *The Handbook of Qualitative Research,* pp. 70–82. London: Sage.

Finley, S. (2003) 'Arts-based inquiry in QI: Seven years from crisis to guerrilla warfare', *Qualitative Inquiry*, 9 (2): 281–296.

Flewitt, R. (2003) 'Is every child's voice heard? Longitudinal case studies of 3-year-old children's communicative strategies at home and in a pre-school playgroup'. PhD thesis, University of Southampton, England.

Flewitt, R. (2005a) 'Conducting research with young children: some ethical considerations', *Early Child Development and Care,* 175 (6): 553–565.

Flewitt, R. (2005b) 'Is every child's voice heard? Researching the different ways 3-year-old children communicate and make meaning at home and in a pre-school playgroup', *Early Years*, 25 (3): 207–222.

Flick, U. (1998) *An Introduction to Qualitative Research.* London: Sage.

Flick, U. (ed.) (2007) *The Sage Qualitative Research Kit.* London: Sage.

Flyvbjerg, B. (2006) 'Five misunderstandings about case-study research', *Qualitative Inquiry*, 12 (2): 219–245.

Frank, A. (1997) 'Enacting illness stories: When, what, why?', in H.L. Nelson (ed.), *Stories and Their Limits,* pp. 31–49. London: Routledge.

Fry, H., Maw, J. and Simons, H. (eds) (1991) *Dealing with Difference: Handling Ethnocentrism in History Classrooms.* London: University of London Institute of Education.

Geertz, C. (1973) 'Thick description: Toward an interpretive theory of culture', in C. Geertz, *The Interpretation of Cultures*, pp. 3–30. New York: Basic Books.

Gibbons, M. and Simons, H. (2002) 'In four movements: Using the creative arts in evaluation'. Paper presented at the United Kingdom Evaluation Society's Annual Conference, The Art of Evaluation: Artistry, Discipline and Delivery. South Bank Centre, London, 12–13 December.

Gilligan, C. (1982) *In a Different Voice.* Cambridge, MA: Harvard University Press.

Glaser, B.G. and Strauss, A.L. (1967) *The Discovery of Grounded Theory: Strategies for Qualitative Research.* Chicago, IL: Aldine.

Glen, S. (2000) 'The dark side of purity or the virtues of double-mindedness?', in H. Simons and R. Usher (eds), *Situated Ethics in Educational Research*, pp. 12–21. London: Routledge/Falmer.

Goldberg, N. (1986) *Writing Down the Bones.* London: Shambhala.

Goldberg, N. (1991) *Wild Mind.* London: Rider.

Gomm, R., Hammersley, M. and Foster, P. (eds) (2004) *Case Study Method: Key Issues, Key Texts.* London: Sage (first published 2000).

Goodson, I. and Sikes, P. (2001) *Life History Research in Educational Settings: Learning from Lives.* Buckingham: Open University Press.

Graham, J. (1971) 'There are no simple solutions: Frederick Wiseman on viewing films', *Film Journal,* 1 (1): 44.

Greene, J.C. (1994) 'Qualitative program evaluation: Practice and promise', in N.K. Denzin and Y.S. Lincoln (eds), *The Handbook of Qualitative Research,* pp. 530–544. London: Sage.

Greene, J.C. (2000) 'Understanding social programs through evaluation', in N.K. Denzin and Y.S. Lincoln (eds), *Handbook of Qualitative Research,* 2nd edn, pp. 981–999. London: Sage.

Greene, J.C. (2007) *Mixing Methods in Social Inquiry.* San Francisco, CA: Jossey–Bass.

Greene, J.C. and McClintock, C. (1991) 'The evolution of evaluation methodology', *Theory Into Practice*, 30 (1): 13–24.

Greene, J.C. and Caracelli, V.J. (1997) 'Defining and describing the paradigm issue in mixed-method evaluation', in J.C. Greene and V.J. Caracelli (eds), *Advances in Mixed-Method Evaluation: The Challenges and Benefits of Integrating Diverse Paradigms, New Directions for Evaluation*, 74, pp. 5–17. San Francisco, CA: Jossey–Bass.

Greenhalgh, T. (1999) 'Narrative-based medicine in an evidence-based world,' *British Medical Journal*, 318 (7179): 323–325.

Greenhalgh, T. and Worrall, J.G. (1997) 'From EBM to CSM: The evolution of context-sensitive medicine', *Journal of Evaluation in Clinical Practice*, 3 (2): 105–108.

Guba, E.G. and Lincoln, Y.S. (1981) *Effective Evaluation*. San Francisco, CA: Jossey–Bass.

Guba, E.G. and Lincoln, Y.S. (1985) *Naturalistic Inquiry*. Beverly Hills, CA: Sage.

Guba, E.G. and Lincoln, Y.S. (1989) *Fourth Generation Evaluation*. Newbury Park, CA: Sage.

Gutkind, L. (1997) *The Art of Creative Nonfiction: Writing and Selling the Literature of Reality*. New York: Wiley.

Harrington, W. (2003) 'What journalism can offer ethnography', *Qualitative Inquiry*, 9 (1): 90–114.

Hicks, J. and Simons, H. (2006) 'Opening doors: Using creative arts in learning and teaching', *Arts and Humanities in Higher Education*, 5 (1): 77–90.

Hood, L. (1989) *Sylvia: The Biography of Sylvia Ashton-Warner*. London: Viking.

Holly, M.L. (1989) *Writing to Grow: Keeping a Personal-Professional Journal*. Portsmouth, NH: Heinemann.

Holly, M.L. (1993) 'Educational research and professional development: On minds that watch themselves', in R.G. Burgess (ed.), *Educational Research and Evaluation: for Policy and Practice?* pp. 157–179. London: The Falmer Press.

House, E.R. (1973) 'The conscience of educational evaluation', in E.R. House, *School Evaluation: The Politics and Process*, pp. 125–135. Berkeley, CA: McCutchan.

House, E.R. (1980) *Evaluating with Validity*. London: Sage.

House, E.R. (1993) *Professional Evaluation: Social Impact and Political Consequences*. Newbury Park, CA: Sage.

House, E.R. and Howe, K.R. (1999) *Values in Evaluation and Social Research*. Thousand Oaks, CA: Sage.

Humble, S. and Simons, H. (1978) *From Council to Classroom: An Evaluation of the Diffusion of the Humanities Curriculum Project*. Schools Council Research Studies. London: Macmillan Education.

Ioannidou, E. (1999) 'An exploration of different forms of uncovering my values and subjective 'I's in the course of my research'. Research Training Programme Assignment. Unpublished manuscript. University of Southampton, England.

Ioannidou, E. (2002) '"This ain't my real language, miss": On language and ethnic identity among Greek Cypriot students'. PhD thesis, University of Southampton, England.

Janesick, V.J. (1999) 'A journal about journal writing as a qualitative technique: History, issues, and reflections', *Qualitative Inquiry*, 5 (4): 505–524.

Janesick, V.J. (2002) 'Problems for qualitative researchers with Institutional Review Boards'. Paper presented to the Annual Meeting of the American Educational Research Association, April.

Janesick, V.J. (2004) *'Stretching' EXERCISES for Qualitative Researchers*, 2nd edn. London: Sage.

Jones, K. (2000) 'A regrettable oversight or a significant omission? Ethical considerations in quantitative research in education', in H. Simons and R. Usher (eds), *Situated Ethics in Educational Research*, pp. 147–161. London and New York: Routledge/Falmer.

Jones, S. (1985) 'The analysis of depth interviews', in R. Walker (ed.), *Applied Qualitative Research*, pp. 56–70. Aldershot: Gower.

Kelle, U. (2004) 'Computer-assisted qualitative data analysis', in C. Seale, G. Giampietro, J.F. Gubrium and D. Silverman (eds), *Qualitative Research Practice*, pp. 473–498. London: Sage.

Kushner, S. (2000) *Personalizing Evaluation*. London: Sage.

Kvale, S. (1996) *Interviews: An Introduction to Qualitative Research Interviewing*. Thousand Oaks, CA: Sage.

Lather, P. (2004) 'This *IS* your father's paradigm: Government intrusion and the case of qualitative research in education', *Qualitative Inquiry*, 10 (1): 15–34.

Lee-Treweek, G. and Linkogle, S. (eds) (2000) *Danger in the Field: Risks and Ethics in Social Research*. London: Routledge.

BIBLIOGRAPHY

Lincoln, Y.S. (1995) 'Emerging criteria for quality in qualitative and interpretive research', *Qualitative Inquiry*, 1 (3): 275–289.

Lincoln, Y.S. and Canella, G.S. (2004) 'Dangerous discourses: Methodological conservatism and governmental regimes of truth', *Qualitative Inquiry*, 10 (1): 5–14.

Lincoln, Y.S and Tierney, W.G. (2004) 'Qualitative research and institutional review boards', *Qualitative Inquiry*, 10 (2): 219–234.

Loader, D. (1997) *The Inner Principal*. London: The Falmer Press.

Louden, W. (1991) *Understanding Teaching: Continuity and Change in Teachers' Knowledge*. London: Cassell, and New York: Teachers College Press.

MacDonald, B. (1971) 'The evaluation of the Humanities Curriculum Project: A holistic approach', *Theory in Practice*, June 1971. Also in Tawney, D. (ed.) (1973) *Evaluation in Curriculum Development: Twelve Case Studies*, pp. 80–90. London: Macmillan; and as 'Briefing decision-makers', in E.R. House (ed.) (1973) *School Evaluation: The Politics and Process*, pp. 174–187. Berkeley, CA: McCutchan.

MacDonald, B. (1976) 'Evaluation and the control of education', in D. Tawney (ed.), *Curriculum Evaluation Today: Trends and Implications*, pp. 125–136. Schools Council Research Studies. London: Macmillan.

MacDonald, B. (1977) 'The portrayal of persons as evaluation data', in N. Norris (ed.), *Safari 2: Theory in Practice*, pp. 50–67. Occasional Publications No. 4. Norwich: University of East Anglia, Centre for Applied Research in Education.

MacDonald, B. (1981) 'Interviewing in case study evaluation', *Phi Delta Kappa CEDR Quarterly*, 14 (4).

MacDonald, B. and Parlett, M. (1973) 'Rethinking evaluation: Notes from the Cambridge conference', *Cambridge Journal of Education*, 3 (2): 74–82.

MacDonald, B. and Sanger, J. (1982) 'Just for the record? Notes towards a theory of interviewing in evaluation', in E.R. House, S. Mathison, J.A. Pearsol and H. Preskill (eds), *Evaluation Studies Review Annual*, 7, pp. 175–198. Beverly Hills, CA: Sage.

MacDonald, B. and Walker, R. (eds) (1974) *Safari I: Innovation, Evaluation and the Problem of Control*. Norwich: University of East Anglia, Centre for Applied Research in Education.

MacDonald, B. and Walker, R. (1975) 'Case study and the social philosophy of educational research', *Cambridge Journal of Education*, 5 (1): 2–12.

MacDonald, B. and Walker, R. (1976) *Changing the Curriculum*. London: Open Books.

Malinoswki, B. (1922) *The Argonauts of the Western Pacific*. London: Routledge.

Mansfield, K. (1987) *The Collected Stories of Katherine Mansfield*. London: Penguin Books. (First published by Constable, 1945 and by Penguin Books 1981.)

Mason, J. (1996) *Qualitative Researching*. London: Sage.

Mataira, P. (2003) 'Maori evaluation research, theory and practice: Lessons for native Hawaiian evaluation studies'. Paper presented at June meeting of the Evaluation Hui, Kamechameha Schools, Honolulu, HI. Available at www.ksbe.edu/pase/pdf/EvaluationHui/Mataira.pdf.

Mathison, S. (1988) 'Why triangulate?', *Educational Researcher*, 17 (2): 13–17.

McCulloch, G. (2004) *Documentary Research in Education, History and the Social Sciences*. London: Routledge/Falmer.

McKeever, M. (2000) 'Snakes and ladders: Ethical issues in conducting educational research in a postcolonial context', in H. Simons and R. Usher (eds), *Situated Ethics in Educational Research*, pp. 101–115. London: Routledge/Falmer.

Merriam, S.B. (1988) *Case Study Research in Education: A Qualitative Approach*. San Francisco, CA: Jossey–Bass.

Miles, M.B. and Huberman, A.M. (1994) *Qualitative Data Analysis: A Sourcebook of New Methods*, 2nd edn. Thousand Oaks, CA: Sage.

Miller, C.M.L. and Parlett, M. (1974) *Up to the Mark: A Study of the Examination Game*. London: Society for Research into Higher Education.

Morris, M. and Cohn, R. (1993) 'Program evaluators and ethical challenges: A national survey', *Evaluation Review*, 17: 621–642.

Mullen, C.A. (2003) 'Guest editor's introduction: A self-fashioned gallery of aesthetic practice', *Qualitative Inquiry*, 9 (2): 165–181.

Mullen, C.A. and Finley, S. (eds) (2003) 'Arts-based approaches to qualitative inquiry', *Qualitative Inquiry*, 9 (2) [Special Issue].

NHMRC (2003) *Values and Ethics: Guidelines for Ethical Conduct in Aboriginal and Torres Strait Islander Health Research*. Canberra: National Health and Medical Research Council.

Nias, J. (1981) 'The nature of trust', in J. Ellliot, D. Bridges, D. Ebbutt, R. Gibson and J. Nias, *School Accountability*, pp. 211–223. London: Grant McIntyre.

Nias, J. (1993) 'Changing times, changing identities: Grieving for a lost self', in R.G. Burgess (ed.), *Educational Research and Evaluation: For Policy and Practice?*, pp. 139–156. London: The Falmer Press.

Nisbet, J. (2006) 'Transcribing interviews: some heretical thoughts', *Research Intelligence*, 97: 12–13. (Nottingham: British Educational Research Association.)

Noddings, N. (1984) *Caring: A Feminine Approach to Ethics and Moral Education*. Berkeley, CA: University of California Press.

Norris, N. (ed.) (1977) *Safari 2: Theory in Practice*. Occasional Publications No. 4. Norwich: University of East Anglia, Centre for Applied Research in Education.

Norris, N. (1993) *Understanding Evaluation*. London: Kogan Page.

Northcott, N. (1996) 'Cognitive mapping: An approach to qualitative data analysis', *Nursing Times Research*, 1 (6): 456–463.

Oakley, A. (1981) 'Interviewing women: A contradiction in terms', in H. Roberts (ed.), *Doing Feminist Research*, pp. 30–61. London: Routledge and Kegan Paul.

Okri, B. (1997) *A Way of Being Free*. London: Phoenix.

Oliver, P. (2003) *The Student's Guide to Research Ethics*. Maidenhead: Open University Press.

Parlett, M. and Hamilton, D. (1976) 'Evaluation as illumination: A new approach to the study of innovatory programmes', in G. Glass (ed.), *Evaluation Studies Review Annual, I*, pp. 140–157. Beverly Hills, CA: Sage. (First published 1972 as Occasional Paper 9, Centre for Research in the Educational Sciences, University of Edinburgh.)

Patton, M.Q. (1980) *Qualitative Evaluation Methods*. Beverly Hills, CA: Sage.

Patton, M.Q. (1997) *Utilization-Focused Evaluation*, 3rd edn. Thousand Oaks, CA: Sage.

Payler, J.K. (2005) 'Exploring foundations: Sociocultural influences on the learning processes of four year old children in a pre-school and reception class'. PhD thesis, University of Southampton, England.

Peshkin, A. (1985) 'Virtuous subjectivity: In the participant-observer's I's', in D. Berg and K. Smith (eds), *Exploring Clinical Methods for Social Research*, pp. 267–282. Beverly Hills, CA: Sage.

Peshkin, A. (1986) *God's Choice: The Total World of a Fundamentalist Christian School and Community*. Chicago, IL: Chicago University Press.

Peshkin, A. (1988) 'In search of subjectivity – one's own', *Educational Researcher*, 17 (7): 17–22.

Piper, H. and Simons, H. (2005) 'Ethical responsibility in social research', in B. Somekh and C. Lewin (eds), *Research Methods in the Social Sciences*, pp. 56–63. London: Sage.

Plummer, K. (1983) *Documents of Life: An Introduction to the Problems and Literature of a Humanistic Method*. London: George Allen & Unwin.

Plummer, K. (2001) *Documents of Life 2: An Invitation to a Critical Humanism*. London: Sage.

Polkinghorne, D.E. (1995) *Narrative Knowing and the Human Sciences*. Albany, NY: State University of New York Press.

Prior, L. (2004) 'Doing things with documents', in D. Silverman (ed.), *Qualitative Research: Theory, Methods and Practice*, 2nd edn, pp. 76–94. London: Sage.

Prosser, J. (2000) 'The moral maze of image ethics', in H. Simons and R. Usher (eds), *Situated Ethics in Educational Research*, pp. 116–132. London: Routledge/Falmer.

Punch, M. (1994) 'Politics and ethics in qualitative research', in N.K. Denzin and Y.S. Lincoln (eds), *The Handbook of Qualitative Research*, pp. 83–97. Thousand Oaks, CA: Sage.

Punch, K.F. (1998) *Introduction to Social Research: Quantitative and Qualitative Approaches*. London: Sage.

Ramcharan, P. and Cutliffe, J. (2001) 'Judging the ethics of qualitative research: Considering the "ethics as process" model', *Social Care in the Community*, 9 (6): 358–366.

Reissman, C.K. (1993) *Narrative Analysis*. London: Sage.

Richardson, L. (1990) *Writing Strategies: Reaching Diverse Audiences*. Qualitative Research Methods Series, 21. Newbury Park, CA: Sage.

Richardson, L. (1994) 'Writing: A method of inquiry', in N.K. Denzin and Y.S. Lincoln (eds), *The Handbook of Qualitative Research*, pp. 516–529. London: Sage.

Richardson, L. (1997) *Fields of Play (Constructing an Academic Life)*. New Brunswick, NJ: Rutgers University Press.

Ricoeur, P. (1981) 'Narrative time', in W.T.J. Mitchell (ed.), *On Narrative*, pp. 165–186. Chicago, IL: University of Chicago Press.
Rippey, R.M. (ed.) (1973) *Studies in Transactional Evaluation*. Berkeley, CA: McCutchan.
Ritchie, J. and Lewis, J. (eds) (2003) *Qualitative Research Practice: A Guide for Social Science Students and Researchers*. London: Sage.
Robinson, J. (1998) 'Implementing Project 2000: A study of a period of change in nurse education in one Project 2000 demonstration district'. PhD thesis, University of East Anglia, England.
Rogers, P. and Williams, B. (2006) 'Evaluation for practice improvement and organizational learning', in I.F. Shaw, J.C. Greene and M.M. Mark (eds), *The Sage Handbook of Evaluation*, pp. 76–97. London: Sage.
Rubin, H.J. and Rubin, I.S. (1995) *Qualitative Interviewing: The Art of Hearing Data*. Thousand Oaks, CA: Sage.
Rugang, Lu (2006) 'Chinese culture in globalisation: A multi-modal case study on visual discourse'. PhD thesis, University of Southampton, England.
Russell, C. (1993) *Academic Freedom*. London: Routledge.
Sammons, P. (1989) 'Ethical issues and statistical work', in R.G. Burgess (ed.), *The Ethics of Educational Research*, pp. 31–59. Lewes: The Falmer Press.
Sanger, J. (1996) *The Compleat Observer? A Field Research Guide to Observation*. London: The Falmer Press.
Sarason, S.B. (1988) *The Making of an American Psychologist*. San Francisco, CA: Jossey–Bass.
Schwandt, T.A. (1998) 'How we think about morality: Implications for evaluation practice'. Paper presented at the annual meeting of the American Evaluation Association Conference, Chicago, November.
Schwandt, T.A. (2001) *Dictionary of Qualitative Inquiry*, 2nd edn. Thousand Oaks, CA: Sage.
Schostak, J. (2002) *Understanding, Designing and Conducting Qualitative Research in Education: Framing the Project*. Milton Keynes: Open University Press.
Schutz, A. and Luckman, T. (1973) *The Structures of the Life-World*. London: Heinemann.
Scott, J. (1990) *A Matter of Record*. Cambridge: Polity Press.
Seale, C. (1999) *The Quality of Qualitative Research*. London: Sage.
Seale, C. (2000) 'Using computers to analyse qualitative data', in D. Silverman (ed.), *Doing Qualitative Research*, pp. 154–174. London: Sage.
Seale, C., Gobo, G., Gubrium, J.F. and Silverman, D. (eds) (2004) *Qualitative Research Practice*. London: Sage.
Shaw, I. and Gould, N. (2001) *Qualitative Research in Social Work: Context and Method*. London: Sage.
Shaw, I.F., Greene, J.C and Mark, M.M. (eds) (2006) *The Sage Handbook of Evaluation*. London: Sage.
Silverman, D. (ed.) (2000) *Doing Qualitative Research: A Practical Handbook*. London: Sage.
Simons, H. (1971) 'Innovation and the case study of schools', *Cambridge Journal of Education*, 3: 118–123.
Simons, H. (ed.) (1980) *Towards a Science of the Singular: Essays about Case Study in Educational Research and Evaluation*. Occasional Papers No. 10. Norwich: University of East Anglia, Centre for Applied Research.
Simons, H. (1981) 'Conversation piece: The practice of interviewing in case study research', in C. Adelman (ed.), *Uttering Muttering,* pp. 27–50. London: Grant McIntyre. Previously published in Norris, N. (ed.) (1977) *Safari 2: Theory in Practice*, pp. 110–135. Occasional Publications No. 4. Norwich: University of East Anglia, Centre for Applied Research in Education.
Simons, H. (1984) 'Principles and procedures for the conduct of independent evaluation', in C. Adelman (ed.), *The Politics and Ethics of Evaluation*, pp. 56–68. London: Croom Helm.
Simons, H. (1987) *Getting to Know Schools in a Democracy: The Politics and Process of Evaluation*. Lewes: The Falmer Press.
Simons, H. (1989) 'Ethics of case study in educational research and evaluation', in R. Burgess (ed.), *The Ethics of Educational Research*, pp. 114–140. Lewes: The Falmer Press.
Simons, H. (1996) 'The paradox of case study', *Cambridge Journal of Education*, 26 (2): 225–240.
Simons, H. (ed.) (1997) *Training for Education Reform Management (TERM) Final Report External Evaluation 1995–7*. Warsaw: Term Programme, Foundation for the Development of the Education System, Ministry of National Education (MoNE).
Simons, H. (1998) '"Give me an insight": Training and reporting in naturalistic evaluation', in R. Davis (ed.), *Proceedings of the Stake Symposium on Educational Evaluation*, pp. 141–154. Urbana, IL: University of Illinois.

Simons, H. (2000) 'Damned if you do, damned if you don't: Ethical and political dilemmas in evaluation', in H. Simons and R. Usher, *Situated Ethics in Educational Research*, pp. 39–55. London: Routledge/Falmer.

Simons, H. (2002) 'School-self evaluation in a democracy', in D. Nevo (ed.), *School Based Evaluation: An International Perspective. Advances in Program Evaluation 8*, pp. 17–34. Greenwich, CT: JAI.

Simons, H. (2005) 'Key concepts', in H. Piper and H. Simons, 'Ethical responsibility in social research', in B. Somekh and C. Lewin (eds), *Research Methods in the Social Sciences*, pp. 56–63. London: Sage.

Simons, H. (2006) 'Ethics and evaluation', in I.F. Shaw, J.C. Greene and M.M. Mark (eds), *The International Handbook of Evaluation*, pp. 243–265. London: Sage.

Simons, H. and McCormack, B. (2007) 'Integrating arts-based inquiry in evaluation methodology', *Qualitative Inquiry*, 13 (2): 292–311.

Simons, H. and Usher, R. (2000) *Situated Ethics in Educational Research*. London: Routledge/Falmer.

Simons, H., Clarke, J.B., Gobbi, M., Long, G. (with Mountford, B. and Wheelhouse, C.) (1998) *Nurse Education and Training Evaluation in Ireland: Independent External Evaluation*. Commissioned by the Department of Health, Dublin, in collaboration with An Bord Altranais, Final Report. Dublin: Department of Health and Children.

Simons, H., Kushner, S., Jones, K. and James, D. (2003) 'From evidence-based practice to practice-based evidence: the idea of situated generalisation', *Research Papers in Education: Policy and Practice*, 18 (4): 347–364.

Smith, L.M. (1978) 'An evolving logic of participant observation, educational ethnography and other case studies', *Review of Research in Education*, 6 (1): 316–377.

Smith, L.M. and Pohland, P.A. (1974) 'Education, technology, and the rural highlands', in R.H.P. Kraft, L.M. Smith, P.A. Pohland, C.J. Brauner and C. Gjerde (eds), *Four Evaluation Examples: Anthropological, Economic, Narrative and Portrayal*, pp. 5–54. AERA Monograph Series on Curriculum Evaluation 7. Chicago: Rand McNally.

Sparkes, A. (2002) *Telling Tales in Sport and Physical Activity: A Qualitative Journey*. Champaign, IL: Human Kinetics Press.

Sparkes, A.C. and Douglas, K. (2007) 'Making the case for poetic representations: An example in action', *The Sport Psychologist*, 21: 170–190.

Spouse, J. (2000) 'Talking pictures: Investigating personal knowledge through illuminating art-work', *Nursing Times Research Journal*, 5 (4): 253–261.

Stake, R.E. (1967a) 'Toward a technology for the evaluation of educational programs', in R.W. Tyler, R.M. Gagne and M. Scriven (eds), *Perspectives of Curriculum Evaluation*. AERA Monograph Series on Curriculum Evaluation, No. 1. Chicago: Rand McNally.

Stake, R.E. (1967b) 'The countenance of educational evaluation', *Teachers College Record*, 68 (7): 523–540.

Stake, R.E. (1972) 'An approach to the evaluation of instructional programs (program portrayal versus analysis)'. Paper delivered at the Annual Meeting of the American Educational Research Association, Chicago. Extracts reprinted in Hamilton, D. Jenkins, D., King, C., MacDonald, B. and Parlett, M. (eds) (1977) *Beyond The Numbers Game: A Reader in Educational Evaluation*. London: Macmillan Educational.

Stake, R.E (ed.) (1975) *Evaluating the Arts in Education: A Responsive Approach*. Columbus, OH: Charles E. Merrill.

Stake, R.E. (1980) 'The case study method in social inquiry', in H. Simons (ed.), *Towards a Science of the Singular: Essays about Case Study in Educational Research and Evaluation*, pp. 64–75. Occasional Papers No. 10. Norwich: University of East Anglia, Centre for Applied Research. (First published 1978 in *Educational Researcher*, 7: 5–8.)

Stake, R.E. (1986) *Quieting Reform: Social Science and Social Action in an Urban Youth Program*. Urbana, IL: University of Illinois Press.

Stake, R.E. (1995) *The Art of Case Study Research*. Thousand Oaks, CA: Sage.

Stake, R.E. and Easley, J. (eds) (1978) *Case Studies in Science Education*. Urbana, IL: University of Illinois, CIRCE.

Stake, R.E. and Kerr, D. (1994) 'Rene Magritte, constructivism and the researcher as interpreter'. Paper presented at the Annual Meeting of the American Educational Research Association, New Orleans, LA, April.

BIBLIOGRAPHY

Strauss, A.L. and Corbin, J. (1990) *Basics of Qualitative Research: Grounded Theory, Procedures and Techniques*. Newbury Park, CA: Sage.

Strauss, A.L. and Corbin, J. (1998) *Basics of Qualitative Research: Grounded Theory, Procedures and Techniques*, 2nd edn. Newbury Park, CA: Sage.

Terkel, S. (1967) *Division Street: America*. New York: Avon Books.

Terkel, S. (1970) *Hard Times*. New York: Avon Books.

Terkel, S. (1975) *Working*. New York: Avon Books.

Thomas, G. and James, D. (2006) 'Reinventing grounded theory: Some questions about theory, grounded and discovery', *British Educational Research Journal*, 32 (6): 767–795.

Thurman, J. (1984) *Isak Dinesen: The Life of Karen Blixen*. Harmondsworth: Penguin. (First published London: Weidenfield & Nicolson, 1982.)

Tillmann-Healy, L. (2003) 'Friendship as method', *Qualitative Inquiry*, 9 (5): 729–749.

Torres, R.T. and Preskill, H. (1999) 'Ethical dimensions of stakeholder participation and evaluation use', in J.L. Fitzpatrick and M. Morris (eds), *Current and Emerging Ethical Challenges in Evaluation. New Directions for Evaluation, 82,* pp. 57–66. San Francisco, CA: Jossey–Bass.

Treacy, M.P. and Hyde, A. (1999) *Nursing Research: Design and Practice*. Dublin: University College Dublin Press.

Van Maanen, J. (1988) *Tales of the Field: On Writing Ethnography*. Chicago, IL: University of Chicago Press.

van Manen, M. (1990) *Researching Lived Experience: Human Science for an Action Sensitive Pedagogy*. New York: State University of New York Press.

Von France, M.L. (1968) 'The process of individuation', in C. Jung, *Man and His Symbols*, pp. 157–254. New York: Dell.

Walford, G. (2005) 'Research ethical guidelines and anonymity', *International Journal of Research and Method in Education*, 28 (1): 83–93.

Walker, R. (1974) 'The conduct of educational case study', in B. MacDonald and R. Walker (eds), *Safari I: Innovation, Evaluation and the Problem of Control*, pp. 75–115. Norwich: University of East Anglia, Centre for Applied Research in Education.

Walker, R. (1980) 'Making sense and losing meaning', in H. Simons (ed.), *Towards a Science of the Singular: Essays about Case Study in Educational Research and Evaluation*, pp. 224–235. Occasional Papers No. 10. Norwich: University of East Anglia, Centre for Applied Research.

Walker, R. (1986) 'Three good reasons for not doing case studies in curriculum research', in E.R. House (ed.), *New Directions in Educational Evaluation*, pp. 103–116. Lewes: The Falmer Press.

Walker, R. (1993) 'Finding a silent voice for the researcher: Using photographs in evaluation and research', in M. Schratz (ed.), *Qualitative Voices in Educational Research*. Lewes: The Falmer Press. pp. 72–92.

Walker, R. and Adelman, C. (1975) 'Interaction analysis in informal classrooms: A critical comment on the Flanders' system', *British Journal of Educational Psychology*, 45: 73–76.

Waters, P. (2004) *Writing Stories with Feeling: An Evaluation of the Impact of Therapeutic Storywriting Groups on Learning*. Kingston, Surrey: South East Region SEN partnership (SERSEN). Available at: www.therapeutic.storytelling.com.

Weitzman, E.A. (2003) 'Software and qualitative research', in N.K. Denzin and Y.S. Lincoln (eds), *Collecting and Interpreting Qualitative Materials,* 2nd edn. pp. 310–339. London: Sage.

Wilby, P. (1980) 'Illumination of the relevant particular', in H. Simons (ed.), *Towards a Science of the Singular: Essays about Case Study in Educational Research and Evaluation*, pp. 212–221. Occasional Papers No. 10. Norwich: University of East Anglia, Centre for Applied Research.

Wolcott, H.F. (1994) *Transforming Qualitative Data: Description, Analysis and Interpretation*. London: Sage.

Wolcott, H.F. (1995) *The Art of Fieldwork*. Walnut Creek, CA: Alta Mira Press.

Wolcott, H.F. (2001) *Writing Up Qualitative Research*, 2nd edn. Thousand Oaks, CA: Sage.

Wolfe, T. (1973) 'The new journalism', in T. Wolfe and E.W. Johnson (eds), *The New Journalism: An Anthology,* pp. ix–52. New York: Harper & Row.

Woods, P. (2006) *Successful Writing for Qualitative Researchers,* 2nd edn. London: Routledge.

Woodward, B. and Bernstein, C. (1974) *All the President's Men*. London: Quartet Books.

Woodward, B. and Bernstein, C. (1976) *The Final Dans*. New York: Simon and Schuster.

Yin, R.K. (1994) *Case Study Research: Design and Methods*. Thousand Oaks, CA: Sage.

INDEX

Abma, T.A. 75
access, gaining 7 38–42
access letter 39
access to documents 102
accessibility
    to different audiences 13, 18
    of language 16, 23
    methods 6, 7
acountability 17
accuracy 102, 103, 128, 131, 132, 137
action research 18, 166
active listening 47
Adelman, C. 5, 19, 59, 64 n.4
affect *see* emotions
agricultural botany model 17
Alderson, P. 104
All the President's Men (Woodward and Bernstein) 155
American Evaluation Association (AEA) 100
Analysis *see* data analysis and interpretation
anecdote, authenticated 4, 76, 77
anecdotal narrative 76–7
anonymity 99, 103, 106–8
anthropology 3, 70
apology, openness to 103, 109–10
artistic forms
    insights from 167
    use in
        exploring the self 85–7, 89–90
        interpretation of data 89, 117, 118, 126, 139–44
        reporting and writing 89, 151–2, 157–9
Ashton-Warner, S. 69, 150
attributed judgements 102, 105
audiences 56, 132, 135, 148
audio-recordings 37, 41, 50, 51–2, 53
    cognitive mapping from 123
    re-listening to 136–7
authenticated anecdote 4, 76, 77
authenticity 128–9, 158
autobiography 70
autocratic evaluation 101

background and prior knowledge 57, 89
Bagley, C. 141, 151
Ball, S.J. 22

Bassey, M. 21
Bellah, R.N. 44, 45
Bentz, V.M. 81–2
Berger, J. 37
Bernstein, C. 155
bias 57, 88–9, 91–2, 94, 130, 132, 137–8, 163–4
biography/biographical data 70, 71–3, 74, 155–7
Blixen, K. 72–3, 155–7
Bochner, A.P. 90
body language 53, 55, 61, 150
boundaries of the case 29
Bounded system 3, 4, 23, 29
British Educational Research Association (BERA) 100
bureaucratic evaluation 101
Burgess, R.G. 44

cameos 72–3, 117, 149, 155–7
Campbell, D.T. 16, 25–6 n.3, 130
Cancienne, M.B. 117, 140, 141, 151
Canella, G.S. 14
Caracelli, V.J. 130
case profiles 73–4, 78, 135
case study in medicine, 3, 13
categorizing of data 117, 118, 119, 121–2, 123, 124 135
Cathy Come Home (film) 169
Caulley, D.N. 154, 160 n.5
Centre for Applied Research in Education (CARE) 6, 15
Centre for British Teachers (CfBT) 170 n.3
change, process and dynamics of 23, 30–1
Charmaz, K. 22, 125, 126
Chelimsky, E. 17
children
    anonymity of 108
    communication strategies 61, 163–4
    informed consent with 104
    observing with video 61
    policy on services relating to 170
choice of methods 33–34
    document analysis 63–4
    interviewing, 43-8
    observing, 61–2
Christians, C.G. 97
Cities-in-Schools (CIS) programme 64

INDEX

Clandinin, D.J. 75, 76, 81, 82, 154
Clarke, J. 74, 139
Clarkson, P. 83
classroom interaction analysis 58, 59, 64 n.4
coding 117, 119, 121–2, 124
Coffey, A. 81, 82, 94 n.5, 95
cognitive mapping *see* concept mapping
Cohn, R. 98
collage 89–90, 142
collective case studies 21, 30–1, 164
Collier, J. Jr. 48
comparison with other research approaches 19, 28, 42 n.2
complex integrity 110
complex reality 20, 21, 23, 170
computer-assisted qualitative analysis 120, 123 n.2 136
concept of case study research 3, 4, 5, 7, 20, 25, 26
  in educational research and evaluation 13, 14–16
concept generalization 164, 165
concept mapping 122–4, 136, 140
conclusion-led reporting 149
confidentiality 99, 102, 106, 108
confirmability 128
Connelly, M.F. 75, 76, 81, 82, 154
constructivism 35,
constructivist, 119, 129, 141
constructivist grounded theory 22, 125, 126
context, 19, 21, 22, 137, 158
  close descriptions of 23
  of people's lives 158, 72
  institutional 70, 71, 72, 137
  interpretation in 4–5, 13, 16, 58, 59
  policy 169–170
  real-life 20, 21, 28,
  socio-political 1, 70, 72
context-dependent knowledge 164, 165
Cook, T.D. 16
Corbin, J. 124, 125
correlational research 16
Creative nonfiction 154, 160 n.5, 158, 174, 176
credibility 128, 131, 132
critical social science 35
criteria
  for negotiation of data 102, 103, 110, 137
  for validity of evaluation 128–9
Cronbach, L. J. 16, 119
cross-case analysis 31, 148, 152, 164, 169
cross-case generalization 164
crystal metaphor 131
cultural difference 30–1, 99, 104, 105, 111 n.4
curriculum innovation
  in schools 13, 15, 29, 30–1 137–8
  in nurse education and training 138–9, 170
Cutliffe, J. 103

dance and movement 151, 152
  use in data analysis and interpretation 89, 140–1
dancing *the* data 141
dancing *with* the data 121, 140–1
data, ownership of 101, 104, 105
data analysis and interpretation, 112, 117–33, 135–44
  artistic forms, use of 117, 126, 139–44
  coding and categorizing 121–2, 135
  concept mapping 122–4, 136, 140
  cross-case 31, 148, 152, 164, 169
  emotions (affect), engagement of 88, 90–91, 125, 126, 142
  grounded theory 112, 121, 123, 124–6
  interim interpretation, example of 137–8
  interviews 123–4, 135–7, 140–1
  intuition in 117, 126, 127, 142
  issue-theme generation 122, 135–6, 142
  mixed mode, example of 138–9
  progressive focusing 33, 122
  use of theory in 122, 124–5, 168
  transforming data 121, 141, 142–3
  validation *see* validity
  writing and re-writing as interpretation 142–3
data collection, 43–66
  participant involvement in 40, 41–3
data conclusion and verification 120
data display 120
data reduction 120, 122
data retrieval system 153
data sets 141,143
data triangulation 129,130
database
  broadening of 15–16
  making explicit 148
defining the case 28–9
definitions of case study 19–21
deliberative dialogue 103
democratic model 18, 22, 33, 36 42 n.4, 101–3, 131, 137, 144 n.2
democratic process 128
Denny, T. 44, 46, 47, 136, 151
Denzin, N.K. 13, 14, 70, 82, 118, 154
dependability 128
description 121, 149, 154, 57, 60–1
  close description 22, 37
  rich description 153, 154
  thick description 3
descriptive case study 21, 32,
  observations 59–61
design of case study 31, 38
  emergent 31, 33, 103
  ethical issues in 38, 98–9
  foreshadowed issues 32
  open-ended 31, 33
  research questions 31

dialogue 22, 36, 108–9,
deliberative 103
  Socratic 45, 48, 149

Dinesen, I. 72–3, 155–7
dis-identification 83
document analysis 3, 5, 7, 33, 43, 54, 63–4
documentary detail 154, 155, 71–2
documentary film 37, 151, 159, 168
'doing no harm', principle of 96–7
Douglas, K. 118, 129
Dowell, J. 13
drama 151
dramatic structure 158, 159
drawing 89, 118, 152
Duke, S. 35, 59–61, 89–90, 92, 123, 141–2, 143, 152

Ellingson, L.L. 90
Elliott, Jenny 152
Elliott, John 17, 166, 169
Ellis, C. 90, 92
emotions (affect) 90–1, 122, 126, 127, 129, 142, 150, *163*
epistemology 14, 18, 23, 35
Erben, M. 70
Etherington, K. 97
ethical committees 99, 100
ethics 8, 40, 41, 44, 96–111
  democratic 101–3
  in designing research 38, 98–9
  doing no harm, principle of 96–7
  and fictionalized reporting 158–9
  observing with video 61
  portrayal of individuals 78–9
  principles and procedures, 99, 102
  and reflections on 103–110
  relational 97
  the self in research 81, 94
  as a situated practice 8, 96
ethnographic case study 22–3, 78
ethnographic research 13, 22
evaluation 9, 17 n.5, 158
  autocratic 101
  bureaucratic 101
  democratic model 18, 33, 36, 42 n.4, 101, 131, 137
  evolution of case study in educational research and evaluation 14–16
  illuminative 16, 17
  judgement in 17–18
  responsive 16, 18, 33
  transactional 16
  validity criteria in 128–9
evaluation case study 21, 22, 131
Every Child Matters 170

evolution of case study research 14–18
  in educational evaluation 14–16
  Nuffield conferences 16–17
  political dimension 17–18, 70
experimental design 6, 14, 17, 24
explanatory case study 21, 32
exploratory case study 21

fairness 78, 87–8, 101, 102, 103, 128, 131, 137
Faulks, S. 158
feelings *see* emotions
fictionalization 154, 157–9
field relationships, management of 54, 59–61
  see relationships in the field
field theory 83
The Final Days (Woodward and Bernstein) 155
Fine, M. 82
Finley, S. 129
Flanders' system 58, 59, 64 n.4
Flewitt, R. 61, 103, 104, 163–4
flexibility 23
  of design 31
  of methods/methodology 23
  in interviewing, 48
  in observing 57, 62
Flick, U. 14
Flyvbjerg, B. 164, 165
foreshadowed issues 32–3, 56, 122, 136
formal reporting 148–9, 152
Frank, A. 75
friendship with participants 91–2
Fry, H. 64

Geertz, C. 3
generalization 16, 20, 24, 27, 162, 164–7
gestalt tradition 56, 83
Gilligan, C. 97
Glaser, B.G. 22, 124, 125
Glen, S. 110
Gobbi, M. 139
Goldberg, N. 160
Gomm, R. 19, 169
Goodson, I. 70, 75, 77
Gould, N. 13
Graham, J. 151, 168
Greene, J.C. 5, 17, 18, 130
Greenhalgh, T. 13
grounded theory 22, 112, 121, 123, 124–6, 168
  constructivist 22, 125, 126
group interviews 49
Guba, E.G. 14, 18, 128–9, 163

Hamilton, D. 16, 17, 122
Harrington, W. 154–5
Health care 13, 75, 151
  see also Duke, S., nursing research

INDEX

Hermeneutic analysis, 119, 133 n.1, 141, 144 n.3
Hicks, J. 48, 89, 151
historical case study 5, 19
historical data 71
holism 83
Holly, M.L. 83, 88
Hood, L. 69
House, E.R. 14, 18, 103, 155, 158
Howe, K.R. 103
Huberman, A.M. 112, 120
Human Traces (Faulks) 158
humanistic research 13
Humanities Curriculum Project (HCP) 6, 15, 42 n.3
Humble, S. 7
Hyde, A. 13

illuminative evaluation 16, 17
illustrative case study 21
imaging 117, 118, 126, 154, 158
individuals, study of 8, 69–80
    biography/biographical data 70, 71–3, 74
    cameos 72–3
    ethical issues 78–9
    historical data 71
    life histories 70, 77, 78
    life stories 70, 77, 78, 135
    lived experience 75–7
    narrative, use of 75–8
    personal portrayals 74–5, 105
    profiles 73–4, 78, 135
    purpose 70–1
individuation 83
inferences from the data 5, 24
informed consent 41, 78, 99, 100, 102, 103–4
instance in action 3, 4, 5, 20, 23
institutional/organizational culture 31, 55, 63–4
institutional development 7, 17
institutional Review Boards (IRB) 100
instrumental case study 21, 30
integrity, simple and complex 110
interpretation in context 1, 4–5, 13, 16, 17
    examples of 58–9, 137
    partial nature of 24
    see also data analysis and interpretation
interpretative asides 119
interpretative case study 21, 105, 150, 152
interpretivism 35
interviews 3, 6, 7, 33, 34
    analysis and interpretation of 123–4, 135–7
    active listening 47, 48, 50
    audio-recording *see* audio-recordings
    cognitive mapping from 123–4
    as conversations 44–6, 50–1
    group 49

interviews *cont.*
    in-depth (unstructured or open-ended) 43–51, 104–5, 135
    interactive/interpersonal 44–6
    observation as companion method 55, 58
    post and telephone 49–50
    proactive 48, 50, 78
    questions 32, 47–9
    rapport, establishment of 47
    responses to reports of 53, 105
    sampling choices 34
    skills development 51
    transcripts of 52, 53, 123, 135–6, 140–1
intrinsic case study 21, 30
intuition 117, 126, 127
intuitive processing 119, 142, 144 n.3
investigative journalism 154
investigator triangulation 130
Ioannidou, E. 85–6, 95
issue generation 122, 139

James, D. 124, 126
Janesick, V.J. 88, 100
Jones, S. 123
Jones, K. 111 n.1
journalism 154–5
    documentary 37, 155
    investigative 154
    'new' journalism 74, 154
Judgement(s)
    alternative or contending 148
    in evaluation 17–18, 22
    participants' 15, 18, 105
    pre-formed 57, 62, 89
    in selecting and interpreting data 81, 148, 163
    stakeholders' 36
Justice 101, 128

Kelle, U. 120, 133 n2
Kerr, D. 58
Kushner, S. 17, 18, 70–1, 74–5, 79 n.3, 107, 142–4
Kvale, S. 44

Language
    accessible 16, 23, 36, 102
    clarity in writing 154–5
    emotive, effect of 155, 158
Lather, P. 14
Leetreweek, G. 111
life histories 70, 77, 78
life stories 70, 77, 78, 135
'Lifeworld' 82, 94 n.2
limitations of case study research 23–4
Lincoln, Y.S. 13, 14, 18, 100, 128–9, 163
lived experience 33, 69, 75–7, 124, 125, 141, 142
Loach, K. 169

Loader, D. 69
Louden, W. 69
Luckman, T. 94 n.2

McClintock, C. 18
McCormack, B. 89, 129, 154
MacDonald, B. 3–4, 16, 44, 154
McKeever, M. 105
Malinowski, B. 32
Mansfield, K. 3
Mason, J. 130
Mataira, P. 104, 111 n.4
Mathison, S. 131
Making meaning 118, 120, 121, 125, 155
  context-embedded 58
  co-construction of 94
  negotiation of 36, 22, 36, 102,
  non-verbal clues to 61
  tactics for 120
Merriam, S.B. 4, 5, 13, 19, 20, 21
meta-evaluation case study 21
metaphor 5, 117, 126, 131, 153, 154, 157, 158
methods/methodology 3, 5, 7, 43–66
  accessibility of 16, 23, 36, 102
  choice of 17, 33–6
  ethical issues in 99, 100, 104
  mixed methods 5, 35, 130
  political implications 17–18
  triangulation of 55, 120, 130
  see also document analysis; interviews; observation
micro-ethnography 22–3
Miles, M.B. 112, 120
Miller, C.M.L. 165
Mohr, J. 37
Morris, M. 98
Morrow, V. 104
multiple perspectives 4, 15, 20, 21, 167
  alternative or contending 148
  participants' 4–5, 17–18, 33, 43, 123, 125, 128
  stakeholders' 4, 18, 33, 36
Mullen, C.A. 129
music, use in data analysis and interpretation 89, 151
narrative(s) 59–61, 75–8, 117, 118, 119
  construction of narrative 71–3, 74–5, 77, 141–2,
  see also stories; story lines
National Development Programme in Computer Assisted Learning 79 n.2
National Health and Medical Research Council (NHMRC) 104, 105
naturalistic generalization 164, 165, 166
naturalistic inquiry 5, 16
negative instances 132, 148
negotiation
  of research process 22, 40, 109–10

negotiation *cont.*
  of meaning 36, 79, 103, 132
  of data 102, 103,
'New' journalism 74, 154
Nias, J. 83, 100–1
Nisbet, J. 136
Noddings, N. 97
Norris, N. 14, 25–6 n.3
Northcott, N. 123, 124
note-taking 55
  in interviews 52, 53
Nuffield conferences 16–17, 25 n.1
nursing research 13, 64, 138–9, 170
  see also Duke, S.

Oakley, A. 44, 45
objectives model 13
objectivity 127, 128, 163
observation 6, 7, 16, 33, 34, 43, 55–63, 66
  choosing what to observe 34, 56–8
  in the classroom 59, 64 n.4
  context-embedded 58
  to contextualize meaning 58, 59
  interview as companion method 55, 58
  naturalistic 16, 56
  over time 58, 59
  participant 3, 23, 55
  participant control of 105
  process of observing 55–8
  reasons for 55
  sampling choices 34
  skills development 63
  structured and unstructured 56
  video 61
Okri, B. 150
Oliver, P. 111
oral tradition 150
organizational culture 31, 55, 63, 64
ownership of data 101, 105

painting 89, 118, 151
paradox of case study 167
Parlett, M. 16, 17, 122, 165
participant observation 3, 23, 55
participants
  anonymity 99, 103, 106–8, 157
  body language 53, 55
  data gathering by 40, 41
  in different cultures 104, 105
  engagement in research process 23, 40–1, 43
  'equitable relationship in research process' 101
  friendship with 91–2
  informed consent 41, 78, 99, 100, 102, 103, 103–4
  and interpretation of data 123
  judgements 18, 105
  negotiation with 22, 36, 40, 102, 109–10

INDEX

participants *cont.*
   perspectives 4–5, 17–18, 33, 43, 123, 125, 128
   privacy 102, 106
   research relationship with 36, 41, 54
   responses to written reports 53, 97, 104–5
   validation of research 131, 132
participatory research 18, 33, 36, 108
particularity 3, 19, 20, 24, 167
particularization, indepth 164, 166, 167
Patton, M.Q. 18, 43, 44, 46
Payler, J.K. 61
personal involvement of researcher *see* self;
   subjectivity
personal portrayals 74–5, 105
Peshkin, A. 81, 83–4
photographs, use of 48, 63–4, 90, 152
picture-drawing case study 21
Piper, H. 99
planning and designing the case 38
Plummer, K. 37
poetry 86, 93, 151, 157
   use in
      data analysis and interpretation 89, 117,
         118, 141–2, 144
      constructing narrative 141–2
      exploration of the self 85–7, 89
      reporting 89, 151, 152
Pohland, P.A. 32–3, 149
policy-making 4, 24, 162, 165, 167, 169–70
political dimension in evaluation 3, 17–18, 22, 70
political issues in the field 54
Polkinghorne, D.E. 154
portrayal reporting 149
   see also personal portrayals
positivist tradition 13, 119 127, 162, 164, 168
post-positivism 35
Powdermaker, H. 92
pre/post testing 14
precoding 122
Preskill, H. 97
privacy 102, 106, 108, 157
process consent 103, 104
process generalization 164, 166
progressive focusing 33, 122
propositional knowledge 164, 165
provisional consent 103
psychology 3, 13, 16, 83
Punch, K.F. 168
purpose of case study research 3–4, 21, 56
purposes of evaluation 17
purposive sampling 34, 36

qualitative case study 4–5, 13–14, 20
qualitative research, case study distinguished
   from 14, 19–20
quantitative methods 5, 19, 34

questions
   focused 48–9
   interview 32, 47–9
   open 47–8
   research 32–3
quotations, use of in writing reports 153, 159

Ramcharan, P. 103
random sampling 34, 36
rapport 38, 47
Rashomon effect 149
Real-life context 20, 21, 23
records, access to 40
reflexivity, self- 8, 23, 91–3, 122, 129
Reichardt, C.S. 16
Reissman, C.K. 75
relationships in the field 17, 36, 41, 54, 59–61,
   91–2, 100–3, 129
relevance 102, 103
reliability 127, 128
   inter-subjective 130
reporting in case study 147–53
   adequacy and explicitness of database
      for 148
   appropriateness for purpose 148, 152
   artistic forms, use of 89, 151–2
   conclusion-led 149
   documentary film 37, 151
   fictionalizing 154, 157–9
   formal 148–9, 152
   interpretative 21, 105, 150, 152
   making decisions about 112–13
   portrayal 149
   story-telling 21, 150
   see also writing in case study
researcher's diary or journal 88
research problem 28–9
research questions 31–2
respondent validation 129, 131, 132
responsive evaluation 16, 18, 33
rich description 153, 154
   examples of 57, 60–1
Richardson, L. 75, 82, 90, 118, 142, 151
Ricoeur, P. 75
Rippey, R.M. 16
Robinson, J. 92
role(s) of researcher, choice of 36–8
rolling consent 103
Rubin, H.J. and Rubin, I.S. 43, 44, 47
Rugang, Lu 152
Russell, C. 97

Safari project (1973) 42 n.2, 144 n.2
sampling 34
   adequacy of 129
   purposive 34, 36

sampling *cont.*
　random 34, 36
　theoretical 34
Sammons, P. 111 n.1
Sanger, J. 53, 56, 57, 58
Sarason, S.B. 82
School-Based Research Consortium
　Initiative 170 n.3
school self-evaluation, 7, 166
Schostak, J. 169
Schutz, A. 94 n.2
Schwandt, T.A. 97, 163
Seale, C. 120, 130
secondary sources 5, 141
selecting a case 30–1
self 4, 8, 81–95
　artistic forms, use of in exploring 85–7, 89–90
　concept of 82–3
　ethics and the 81, 94
　impact of 4, 81, 94
　situatedness of the 81–2
　subjective 4, 8, 24, 83–8
　writing in the 92–3
self-reflexivity 8, 23, 91–3, 129
Shapiro, J.J. 81–2
Shaw, I. 13
Sikes, P. 70, 75, 77
Silverman, D. 14
simile, use of in writing, 156–7
Simons, H. 7, 15, 17, 18, 64, 84–5, 92, 107,
　138–9, 154, 166, 167
situated generalization 164, 166
skills development
　in-depth interviewing 51
　observation 63
　writing 159–60
Smith, L.M. 3, 32–3, 104, 119, 149
Snowber, C.N. 118, 140, 141
social-anthropological model 17
social justice perspective 22
social work 13
sociology 3, 13, 70
Socratic dialogue 45, 48, 149
Sparkes, A.C. 118, 129, 151
Spouse, J. 118
Stake, R.E. 5, 13, 16, 19, 130
stakeholders 22
　judgement 36
　perspectives 4, 18, 33, 36
　validation of research 131
Stanley, J.C. 16
story of the case 1, 5, 9, 135–44, 147–57
story lines 141, 143, 148–9
Strauss, A.L. 22, 124, 125
strengths of case study research 16, 18, 19–21 23
structural analysis 141, 144 n.3

subjective 'I's 83–7
subjectivity 4, 8, 24, 83–8, 128, 129
　as negative 162–3
　as strength of qualitative inquiry 162–4
subsequent coding 122
Success and Failure and Recent Innovation
　(Safari project, 1973) 42 n.2, 144 n.2
surveys 14, 34
symbolic interactionism 125
systems analysis 13

tacit knowledge 154, 165
Teacher Training Agency (TTA) 170 n.3
Terkel, S. 37
theme-generation 122, 135–6, 142
theory, different uses of 168
theoretical framework 33, 112, 168–9
　see also grounded theory
theoretical sampling 34
theory-generation 22, 162, 167–9
theory-led case study 21–2
theory-testing case study 21, 22
theory triangulation 130
theory-verification 168
thick description 3
Thomas, G. 124, 126
Thurman, J. 72–3, 155–7
Tierney, W.G. 100
Tillmann-Healy, L. 92
Torres, R.T. 97
transactional evaluation 16
transcripts 52, 53, 123, 135–6, 140–1
transferability 128
transforming data 121
Treacy, M.P. 13
triangulation 55, 120, 129–31, 132, 133
trust 38, 97, 100–1
trustworthiness 128
'truth' 92, 130, 132, 133
types of case study 21–3
typicality 30

UNCAL (understanding computer assisted
　learning) 79 n.2
usability of findings 24, 164
Usher, R. 107
utilitarian pragmatism 35

validity 78, 127–33, 166
　impact of self-reflexivity on 81, 90, 91, 92
　internal/external 127–8, 132
　observation and 55
　and policy determination 24
　strategies for respondent validation
　　129, 131, 132
　triangulation 55, 120, 129–31, 132, 133

Values
   methodology and epistemology 34, 35
   personal, awareness of and impact on research 81, 89, 94
   of programme/project 17, 34,
Van Maanen, J. 37, 161
van Manen, M. 75, 76–7, 142
verification of data 120, 121
video observation 61, 163
vignettes 56, 57, 117, 119, 149, 155, 156, 160
Von Franz, M.L. 83
vulnerable groups informed consent with 104

Walford, G. 106
Walker, R. 3, 5, 46, 92, 118
Waters, P. 108
Weitzman, E.A. 120
Wilby, P. 155

Wiseman, F. 37, 151, 168
Wolcott, H.F. 118, 121, 128
Wolfe, T. 74, 154
Woods, P. 89, 90
Woodward, B. 155
working hypotheses 119, 122, 139
Worrall, J.G. 13
writing in case study 152–60
   improving skills of 159–60
   inspirations for developing skills of 153–7
   biography 155–7
   journalism 154–5
   literary tradition 154
   and re-writing 118, 142–3
   'self' into the text 92–3
   see also reporting in case study

Yin, R.K. 4, 5, 20, 21, 28

ABOUT THE AUTHOR

Helen Simons is Professor Emeritus of Education and Evaluation at the University of Southampton, Honorary Professor at London Metropolitan and Westminster Universities, and an independent consultant in research and evaluation incorporating the creative arts.

Initially a teacher and educational psychologist since arriving in England in 1970, she has specialized in evaluation and educational research at the Universities of East Anglia, London Institute of Education and Southampton. She has also been a Visiting Scholar at the Universities of Malaga and Almeria Spain; Rejakvik, Iceland; and in Norway, New Zealand and Australia. In 2001 she was elected an academician of the Academy of Social Sciences, UK and from 2004 to 2006 was President of the United Kingdom Evaluation Society (UKES).

Helen has actively pursued a democratic approach to research and teaching of case study and advocated qualitative and artistic forms of inquiry to represent and communicate experience. She has also played a major role in promoting professional ethics. As ethics convenor of the UKES and the British Educational Research Association, she co-authored the first edition of each society's ethical guidelines.

Helen Simons is the author of *Getting to Know Schools in a Democracy* and 'The Paradox of Case Study', co-editior of *Situated Ethics in Educational Research* (with R. Usher) and editor of *Towards a Science of the Singular: Essays about Case Study in Educational Research and Evaluation*.